UTILITARIANISM: RESTORATIONS; REPAIRS; RENOVATIONS

DAVID BRAYBROOKE

Utilitarianism: Restorations; Repairs; Renovations

Variations on Bentham's Master-Idea,

That disputes about social policy should be settled by statistical evidence about the comparative consequences for those affected

UNIVERSITY OF TORONTO PRESS
Toronto Buffalo London

© University of Toronto Press Incorporated 2004
Toronto Buffalo London
Printed in Canada

ISBN 0-8020-8732-9

Printed on acid-free paper

Toronto Studies in Philosophy
Editors: Donald Ainslie and Amy Mullin

National Library of Canada Cataloguing in Publication

Braybrooke, David
    Utilitarianism : restorations; repairs; renovations : variations
    on Bentham's master-idea, that disputes about social policy
    should be settled by statistical evidence about the compara-
    tive consequences for those affected / David Braybrooke.

(Toronto studies in philosophy)
Includes bibliographical references and index.
ISBN 0-8020-8732-9

1. Utilitarianism.   I. Title.   II. Series

B843.B72 2004   144'.6   C2004-901558-3

University of Toronto Press acknowledges the financial assistance to its
publishing program of the Canada Council for the Arts and the
Ontario Arts Council.

University of Toronto Press acknowledges the financial support for its
publishing activities of the Government of Canada through the Book
Publishing Industry Development Program (BPIDP).

To two deeply valued friends –

Ed Lindblom,
who gave a direction and extra momentum
to my thinking at an early stage, and

Jim Fishkin,
who gave the thinking and the momentum
a chance to keep going for years
beyond the conventional age for retirement

Contents

in hand with the concept of needs, but goes further, might come in to deal with questions remaining after needs have been met; so might utility in some guise, and the pursuit of pleasure.

These restorations, repairs, and renovations give the attractions of Bentham's Master-Idea a more convincing cast than ever and bring its unhappy career to a happy end.

UTILITARIANISM: RESTORATIONS; REPAIRS; RENOVATIONS

Introduction

In this book, I bring together for revision and supplementation my chief writings, early and late, on the subject of utilitarianism. The result is an account that gives utilitarianism a new look. What is new about the new look?

By 'new,' I have in mind not so much the dates of my writings, or even the date of bringing them together, as the fact that the chief ideas that shape my view of utilitarianism have not so far established an easily visible place for themselves in the standard literature. Though I have had some success with the separate writings, I have not until now presented a consolidated view of utilitarianism and demonstrated how different it is from the standard one, both in particular aspects and as a whole. So bringing things together is something new, though it relates, somewhat obliquely, to the standard literature, including the current disputes about consequentialism associated with the work of Samuel Scheffler.[1]

New, too, in the sense defined, is the emphasis that the things brought together give to the politics of utilitarianism and, in particular, to the process of public policy-making. These things are barely touched upon in the current disputes just cited, which tend to concentrate upon the bearing of utilitarianism upon personal choices, and on the threat that Bernard Williams and others have held that it poses in such choices to the integrity of moral agents.[2] My emphasis on policy-making is especially distinctive in giving due weight to the operation there in modern democracies and elsewhere of the ubiquitous, continuing sub-process that constitutes what I call 'the Revisionary Process.' Here, policy proposals are continually being revised to win greater support; here, policies themselves are continually being revised to obtain more success with more people. Attention to the Revisionary Process disposes of objections that arise from trying misguidedly to assess utilitarianism, assuming that all options are given and a once-for-all solution to the problem of choosing them is to take final shape in the near future (chapter 1, 40; chapter 2, 45). Attention to the Revisionary Process disposes, too, of the objection that when (as utilitarianism would insist) decisions about social policies must turn on consequences we cannot know enough about consequences to know what decision to take. Given a continuing process, we do not have to know everything about consequences to make prudent decisions; the decisions are normally, continually, followed by opportunities for revision (see chapter 2). Some decisions about life-sacrifices that we may encounter during the process of public policy-making are ruled out by an elementary statistical consideration, namely, keeping in view the same population when we are comparing two policies for their effect upon it (see chapter 3). Other decisions, about sacrifices maybe very painful, but short of being life-sacrifices, are ruled out by judicious use of the notion of a comparative census, under which, instead of resorting to an interpersonal calculus of utility, we establish two or three categories and count the persons who fall into each of them under the policies to be compared (see chapter 4). Adverse consequences for some people do not then get masked by an overall utility score. Utility, personal and interpersonal, is not even the way to go in applying utilitarianism with the census-notion in real-world comparisons of policies. The way to go (see chapter 5) is to make careful systematic use of the concept of needs, making sure, before turning to more elusive subjects, of provisions for vital needs like food, clothing, and shelter. (The more elusive subjects are covered, along with needs, by Amartya Sen's 'capabilities' approach, with which I consider mine allied.) In its various applications the concept of needs has supplied surrogates for utility and by doing so accounts for the effectiveness that utilitarianism has had as a 'public philosophy,' to use Robert Goodin's phrase.[3]

None of these ideas has a visible place in Goodin's own presentation of utilitarianism, except for his attention, short of a careful systematic use, to the concept of needs. I agree, however, with his insistence that utilitarianism is more convincing as a public philosophy, for use in deciding upon social policy, than as a private ethics. Without renouncing every opportunity to defend utilitarianism as a private ethics, for the most part I, too, treat utilitarianism as a public philosophy. At the very least, utilitarianism depends less awkwardly on multiple special defences in public connections than it does in private ones.

Goodin is not alone in neglecting the ideas that give the present book its special character. The neglect is a common feature of the standard literature. For evidence supporting this assertion I can cite the disputes about consequentialism and integrity. I also rely on the acute, judiciously balanced, and comprehensive synopsis of the received standard literature to be found in William H. Shaw's *Contemporary Ethics: Taking into Account Utilitarianism*. This book, I think, does as well as any book could do in setting forth, with all the virtues and vices pertaining thereto, an insider's synopsis. A mark of its being an insider's synopsis is that Shaw, conforming in this to the common, unthinking assumption of philosophers writing on utilitarianism, sees no alternative to an interpersonally additive calculus of utility as an interpretation of the principle 'that we can [only] derive an overall welfare assessment of a given state of affairs based on the welfare or happiness or utility of each individual person.'[4] He rightly takes this principle to be centrally defining of utilitarianism. We can spell out the point of making such an assessment as being to compare it to other assessments, pertaining to other options in social policy; and on the basis of the comparison to decide on one option or the other. It is another way of formulating what, wording it differently on my title page, I call (there and in the table of contents as well as thereafter) 'Bentham's Master-Idea' (in French, his *idée mère*). However, the principle is not tied logically to the notion of an interpersonally additive calculus of utility. The census-notion supplies an alternative – more effective; more practical; less objectionable – way of carrying out the assessments, and does so in keeping with the intentions of utilitarianism, as expressed in Bentham's Master-Idea.

'Correctly understood,' Shaw says, 'utilitarianism tells us to do only one thing, maximize happiness ... it is the total amount of happiness, not the number of people ... that matters.'[5] Concern with the number of people – with seeing to it that more people are made happier rather than fewer – has been a feature of utilitarianism, correctly understood, if not fully incorporated, from the beginning. Bentham himself was sometimes a categorically 'greatest number' utilitarian.[6] The concern was expressed with moving eloquence by John Stuart Mill: morality itself, Mill held, if it is to conform to the greatest happiness principle, consists of 'the rules and precepts for human conduct, by the observance of which an existence ... exempt as far as possible from pain, and as rich as possible in enjoyments ... might be, to the greatest extent possible, secured to all mankind.'[7] The census-notion offers guidance that an aggregative calculus does not offer to bringing this sort of extension about.

The census-notion, moreover, supplies an alternative interpretation of Bentham's Master-Idea that, like the other ideas advanced in this book, combine to give a decisive and complete answer to the objections to utilitarianism that I take up. The ideas belong to a very different style of argument from the one that Shaw characteristically uses. Shaw emphasizes and discounts the fantastic assumptions that generate the objections. Discounting the objections as resting on mere fantasies is a very sensible way to argue on these points; occasionally I myself argue in this style. Generally, however, I try for something different, something more trenchant than results like Shaw's, which are somewhat inconclusive. I try to show that even in principle, with fantastic assumptions in place, utilitarianism does not have to concede anything substantial to the objections.

Are the census-notion and the other new ideas decisive only because they leave anything that can plausibly be called 'utilitarianism' behind? I do not think so. The ideas connect surprisingly closely with the utilitarianism of Bentham and his followers. If we regard the slogan 'The Greatest Happiness of the Greatest Number' as occupying, officially or unofficially,[8] a central place in the utilitarian tradition, we should be impressed by the fact that the census-notion has a better claim than the calculus to making sense of the slogan. It does not lead to breakdown, as the calculus combined with the slogan does, in the face of a choice between a policy that achieves the greatest sum of happiness and another policy that advances a greater number to a higher level of happiness. It is true that Bentham did not constantly adhere to the slogan any more than he did to the calculus. The presence of the slogan in the literature nevertheless gives evidence of the implicit presence and operation of the census-notion. So do the instances of Bentham's moving away from the combination of the slogan and the calculus when he is specially concerned with distributive considerations.

The census-notion does have troubles of its own: in some sorts of mixed comparisons, it fails to deliver a clear answer favouring one policy against another. In particular, it fails to deliver where the calculus (in some disregard of the slogan) would (were it feasible) press forward a recommendation, namely, for a policy that makes some people very happy even if it also makes some people somewhat unhappy. But the policy-making process does not stand still before such a conflict: I present the census-notion as keeping company always with the Revisionary Process, in which a failure to deliver a recommendation is taken as a challenge to invent a revised policy that can be firmly recommended.

Theoretical attention to the process of making policies and with it to the Revisionary Process is wholly utilitarian, even if few utilitarian writers have seen the importance of giving it prime attention.[9] For I suppose that champions of utilitarianism would never have denied that applications of their theory would take place in the midst of a social process of dispute and deliberation and that in application the theory would have to make the best of the advantages and disadvantages of the process. In the process, as it is carried on in the real world, the theory had to come to terms with the claims of human needs; with the census-notion in hand, it can deal with these claims effectively. In the absence of a practical calculus of utility, that is the way, through the surrogates for questions about utility supplied by questions about needs and questions about other matters less basic, that utilitarianism has had whatever effect it has had on real-world policy-making. So I do not go outside utilitarianism when I shift, in practical applications, from utilities to needs.[10] Moreover, I treat priority for meeting needs as a foundation on which utilitarians can superimpose provisions for matters less basic. Throughout my restorations, repairs, and renovations, I present a utilitarianism that remains true to Bentham's Master-Idea, that moral disputes about social policy should be settled by statistical evidence about the consequences for human beings.[11]

I use the appellation 'Bentham's Master-Idea' without perfect textual warrant, but with good warrant by analysis and argumentation nevertheless. Bentham does not, so far as I know, give it separate formulation, as Shaw does, calling it 'the centrally defining principle of utilitarianism' (see above). It comes in the first chapters of his *Introduction* implicitly combined with attention to pleasure and pain as the way of giving attention to happiness and with the calculus as the means of giving pleasure and pain systematic attention. But the combination is not logically indissoluble.[12] There are three ideas in the combination. Settling disputes by statistical evidence about the consequences for those affected is the most fundamental of the three, since there are various aspects of the consequences that evidence may be sought for (even various conceptions of happiness), and there is an alternative to the calculus as a systematic means of organizing the evidence. If Bentham did not see this, it might be held that he does not deserve full credit for the Master-Idea, but I say that if the full signifi-cance of his purpose and his teaching is appreciated, he does deserve credit, and we should give it him.

Part One

Restorations and Repairs That Leave
Utility and the Calculus in Place

1

Does Utilitarianism (Bentham's Master-Idea, Applied as Hedonic Act-Utilitarianism or Otherwise) Undermine Reliable Adherence to Moral Rules? No*

Reliable adherence to rules comes in, endorsed by hedonic act-utilitarianism, with rules set up to govern actions in the presence of imperfect information about what individual agents, acting by themselves, would otherwise do. The case for rules extends, moreover, from imperfect agents to quasi-perfect ones, who lack only the information to coordinate their actions when they are out of communication.

Hedonic Act-Utilitarianism (a name I owe to Judith Jarvis Thomson[1]) is an interpretation of Bentham's position that captures the features of utilitarianism most commonly ascribed to it in the literature. It assumes that it is possible to calculate the pleasures and pains attributable to individual persons affected by given actions and to add up those pleasures and pains across all the persons affected. It prescribes that those actions the effects of which so calculated and so added up bring about a net sum of pleasure greater than would be brought about by any action alternative to them (or at least as great as any alternative) should be chosen. Thus, it says, the Greatest Happiness of the whole group of persons affected will be attained.

I shall not, in this chapter or in the next two chapters, set aside the assumptions about calculation and adding up across persons, both of which remain very doubtful even to this day. What I shall aim to show is that even in this question-begging form, utilitarianism is not

---

* Based on and in part reprinted from my article 'The Choice between Utilitarianism,' *American Philosophical Quarterly*, 4 (January 1967), 28–38. So far as reprinted, copyright © 1967 by *American Philosophical Quarterly* and reprinted with its permission.

My chapter titles in this book imitate Locke's headings in his *Questions about the Law of Nature* and are intended as a tribute to the brisk style of his headings.

vulnerable to some of the most familiar objections that have arisen against it. In this chapter I shall be concerned with the objection that utilitarianism undermines reliable adherence to moral rules, for example, the rule that every promise is to be kept. For if the promise was made on a desert island from which only you have returned, or at a deathbed where only you were present with the dying person, why should it be kept if you now have an opportunity to create more net pleasure by breaking the promise? To insist on obeying the rules in these instances is not, it seems, something that utilitarians can be expected to do.

Hume offers an even more unsettling example: you are bound (in justice, he says) to return some property to its rightful owner, even if in his hands the property will be used to promote sedition and thus impair the general welfare. You have more use for the property, applied to innocent uses, than the rightful owner does anyway. So, heeding the rule of justice in this case will run contrary both to the private interest (your private interest, compared with the owner's) and to the public interest. Yet Hume thinks, and for purposes of argument I shall assume, that you should obey the rule calling for the return of the property and, I add, you should do so even if (because of limited public provisions for detection) you might get away with disobeying it.[2] Can a utilitarian take such an inflexible stand on justice?

Act-utilitarians want to push as far as possible the application of the Principle of Utility action by action, in calculations and choices that are unaffected by deference to moral rules. (I assume, to fix ideas, the principle as understood in Hedonic Act-Utilitarianism.) Act-utilitarians begin, at least, by hypothesizing that there are no possible circumstances in which the Principle of Utility, applied to single actions with full consideration of everything that is at stake, ought to be to any degree qualified in favour of heeding moral rules. Everything that is at stake includes the features of the circumstances contributed by previous actions and the influence that the actions now contemplated may have on future actions. According to rule-utilitarianism, as I conceive it, full consideration is in practice impossible, so that even utilitarians by conviction must bind themselves to act in deference to rules. This is the basis – imperfect information – for a strong defence of rule-utilitarianism, and it operates even if we suppose that the rules always apply simply to make as sure as possible of utilitarian actions and discourage counter-utilitarian ones.

A basis for a stronger defence lies in taking special notice in addition of circumstances in which moral rules ought to be upheld and upheld, moreover, on utilitarian grounds, even though the harm done by some single violations, taking them as single instances, independently of actions done independently from them, would be outweighed by the good that would ensue from the violations. The rules themselves must be justified by utilitarian considerations; but they are rules that sometimes in individual cases taken by themselves may preclude utilitarian actions and require counter-utilitarian ones.[3]

It may be helpful to think that we are dealing with two sorts of rules, both of which will have a place in rule-utilitarianism: first, rules designed simply to check people in every case that falls under the rule from acting against the principle of utility, that is to say, from making counter-utilitarian choices; second, rules designed to check them in certain circumstances from acting (on their own) on the principle of utility, that is to say, from making (on their own) utilitarian choices, though in other circumstances the rule may straightforwardly prescribe utilitarian choices. The grounds for rules of the latter sort lie in benefits that can be obtained only by the coordination of agents and actions that they make possible. The two sorts of rules seem to be mutually exclusive, but it does not matter for my purposes whether they are or are not. Nor is the usefulness of the distinction undermined by having both sorts fall under the same general definition of rules, for example, the one given by D. Braybrooke, B. Brown, and P.K. Schotch in *Logic on the Track of Social Change*,[4] where a rule is said to be 'a system of imperatives, that is to say, of action types that are blocking operations that target (**nono**ing, more or less precisely) specified other action types (by given agents – falling under **volk** – in circumstances specified under **wenn**)'; 'nono,' 'volk,' and 'wenn' are operators in a general logic of rules set forth in the same book. (Actions, like bowing to a specified person, are instances of action-types – for example, bowing to some person. Blocking operations range from frowns through negative commands to physical restraint.)

Of the two views, rule-utilitarianism is the one more difficult to state without paradox; yet it is also the view that matches traditional morality more closely. Does it involve 'rule-worship,' a merely sentimental attachment to rules?[5] The support that it may gain from traditional morality cannot be decisive for accepting rule-utilitarianism as a theory of ethics. Utilitarianism in the Benthamite tradition has always meant to be, not just an account of traditional morality, certainly not an account committed to endorsing traditional morality, but a theory prepared to be innovative in departing from traditional prescriptions.[6] However, rule-utilitarianism can be innovating, too: the rules that it justifies may not be traditional ones.

I shall assume for the time being that whatever rules are in question when rules have a place are inflexible, allowing neither explicitly nor tacitly for exceptions, and that agents are never to make any exceptions from them. These assumptions enormously exaggerate the degree to which ordinary moral rules are inflexible. However, inflexibility of the rules and inflexible attachment are not irrational, given certain political conditions, that is to say, given certain arrangements (or lack of arrangements) for observation by other agents and given certain imperfections of information and outlook on the part of the agents who are to heed the rules.

There are circumstances – other forms of social life within which policies about morality may be developed – in which rational grounds for applying rule-utilitarianism in preference to act-utilitarianism disappear. They supply an instructive contrast and I shall take them up first.

With Continuous Access to the Authority of the Community, No Occasion for Rule-Utilitarian Reasoning

The Community-in-Session

Imagine a society small enough that all its members can be gathered in one arena. There, in public, the members spend their whole lives, exposed to public scrutiny whatever they might do or whenever they might do it. No one can escape scrutiny. If two people should turn their backs on the rest of the community, they find themselves facing mirrors visible throughout the arena. If they whisper together, their words are picked up by a microphone and broadcast.

In such a society, one might infer, it would be sensible for anyone proposing to do anything about which moral questions arise to seek community approval first. Let us suppose that it is a universal custom for everyone in the community to do this, so that every decision about which even minor moral doubts are raised becomes a public decision in which the whole community, which I shall call 'the Community-in-Session,' takes part. Many, maybe most, of the actions taken in the

Community will go unquestioned. They are not questioned, perhaps, because no actions of those types have ever been questioned in the past; or they have been questioned, but they were then approved, setting a rebuttable precedent for expecting them to be approved now. This is not to say that a rule has been adopted permitting them, just that nothing is thought to stand in the way of doing them. There is not even what von Wright calls a 'weak permission,' that is to say, the absence in the going set of prohibitions of any prohibition against doing them.[7] There is no such set of prohibitions present in the Community-in-Session.

I might note that, notwithstanding, I could run essentially the same argument even if I allowed that permissive rules, along with rules prescriptive and prohibitive, were present in the Community-in-Session. This is what I did in the article from which this chapter derives.[8] Then it would be the rules that would in many cases be brought into question, not actions without rules. However, the rules would always be subject to immediate change; they would continue from moment to moment only if (when asked for, which might be continually) act-utilitarian endorsement were available for any action taken under them. They would have not the least independent force as rules, and this is true even of rules that the Community might newly adopt to deal with moral problems. I achieve, I believe, a more trenchant effect in portraying the Community-in-Session as something that gives act-utilitarianism maximum scope if I do without even these perpetually contingent rules. Thus, I consider only actions directly questioned under the Principle of Utility or left unquestioned.

Some intended actions will be questioned in the Community-in-Session, either because circumstances have changed, and with them the consequences of those actions, or because something hitherto unrecognized has come to light in their consequences.

Besides providing against concealment, the Community-in-Session provides, let us suppose, against the formation of factions or coalitions that seek to promote some members' selfish interests at the expense of others.[9] The provisions against concealment will themselves operate against factions. We can go further by assuming that the Community is sufficiently homogeneous to forestall having factions form on ethnic, religious, or any other lines. We shall assume also that the decision-making of the Community relies on reaching the Quakers' 'sense of the meeting,' that is, in effect, relying on unanimity. No approval will be forthcoming unless it is unanimous approval, but if we assume that all questions about actions can be settled without a division of opinion on the information available, unanimity may not be impossibly hard to come by.

Finally – simply to avoid having to take up a certain set of problems – let us suppose that the Community-in-Session is so fortunate as to escape any military threats or natural emergencies substantial enough to require sacrificing the lives or fortunes of some members as a means of preserving the lives or fortunes of the rest.

Soaring over the difficulties of elaborating the principle of utility,[10] I shall assume that agents do frequently know what the net undistributed benefits of given actions will be and that, when they know what the net undistributed benefits will be, they can always rank those actions according to the amount of those benefits (whether or not they can measure amounts exactly). I shall also assume that when the net undistributed benefits to be obtained from an action are known to be greater than those to be obtained from alternative actions, there will be a distribution to all the present members of the Community such that every member gets what all members regard as a fair share . (This assumption, of course, brings in considerations of justice, but only to clear the stage for ignoring arguments about them.) The breathtaking scope of these assumptions is a measure of the importance of the problems about meaning and justice which they sweep over.

Act-Utilitarianism in the Community-in-Session

The version of utilitarianism that would prevail in the Community-in-Session is act-utilitarianism. Let us assume that all the members of the Community are utilitarians. In the Community, they will be act-utilitarians, because the Community goes as far toward accommodating act-utilitarianism as can be imagined, and there will be no reason for a utilitarian to adhere to anything else. There would be no point even in keeping up the distinction between act-utilitarianism and rule-utilitarianism; for in the Community-in-Session the grounds for preferring rule-utilitarianism (at least the grounds that I shall be concerned with) disappear. In the Community-in-Session, for one thing, no member can ever choose to act secretly. Brandt's would-be gas-cheat[11] and Smart's (earlier, A.K. Stout's) flower-gardener,[12] if they wished to lay to rest complaints about using excessive gas and water in a time of shortage, would have to produce arguments that would persuade the rest of the Community. They would have to show that their using more gas or more water would lead to a net increase in happiness, given what other people would do or want to do.

In the Community-in-Session, no member is ever in a position where he must act on his own, if he is to act at all. Every member is always in communication with every other member, and every action is an immediate possible subject of approval or disapproval, should anyone wish to raise a question about it. No one is ever closeted with a dying testator; no one makes promises on a desert island to someone who does not return with her. If anyone believes that departing from existing precedents would lead to greater utility, he can seek to have the rule amended. The absence of personal discretion is compensated for by continuous and immediate access to the moral authority of the Community. (This is not to say that authority is infallible, just that it is what must operate to approve or disapprove any questioned action.) No one is ever in the position of the city gatekeeper in St Thomas's example, who has to decide on his own whether to let people in after the city-gate has been closed for the night. Hurrying toward the gate on that exciting evening is a party of the city's own soldiers, hotly pursued by enemy forces.[13] In the Community-in-Session, the gatekeeper could refer immediately to the Community as a whole for a decision about opening the gate.

In the Community-in-Session, with every member committed to utilitarianism, every single action taken in the Community would conform to the Principle of Utility (unless there are untoward consequences that no one recognizes). Were anyone ever to be tempted to deviate from the principle, other members of the Community, all being act-utilitarians, would willingly move to admonish her, which should suffice, since by assumption she is an act-utilitarian, too, and will need only to be reminded of her commitment. Should it not suffice, through some misunderstanding, the others will block the action in question or punish it, assuming (what I shall assume) that the cost of blocking or punishing is negligible.

It has been suggested to me[14] that no one in the Community would have any incentive to monitor other people's actions, much less take the trouble of admonishing, blocking, or punishing. But that no one will take the trouble is excluded by the assumption that all the members are convinced act-utilitarians, and thereby committed to taking the trouble to have the principle of utility always prevail. It also seems wrong anyway. People still stand to lose out if anything goes in the arena occupied by the Community, and some people assault others, steal their goods, enslave them, and so on, in full view of the others. Since these evils might happen to any of them, they all will have a motivation to stop them.

This motivation, however, is first-order motivation. The suggestion brings to light a problem about second-order motivation, in which the free-rider opportunity leads anyone not a committed utilitarian to let others enforce: if others will monitor, block, and punish, why should I? The answer would have to be the imposition of a rule requiring monitoring and checking; and the Community would have to make sure it was enforced. Thus, were it not for the assumption about every member being a committed act-utilitarian, it would appear that it would not be possible to set up the Community-in-Session, and thus give act-utilitarianism maximum scope, without presupposing a rule. This makes even more of rule-utilitarianism than I have aimed to make of it. Whether or not a rule were to come in with the very postulation of the Community-in-Session, however, the Community-in-Session would still serve my purpose in showing how the scope for act-utilitarianism diminishes immediately that we allow for information less perfect than the agents have there. The main route to rule-utilitarianism lies through imperfect information, which is a pervasive feature of the real world commonly neglected by philosophers as much as, often in the past and sometimes in the present, by economic theorists.

The model of thoroughgoing act-utilitarianism offered by the Community-in-Session raises a number of other doubts. Is it feasible? One might imagine a very small community in which it would be feasible: for example, three bachelor brothers wholly committed to making a go of the farm that they jointly possess. They could be continually in each other's presence as they work together.[15] However, even the brothers might soon have occasions to work separately on different tasks or in different parts of the farm. The Community-in-Session would be difficult to set up for any considerable number of people – say, twelve people or more. It would be difficult to keep going. How would the Community feed itself without sending some people out into relatively distant fields to raise crops or out to sea to catch fish?

Suppose, nevertheless, that it turns out to be feasible. Would it be attractive? Some people – I expect the overwhelming majority of people, would find it very unattractive: 'a nightmare scenario.'[16] There is no provision for private pleasures that people – most people, including most act-utilitarians – would want to pursue by themselves or with a few specially chosen intimates. No one can have any intimates. Some people, in special circumstances, like the three farmer brothers, might not be bothered by this fact, at least for a time. But I expect most people, including most act-utilitarians, would be bothered.

Act-utilitarians who find the Community-in-Session unattractive thus immediately face an argument against their project of pushing the use of act-utilitarian reasoning as far as it can go. The Community-in-Session serves as a fair model for what this would result in, namely, social arrangements where no action escapes monitoring. The alternative to this or any other model for thoroughgoing act-utilitarianism is one in which some allowance is made for intermissions in the monitoring during which private pleasures could be pursued. But these intermissions inevitably open up room for abuses. Certain assumptions about the likelihood of such abuses complete the argument for setting a limit to the act-utilitarian project and beginning to rely instead upon rules.

With Intervals between Sessions of the Community and Imperfect Information during the Intervals, Rule-Utilitarianism Makes a Place for Itself

Rule-Utilitarianism in Intermittently Meeting Communities

Let us now imagine that the same people who have been living together as the Community-in-Session disperse throughout the area of a New England town or of a small Swiss canton. They will no longer be continuously ready to pass on the moral character of questioned actions. They will meet only intermittently, perhaps once a day or once a week, perhaps only once a year or once a decade. However frequently the Community meets, there will now be intervals between sessions during which members of the Community may have to act on their own in morally significant cases. These are circumstances that open up an opportunity for the Community, when it does meet, to legislate for what is to go on in the next interval. They also open up a genuine option between act-utilitarianism and rule-utilitarianism (or rather, as will become clear, act-utilitarianism unqualified, by itself, and act-utilitarianism qualified by combining and working through rule-utilitarianism).

Imperfect Agents

The most obvious reasons for preferring rule-utilitarianism in intermittent communities derive from the imperfections of human beings.
Human beings are, notoriously, imperfect in moral attitude and in
knowledge and intelligence as well.[17] Many will not even aim to do
well if they are not checked by rules; they will not be act-utilitarians
unless being monitored makes them so. Even if they aim to do well,
that is to say, here, act on the Principle of Utility, they will not generally have enough information to evaluate the comparative consequences
of heeding the rules and violating them. They may not unreasonably
think in most cases that they are more likely to be acting in accordance
with the Principle of Utility if they heed established rules than if they
do not. The rules, they may well believe (and philosophers will encourage them to believe this), reflect experience with the consequences
of doing otherwise; moreover, other people will expect them to heed
the rules, and if they do not, the plans and the benefits of other people
will be put in jeopardy.[18] Even in cases where they have reason to
suspect that violating the rule will contribute to the Greatest Happiness more than heeding it, they cannot count on having enough information to vindicate the suspicion; and, dealing with the information
that they do have, they are liable to form distorted estimates about
where the Greatest Happiness lies, balancing considerations too hastily or not at all and giving undue weight to the stakes in pleasure and
pain for themselves and people close to them. Moreover, even if these
things do not have any important effect, people generally have imperfect knowledge about what other agents in similar situations are doing or going to do; hence, they do not know what effect their choices
of actions and policies will have in addition to the actions and policies
chosen by others.

It would be very helpful, no doubt, if all agents would make only
those decisions that they could anticipate the Community's ratifying –
when and if the Community ever meets in legislative session and
supposing that only utilitarian arguments would be publicly persuasive when it did. But by the common opinion that human beings have
of themselves, this cannot be counted on. A community in which this
cannot be counted on may have a use for customs or institutions that
are intended to limit – in crucial cases, to remove – the discretion of
individual agents when they are out of communication with the community as a whole. If the dangers of letting them act on their own
discretion are greater than the dangers of binding them, it will con-

form to the Principle of Utility to bind agents by general inflexible rules established in advance. People will be expected, for example, to keep promises as a matter of rule; and the point of having a rule will be precisely to rule out personal discretion about keeping or breaking promises in individual cases.[19]

Traditional morality, at least on a simplified view that often is present when traditional morality is invoked, has stood by inflexible rules and inflexible attachment, giving more weight to the dangers that discretion would be abused than to the advantages of a system allowing some discretion. This weight explains the superior attractions, from the point of view of traditional morality, that rule-utilitarianism offers compared with act-utilitarianism. (Neither traditional moralists nor rule-utilitarians, to be sure, might want to say that rule-utilitarianism does explicate traditional morality.)

The implications of the simplified view of traditional morality go further than this: they explain why the attachment to certain moral rules may appear blind or irrational or intuitive. Such attachment, which Smart seems to endorse in spite of himself when he speaks of abiding by 'habitual and stereotypical rules' rather than run the dangers of delay or personal bias, may be thought to be just the attitude toward moral rules that it is best to inculcate. How otherwise bind people efficaciously when they are out of sight?

The implication would not justify this attitude in the eyes of rule-utilitarians, however, if the attitude prevented changing bad rules or obsolete rules. True rule-utilitarianism cannot be complacent rule-utilitarianism. If rule-utilitarians are to live up to their own professions regarding the Principle of Utility, they must be alert to defects in existing rules. They must also bear in mind the fact that even the most judiciously selected rules are liable to become obsolete. Indeed, they may become obsolete very suddenly, when unexpected circumstances come up; and if there are no clear provisions for re-legislating the rules, or the opportunities for re-legislation come only rarely, a great deal of unnecessary damage may be done by inflexibly heeding rules in the meantime. An adequate system of ethics has an important stake, especially in changing times, in having relatively frequent explicit legislative opportunities for revising the rules. Frequent opportunities for revision will help minimize the damage done in the intervals between them.

In the long run, reasons for revising the rules may arise from the fact that the human imperfections on which the necessity of binding rules supposedly rests are likely to change. If individual agents should become, on the average, more knowledgeable or benevolent, the rules will invite adjustment to allow agents larger spheres of discretion.

Part of the power of arguments like Smart's for preferring act-utilitarianism lies in the fact that alertness to changes in people and in the environment seems more readily associated with act-utilitarianism than with rule-utilitarianism. In fact, both require alertness. In intermittent communities, differences in the speed with which people adhering to the two doctrines respond to perceived changes in conditions could be removed to any degree of approximation by making the intervals between legislative sessions shorter and shorter.

I have just completed a strong defence of rule-utilitarianism, resting on the imperfections of agents' information, of their sagacity in dealing with the information that they do have, and of their arrangements for communication and legislation, as well as on their moral imperfections. The defence is basic, central, and sufficient to make sure of a place for rule-utilitarianism in practice. It also covers both sorts of rules distinguished above, those (like a rule against treating people with cruelty) deviating from which cannot normally be expected to promote the Greatest Happiness on any occasion and those from which such deviations continually seem to offer opportunities to do this. The latter, my second sort of rules, consist of rules set up as devices for coordinating actions to achieve a cumulative effect.

It is not, however, a defence that will satisfy everybody. It is not an in-principle defence that covers every theoretical possibility. It does not cover the possibility touched on by David Lyons in his book *Forms and Limits of Utilitarianism*. Lyons undertakes to show that what he (rather disobligingly) calls 'primitive rule-utilitarianism' is 'extensionally equivalent' to act-utilitarianism, yielding 'equivalent judgments in all cases.'[20] This result depends chiefly on the contention that any discrepancy between on the one hand reckoning the effects of acts separately then adding the effects up and on the other hand reckoning their effects combined when they occur in combination can be removed. It can be removed by redescribing the single acts so as to apportion to each its full share of the combined effect. I think that this contention may be freely admitted. Moreover, it brings to light a theoretical possibility, not tied to the practical assurances of the Community-in-Session, of convinced utilitarian agents in possession of all the information at issue choosing actions in a way that gives no place to rule-utilitarian reasoning. Yet just as soon as we move from ideal possibilities toward the real world no further than to allow that agents, however thoroughly utilitarian in conviction, are likely to have imperfect information, imperfect opportunities for communication, and varying opportunities for legislation, rule-utilitarianism claims attention.

Moreover, there is much to be learned about the relations of act-utilitarianism and rule-utilitarianism if we consider how imperfect arrangements for communication and legislation affect even agents ideal in other ways, including their information and sagacity. The article from which this chapter derives was entitled 'The Choice between Utilitarianisms,' but what I really did there and again do here is show that there is no simple choice between them: act-utilitarianism and rule-utilitarianism are so intertwined that the presence of both is required for a consistent and comprehensive utilitarianism. Some circumstances, even in a nearly ideal world call for rule-utilitarian reasoning or for rule-utilitarian reasoning part of the way; other circumstances call, at least part of the way, for act-utilitarian reasoning.

Quasi-Perfect Agents

The case for preferring rule-utilitarianism to act-utilitarianism in intermittent communities gains strength from the assumptions of traditional morality regarding human imperfections; but the case does not depend on those assumptions. Suppose that all the members of the community can be trusted to act according to the Principle of Utility. Suppose that they are all equally well informed and such accurate reasoners that they never make mistakes, deductive or inductive. Since they are not, we suppose, omniscient, they are not perfect agents; but they are at least quasi-perfect paragons of virtue and wisdom. Yet if the community to which these paragons belong meets at most only intermittently, they may have to accept limits on their discretion that will prevent them from acting as act-utilitarians in every instance. The Principle of Utility may require them to act as rule-utilitarians. Again, I mean to cover all sorts of rules, though the argument will bear most immediately and most plausibly on coordinative rules.

Suppose there is a sort of action, A, that will in the aggregate violate the principle of utility, not just by falling short of the maximum of V (aggregate utility) available, but by turning the aggregate into a negative quantity, if (but only if) n_h or more of the actions are done during a certain interval of time. ('h' stands for 'harm.') The quantity n_h thus represents the minimum number of actions A during that interval such that V, the total net benefit from doing such actions, is negative.

Suppose that the figure n_h is known and known to be greater than one. Suppose, also, that it is known that during the interval n_h (or more) agents will be in a position to do an action A.

Now, this may be the case in every single instance: if the agent considers the actions of every sort, including actions of the sort A, that he knows have occurred previously, and considers the actions of every sort, including actions of the sort A, that would be influenced by his doing action A now (perhaps by taking his doing it as an example, but in other ways as well), he will on the basis of these considerations find himself enjoined to do A by the Principle of Utility. For doing A in each single instance, so considered, offers a certain net benefit, a, greater than the perceived disadvantages.

Suppose, however, that the Community will not come into legislative session at any time during the interval. Suppose, also, that no set of agents s in number, where s is less than n_h, will be able to set up arrangements during the interval for communicating to the rest of the Community that they are doing actions A less than n_h times in time to forestall $(n_h - s)$ agents from doing such actions also.

What does utilitarianism prescribe in this situation? The answer to this question turns out to be exceedingly complex. What utilitarianism prescribes varies according to whether the situation is discovered before or after the interval begins and according to what further information is in the possession of the agents and the Community. It also varies according to whether or not everyone is expected to reason in the same way and act on the same principles (even though their final actions may differ); for the time being, let us assume that they are expected to. Beginning with the further assumptions that the situation regarding actions A is discovered by individual agents during the interval and that their information about the situation is limited to the facts set forth above, let us consider some cases.

DISCOVERY DURING THE INTERVAL: VIRTUAL LEGISLATION

Under the conditions assumed, if every agent reasons and acts as an act-utilitarian, n_h (or more) actions A will be done during the interval and aggregate harm will result. It therefore contravenes the principle of utility for every agent to reason and act as an act-utilitarian. For there is another line of reasoning that would forestall the harm if every agent adopted it. According to this line of reasoning, the proper thing for every agent to do is to impose on himself the requirement of refraining from doing actions A, since otherwise every agent with the opportunity to do A will do A on act-utilitarian grounds. If doing A involves breaking a previously legislated rule, the self-imposed requirement amounts to reaffirming the rule. If doing A does not involve breaking a rule, the universal coincidence of self-imposed requirements may be regarded as virtual legislation. In both cases, the reasoning of the agents (which a utilitarian observer would endorse) is rule-utilitarian, although in the second case the rule has not been communicated, and symmetry of reasoning and conduct takes the place of actually legislating and heeding legislation.

On the present assumptions, Brandt's gas-cheat and Smart's flower-gardener, finding themselves in a community of quasi-perfect utilitarians, yet subject to their familiar temptations, would have to refrain from the actions that they contemplate. For if they found the actions utilitarian by reasoning from certain considerations, so, they must recognize, would every other agent in a position to do the same thing; but if every agent in a position to do these things – to take more gas or use extra water – were to do them, in each case the Community would suffer a net loss in utility or happiness. There is no way of preventing this result except by everyone's considering himself bound to refrain. Therefore, everyone would refrain.

The fact that in these examples the attractions of A depend in part upon A's being a deliberately concealed action is not essential to justifying rule-utilitarianism in the type of situation assumed. What counts in compelling well-meaning agents to adopt rule-utilitarianism in all such situations is the incompleteness of information, the want of communication respecting the actions, and the lack of an opportunity to join in legislation.

The effect of the present assumptions in other examples treated by philosophers is problematic. Would actions breaking promises in those instances where (taking the instances singly) breaking the promises would gain more utility than keeping them aggregate with the instances of keeping promises into a body of actions very distant from achieving a satisfactory overall result? It is not entirely obvious that in any interval of time, even a very long one, the number of such actions would be likely to reach a critical figure n_h. Deviations few and far between over a long period of time would not, for example, do much to shake confidence in the rule about keeping promises. Hume, in his argument for the coordinative rules of justice, assumed that the act-utilitarian deviations would be frequent enough or consequential enough to seriously undermine the rules. However, did he have evidence for this? Even evidence confined, as it should be, to the members of a continuing community (not people living so far apart in space and time as to be out of communication with one another entirely), was not at his disposal. It is even less clear that the subclass of deviant actions that consists of undetected promise-breakings would reach the critical damaging figure. If all the deathbed agreements and desert-island promises that were ever made were broken in those instances in which doing so accorded with the Principle of Utility, would the aggregate effect be counter-utilitarian? I find this difficult to believe.

In the absence of firm evidence, how are we to reason about consequences in this connection? I think we have to reason in terms of plausible precautions. Common experience, one may think, gives us enough evidence of people being tempted, not just to break a coordinative rule like the rule against breaking promises, but to rationalize instances of deviation from the rule, to apprehend that licensing people to deviate on act-utilitarian grounds would lead to quite a lot of deviations, so that these become expected with some probability. That would unsettle expectations about the rule's being heeded and thus would jeopardize the benefits of having the rule.

DISCOVERY BEFORE THE INTERVAL: LEGISLATION BEFOREHAND

The facts about actions A may be discovered before the interval begins, in time for the Community to meet and legislate. If the Community then knew (in addition to the information given above) which number of actions, n_v, would maximize V (the total net benefit from doing actions A), the Principle of Utility would require legislating a special rule. The rule would select a number of agents to do A all of n_v times (and no more) during the forthcoming interval while all other agents were strictly forbidden to do A at all. The collective action of adopting the rule before the interval begins would be act-utilitarian, provided that the rule itself does not introduce new disadvantages that did not figure among those attendant upon doing or failing to do A, like increasing the oppressive effect of being too much bound by too many rules (an effect that is one inspiration for anarchism).

During the interval itself, would it be act-utilitarianism or rule-utilitarianism that prevailed? The rule itself (we are assuming) would be, at bottom, inflexible. Furthermore, every agent with an opportunity to do A would still be in a position, when the opportunity occurred, to reason that neither the actions A (or actions of other sorts) that he knows individual agents have done previously nor the actions A (or actions of other sorts) that would be influenced by his doing A make the benefits of his doing A less than (or even equal to) the disadvantages. The rule therefore contravenes act-utilitarian reasoning carried to this point. On the other hand, given the rule (and the legislation as a previous collective action that must be taken into account), the disadvantages of doing A, except for designated agents doing actions A within their allowance, will outweigh the benefits. Carried to the end, therefore, the reasoning of every agent may be said to be act-utilitarian, though this reasoning is legitimate only because of the acknowledged existence of an inflexible rule. But abiding by the rule will (on the assumptions made) be act-utilitarian in every instance. Thus, of the three 'very serious objections' to rule-utilitarianism that deter T.M. Scanlon from adopting it, the first offers no case to answer. It is that rule-utilitarians are 'hard pressed to explain why, if at base they are convinced utilitarians, they are not thorough-going ones.'[21] Their act-utilitarianism leads them in some circumstances to a collective decision to set up inflexible rules, the hallmark of rule-utilitarianism, but they will be act-utilitarians again in deciding to abide by the rules. (The other two objections have to do, one with justice, the other with a purported dilemma about what rules, ideal or current, to take a stand on. They will be dealt with in due course.)

If n_v were not known, the Community might still be able to arrange to have that number of actions A done (and no more). It might be able to set up a communication centre for use during the interval, legislating beforehand that every agent who did an action A was to report doing it to the centre and every agent considering doing such an action was to obtain from the centre an up-to-date compilation of other agents' reports. Then actions A would be done, one by one, up to the number of n_v such actions each justified by act-utilitarian reasoning; but on the point of doing an $(n_v + 1)$th action A, any agent concerned would refrain. As a quasi-perfect agent in possession (thanks to the communication centre) of the requisite information, she would see that, given all those actions A already done, the harm of doing one more would outweigh the good (and would offset in part the net total benefit, V, previously achieved).

During the interval, every agent will reason as an act-utilitarian about actions A. It is possible for him to justify doing A by such reasoning only so long as every agent is inflexibly following the rule of reporting to the communication centre and seeking information from it. But this makes no difference to the character of his reasoning about actions A. However, what about his reasoning concerning this rule? Here (by contrast with a rule designating n_v agents beforehand) it is by no means obvious that failing to abide by the rule will forfeit some net benefit available to the Community (reduce V from the maximum benefit) or do the Community harm (turn V as an aggregate quantity negative). If the number of actions A reported to the communication centre has not, in fact, yet reached n_v, what harm does an agent do if he disregards how many actions A have occurred? Since the compilation that he would obtain from the centre would not deter him from doing A, what does it matter in his case if he omits to obtain the compilation?

Clearly, an agent would do harm by failing to report doing A when she does it. Failing to report would infallibly lead to more than n_v actions being done by all agents together, so that some agents would be doing net harm, either by reducing V from its maximum or by turning V negative. Abiding by that part of the rule is act-utilitarian in every instance. But the part requiring that information be sought as well as given will rest on another foundation. As regards this part, rule-utilitarianism will prevail. If some agents assume that it is safe to disregard this part of the rule, all agents will assume this (since everyone reasons in the same way). But if all agents act on the basis of this apparent safety, more than n_v actions will be done – in fact, n_h or more, leading to aggregate harm. The only way to prevent this result is for all agents to abide by the second part of the rule. Therefore, all agents will abide by it.

Suppose, finally, that though the situation regarding actions A is discovered before the interval begins, in the sense of knowing that there is some number of actions A after which further such actions move away from the optimum V, but n_v is not known, nor is n_h, and circumstances preclude the community from setting up a communication centre and proceeding as just described. The problem, again, is to modify the situation by legislation so as either to forestall act-utilitarian reasoning during the interval or to supply such reasoning with new premises. What sort of rule should the Community legislate? It might legislate an inflexible rule forbidding every agent to do A. Then rule-utilitarianism would prevail during the interval. In every single instance the attractions of doing A remain unchanged, but if any agent acted upon the attractions, all would do so. The only way available to prevent the aggregate harm consequent upon n_h (or more) agents doing A is for all to abide by the rule and refrain. Therefore all will reason that they must refrain.

Would it not be possible, however, for the Community to obtain some of the benefits of actions A without running the risk that so many such actions would be done as to result in aggregate harm? One way of doing this depends on knowing the range of values in which n_h lies, $n_h - x$ to $n_h + x$ (or at least the lower bound, $n_h - x$, of this range). Suppose the Community legislates that some number of agents are to be designated to do actions A less than $n_h - kx$ times, where kx is some value set prudently larger than x, while other agents are to be forbidden to do A at all. Then, though V, the total net benefit from actions A during the interval, will not necessarily be maximized, it will at least probably be greater than zero. Any rule that had this result would conform better to the Principle of Utility than a rule forbidding every agent doing A. Moreover, experience with situations of the sort assumed might enable the Community to estimate the range of values within which the optimum V falls and in the light of this knowledge stipulate a number of actions A to be done that would have a good chance of falling within that range, as well as falling comfortably short of n_h.

Smart's Mixed Strategies Solution

Smart's Solution

Let us revert to the assumption that the situation regarding actions A is discovered during the interval, while the agents are out of communication with one another. One can hardly help being tantalized by the thought: is there no way, even with this assumption in force, of coordinating the decisions of those quasi-perfect agents so that some actions A are done, in order to reap some of the acknowledged benefits, but fewer than n_h, so that general harm is avoided? Better yet, is there no way of finding and coordinating on the n_v actions that would maximize the total benefit V? Smart has called in game theory to treat the gas-cheat and flower-gardener cases, with results that may come as close to finding n_v and coordinating on n_v actions, when the agents are out of communication with one another, as any approach to the problem is likely to get.

Smart argues that in a society composed entirely of act-utilitarians, individual agents should follow mixed strategies with regard to actions of the sort confronted in the gas-cheat and flower-gardener cases. They should make use of appropriate chance devices to give themselves a certain probability p of doing the action and another probability $(1 - p)$ of refraining from it. Thus:

> Let m be the number of people in the community. Let $f(n)$ be the national damage done by exactly n people disobeying the government's request [not to use excess gas; or not to water gardens]; it will be an increasing function of n. Now if each member of the community gives himself a probability p of disobeying the edict it is easy to determine, as functions of p, the probabilities $p1$, $p2$ ... pm of exactly 1, 2, ... m persons respectively disobeying the edict. Let a be the personal benefit to each person of disobeying the edict. I am, of course, supposing what is perhaps a fiction, that numerical values can be given to $f(n)$ and to a. Then if V is the total benefit to the community we have:
>
> $$V = p1(a - f(1)) + p2(2a - f(2)) + p3(3a - f(3)) + \ldots pm(ma - f(m)).$$
>
> If we know the function $f(n)$ we can calculate the value of p for which $dV/dp = 0$. This will give the value of p which maximizes V.[22]

This argument does open up new possibilities of coordination that are more discriminating in effect than the inflexible, universally prohibitory rule previously discussed. However, the solution to which the argument leads is not quite so attractive from a utilitarian standpoint as it seems at first sight. It certainly seems at first sight that if all agents in the community calculate p and follow the mixed strategy embodying it, that V, the total benefit to the community, will be maximized; that, in other words, n, the number of people disobeying the edict (each once) will probably equal n_v, the number whose disobedience will maximize the total extra benefit to the community of doing any of these acts of disobedience at all (provided at least that a is reinterpreted to include benefits not only to the agent disobeying but also to other people). It seemed so to me, and it would have continued to seem so if I had not taken counsel with a mathematical friend (H. Chandler Davis). His advice enables me to point out that what Smart's solution would maximize is something very different from V, the total benefit, which is a simple function of the number of people disobeying. Smart's solution would maximize E, the expectation of benefit, that is to say, $\sum_{n=0}^{n=m} pnV(n)$. This is the quantity, not V, that is described by the right-hand side of Smart's equation.

Quite consistently with the agents' undertaking to behave so as to maximize E, a chance may remain, perhaps a substantial chance, of so many agents being, in fact, led to disobey that V, far from being maximized, would turn negative. It may be granted that the chances of V's becoming drastically negative – a disaster – would be small.[23] Even so, cautious agents may prefer the no-risk policy of inflexibly obeying the edict.[24] They may be especially inclined to prefer this policy if there are many sorts of actions A_1, A_2, A_3, and so on, all of them avoidable, that would form so many different routes to disaster if a sufficient number were done of any of them. The probabilities of engendering disaster by these different routes may add up to an overall risk large enough to deter the agents from taking the mixed strategies approach to the actions class by class.

These complications are not necessarily unmanageable. However, they are not the only difficulties in accepting Smart's argument, illuminating as it is, as vindicating act-utilitarianism even for agents who are out of communication with one another. In the first place, Smart's assumptions are unrealistic (as he himself freely admits) – indeed staggeringly so. They are several degrees more unrealistic than the assumptions that we worked with above, which led to a rule-utilitarian solution when the situation regarding actions A is discovered during the interval. Smart assumes not merely that a, the benefit to be expected from each action taken singly, is known, but that it is the same amount in the case of every agent. True, the latter assumption is perhaps no more heroic than assuming that a varies between agents (which is by itself more plausible) but that at least some agents know all its values. At least some would have to know, if any were to apply Smart's argument.

The assumption that some agents know the whole function $f(n)$ redoubles the heroism. The most that people are likely to know, in any real situation, are some values of n greater than n_h, which have even stronger implications of disutility, and some values of n at the other end of the range, very much less than n_h. If they expect n_h agents (or more) to be in a position to do actions of the sort in question during a given interval, tempted to do them by various amounts of prospective benefits a, a rule-utilitarian solution emerges; for they cannot undertake Smart's calculations. To be consistent utilitarians they will all have to refrain from doing A.

In the second place, Smart's mixed strategies solution is itself a rule-utilitarian solution.[25] To ward off this judgment, in the revised version of his little book on utilitarianism, Smart has introduced a distinction between rules and conventions (as David K. Lewis understands them).[26] But conventions can be regarded as a variety of rules; and whether rules or conventions figure in the solution, it does envisage circumstances in which the Principle of Utility, as applied to single instances, ought to be set aside and actions done that are counter-utilitarian, taken as single instances. This will happen whenever the chance device dictates that the agent should refrain from doing A. The (virtually legislated) rule or convention that is upheld in such circumstances may be identified as the same rule upheld when the chance device dictates that A is to be done, namely, the rule that the mixed strategy incorporating p is to be followed. It is true (as Smart points out) that this rule is quite unexpectedly different in kind from traditional moral rules. Nevertheless, it is not a rule founded on the Principle of Utility as applied to single instances; it is not a rule liable to variation from instance to instance, considering in each instance actions known to have occurred previously and actions expected to occur subsequently as a result of the one now contemplated. It is a rule founded not merely on those considerations, but also on the application of the Principle of Utility to aggregate effects, including the effects of actions taken independently, parallel to one another but otherwise unconnected.[27]

Improving on Smart's Solution by Prior Legislation

If the situation regarding actions A is discovered beforehand, and the community thus has the opportunity to legislate a rule to take care of the situation, Smart's solution will be discarded. For then we can return to a solution visited earlier in this chapter. Since n_v can be calculated, the community will (as demonstrated above) adopt a rule designating a number of agents to do A all of n_v times during the interval, forbidding other agents to do A at all.[28] This solution (again, as remarked above) would be act-utilitarian in adopting the rule and act-utilitarian in the instances of application, given the presence of the rule. The rule would be adopted on act-utilitarian grounds, and abiding by the rule during the interval would in every instance be justified by act-utilitarian reasoning. However, there is a temptation to act otherwise that the rule forestalls.

Mixtures of Reasoners

Hitherto it has been assumed that every agent would reason in the same way. In circumstances in which act-utilitarianism sufficed, all agents would be act-utilitarians; in other circumstances, for reasons compelling to them all, all would be rule-utilitarians. Among the latter circumstances, however, there are some in which, though the Principle of Utility would be better served by all agents' being rule-utilitarians than it would be by all agents' being act-utilitarians, it would be still better served if some agents were the one and other agents the other. Consider again the circumstances in which the situation regarding actions A is discovered during the interval, without sufficient information coming to light for Smart's mixed strategies solution to be applied. Suppose that in these circumstances it is known that $(n_h - 1)$ or fewer of the agents belonging to the community are convinced act-utilitarians, and so do A, while the rest are convinced rule-utilitarians, who understand the need for a rule to prevent n_h agents from doing A and will virtually legislate for themselves a rule of refraining from doing A, knowing about the others who will do it. More net benefit will be obtained for the community if everyone acts according to these different convictions than will be obtained if all agents are converted to rule-utilitarianism. In the former case, some positive amount of V will be obtained from actions A; while in the latter case, everyone would refrain from doing A, and hence V would be zero.

In such circumstances, Brandt's gas-cheat and Smart's flower-gardener, taking them to be act-utilitarians in a mixed community of act-utilitarians and rule-utilitarians, might go ahead and do A in perfect accord with the Principle of Utility, except insofar as the expectation of their acting contrary to rule might undermine the morale of the rule-utilitarian segment of the community or make social training in ethics less effective.

The exception, of course, is a big one when it applies.

On the point of morale, it does not apply if we preserve our assumption that when the net benefits of an action or policy are greater than the net benefits of the alternative actions or policies contemplated, the benefits will be distributed so that everyone gets what all regard as a fair share. But suppose that the benefits redound exclusively to the act-utilitarians. Then, even if the rule-utilitarians do not suffer any concrete harm, it might well seem to them that the benefits obtained by the act-utilitarians were unjustly obtained; without the uncompensated self-denial of the rule-utilitarians the act-utilitarians could not act.

Moreover, whether or not the rule-utilitarians have this feeling of injustice, would it not damage any system for social training in ethics to discard or flout the premiss that everyone ought to have the same ethics? It may seem obvious that ethical training must be the same for everyone. Yet the circumstances described do suggest that, contrary to the assumptions of philosophers and of traditional morality,[29] uniformity in ethics is not an unmixed good. Moreover, in the circumstances described, though the rule-utilitarians may be under a natural temptation to resent the permission that the act-utilitarians have to do A, would it not be unworthy of them (and their utilitarian principles) to deny that a better social result will, in fact, be obtained by diversity of reasoning and conduct? Are they to be dogs in the utilitarian manger? Furthermore, one might imagine that the special position of the act-utilitarians was not only not resented, but respected. The act-utilitarians might all be retired war heroes, or film stars, or philosophers, granted a franchise to practise act-utilitarianism as people deserving just such a tribute and indulgence.

Extreme Challenges to a Rule

How Judith Dealt with Holofernes

Judith and (the late) Holofernes will appear in a moment. Meanwhile, some preliminary remarks. If the moral community meets to legislate sometime during the minimum interval within which the aggregate effect of agents' freely doing A would be harmful, it may meet in time to recognize that some number of actions A less than n_h have been done, accept without recrimination the good thereby accomplished, and flatly forbid further actions of the same kind until the interval ends (or by some other scheme of limitation, like those discussed earlier, prevent the number from rising to n_h before the end of the interval).

But suppose, as before, that the community will meet again to legislate only at the end of the interval. Then, whatever sorts of agent it consists of, imperfect or quasi-perfect, it will have believed itself compelled, in an act-utilitarian collective decision, to adopt an inflexible rule about actions A before the interval. Now, the case for any such rule will have to be empirical, given that the community is composed of utilitarians. But then, however well-reasoned, it may be a mistaken case. People may discover during the interval that there is no chance that n_h or more actions A will take place during the interval; or that there are no grounds for thinking that greater harm than good would eventuate if they did. On the other hand, suppose that in the instance at hand, it is discovered that doing A will create much greater harm, catastrophic harm. What are these people, acting as individuals, to do?

Their responsibility will be somewhat lightened if the community will soon meet to legislate. Meeting at the end of the interval, the community will be able to weigh the utility gained by adhering to the rule against the utility forfeited by denying any exceptions; it may be expected to correct this and every other rule so far as they need to be modified, in particular usefully modified to incorporate what would otherwise be some exceptions into the rule itself. But this is not an expectation that many people can have in the real world. The large societies characteristic of the real world in modern times do not meet to take up moral legislation. In them, individual agents who have discovered the disutility of rules hitherto thought to be useful cannot be restrained by the promise that the community will legislate on the subject at the earliest opportunity.

There are provisions of sorts for something like moral legislation in such societies – but the provisions are slow, multiple, and confused. Often they will not even be set in motion unless individual moral reformers take the initiative of presenting test-cases of violation. This is how birth control was legitimized during the first part of the twentieth century; and this is how the free choice of abortion has made the progress that it has made toward general acceptance. The old rules are defied; people are punished under the criminal law for defying them; but public clamour mounts until punishing them is no longer popular; then the courts find one way or another of suspending the operation of the old rules.

Now, consider Judith's treatment of Holofernes.[30] Had she not killed him and before killing him deceived him ('Baby, I'll show you a good time!'), her people would have suffered catastrophe at the hands of Holofernes' army: the women and girls raped and enslaved; the men and boys killed, the boy babies dashed to death against the walls. Or let us so suppose. The aggregate gain from having everybody heed the inflexible rules against deceit and murder, Judith might reasonably have judged, was overshadowed in this instance for the whole of any interval reasonable to contemplate (the life of this generation; the life of five, six ... sixteen) by the loss that the decimation or extermination of her people would involve. So she decides to set aside the rules.

Judith herself might have reasoned to her action, not via utilitarian considerations, but thinking as a patriot, with the common good of her people in mind. This is the reasoning typical of all too many cases in which people wage war and inflict death; so it cannot be the conclusion of the reasoning that shocks critics of utilitarianism so much as the calculation of benefits and disadvantages – or at least this would be the case if the critics were more mindful of all the dimensions of traditional moral reasoning displayed in historical issues about life and death. What do the critics offer as an alternative to patriotism or to calculations under the Greatest Happiness Principle? Injury, enslavement, death to hundreds, thousands, millions of innocent people? People uncomfortable about the utilitarian solution to such cases should ask themselves whether there is any solution to the issues posed that they would find entirely satisfactory. The utilitarian cannot find it entirely satisfactory to engage in the torture, deceit, and murder of some people that in one case or another is required to prevent a catastrophe.

Suppose an individual agent like Judith, discounting soberly for her own liability to error, has discovered that a certain inflexible rule is mistaken, and that violating it would do more good than harm – much more good, so much more that it offsets any possible minor mistakes in estimates, even when the scandal of violating it is allowed for. Will she not be bound by the Principle of Utility to violate the rule? But then what, in the end, becomes of rule-utilitarianism? Is not act-utilitarianism finally vindicated? Evidently an agent is bound to heed a rule, however inflexible it purports to be, only so long as acting in accordance with it at least does not make an extreme departure, in the case of any single action, from obtaining more net good. This seems to hold for both sorts of rules distinguished earlier. The rule against murder falls under the first sort of rule, which checks agents from acting (on their own) against the Principle of Utility. The rule against deceit falls under the second sort, which has its justification in bringing about a coordinative effect that would be jeopardized if agents were not checked from acting (on their own) on the Principle of Utility.

Final vindication of act-utilitarianism does not follow. For the discovery that the agent makes, in the circumstances assumed, is not merely a discovery about the alternative actions immediately in prospect. It is also – and more significantly – a discovery about a rule, and about just one rule at that. To discover merely that violating the rule on this occasion would maximize utility, even taking into account the consequences (if any) of the violation in this instance in encouraging violations in subsequent instances and acting accordingly, would not upset the rule. The case for the rule and for the rule's being inflexible stands or falls not on these effects alone, but on the aggregate harm of actions that may be taken quite independently. What the agent discovers, if he discovers that the argument for the rule fails when this instance is taken into account, is that this aggregate harm has been overestimated. His violation can be justified only by proof that upholding the rule in this connection more than offsets the benefit of observing it in other connections. But that proof does not extend to showing that there is never any need for inflexible rules, or even a need for the same inflexible rule in other connections. It does not even extend to bringing into question the validity of such other inflexible rules as may be currently in force. The case for every inflexible rule has to be considered on its own merits.

Let it be noted, furthermore, that the agent's discovery is compatible with either of two very different conclusions respecting future actions of the sort *A* that have hitherto fallen under the discredited rule. At one extreme, it may be the case that in view of the agent's discovery, no inflexible rule can be justified for governing any future actions of this sort. On the other hand, the present inflexible rule may survive in other applications. Or it may be the case that one or more new inflexible rules can be justified as governing one or more subclasses of these actions. It may be better to allow promises to be broken whenever there are utilitarian grounds for breaking them than to have an inflexible rule against breaking promises on any occasion. It may be better still to have an inflexible rule restricted to governing promises (say) in cases in which the harm done by heeding the rule, in the instances where there is harm, never rises above a certain level.

Here, as in other circumstances, utilitarianism reveals a challenge to the adequacy of our institutional means for establishing or ratifying fine discriminations in moral insight. But the position in theory is quite firm. Whatever its difficulties, rule-utilitarianism is not to be surrendered to act-utilitarianism at all times and all places. In some circumstances, depending on the state of the world and on the state of information, act-utilitarianism would displace rule-utilitarianism in circumstances that would otherwise favour rule-utilitarianism. In other circumstances, a consistent utilitarian will have to stand by rule-utilitarianism. So utilitarians will after all support having inflexible rules if those are the only kinds of rules available.

Flexible Rules: Rules Understood as Having Exceptions

Flexible Rules

Are inflexible rules the only kinds of rules available? Ordinary rules – ordinary moral rules – are not inflexible, though people, including philosophers, often talk as if they were. The rule about keeping promises, like moral rules typically, must be supposed to admit of exceptions, some known but cumbersome and distracting to mention in any standard formula, some unknown because never yet encountered. The discretion to make exceptions may be familiar and often used, as it is when commercial contracts call for revision.[31] It is even a virtue to be ready to use the discretion – the virtue that St Thomas calls *epieikeia*.[32]

The presence in the understanding of a given rule of known exceptions (in the case of the rule against homicide, exceptions like self-defence, military action, maybe capital punishment) enables the community, without any resort to new legislation, to capture some of the utility that would otherwise be lost from inflexible adherence to the rule stated in some short, imperatively efficient form ('Do not kill!' 'Keep your promises!'). This does not affect the basic issue. There are rules, and they are to be heeded in the absence of any opportunity to legislate. They are now just more complex rules; and though they demand more sophistication of agents, the sophistication, consisting in the awareness of the known exceptions, is commonly achieved and not especially worrisome in respect to abuse.

Things stand differently with exceptions not anticipated before the demand for making them arises. In a given community, it might be unwise to allow individual agents the discretion to deal with them (except in cases like Judith's of impending catastrophes or the opposite – rare and unrepeatable opportunities for overwhelming benefits). In another community, however, suppose that the agents have become sophisticated in their capacity to allow for known exceptions. They can be trusted, moreover, if they are given the discretion to do so, to make only those unanticipated exceptions that are comparable to the known ones in obtaining net increases in utility or happiness, in some cases actually doing better than not making exceptions in carrying out the purposes of the rules in question. The guard at the city gate may have been the first in the experience of the community to encounter the case in which opening the gate to let in a party of the city's soldiery does more to secure the safety of the city than keeping the gate shut as the rule demands. This case, indeed, shows that contrary to the simplified view of traditional morality, traditional morality does accord agents some discretion in dealing not just with known exceptions, but also with unanticipated ones. If the guard kept the gate closed and the soldiery perished, the city council would be asking the next morning, without thinking they were innovating in morality or common sense, how the guard could have been so foolish.

No doubt incorporating known exceptions into the rules, fully understood or fully set forth, softens the distinction between act-utilitarianism and rule-utilitarianism by capturing some of the benefits that rule-utilitarianism would sacrifice (to gain in the aggregate). Allowing discretion for unanticipated exceptions softens the distinction further, to the point of suggesting that act-utilitarianism is a closer approximation to traditional morality than it might have seemed. The rules become more attractive; but act-utilitarianism becomes more attractive, too, as its objections to rules subside.

Does the distinction between act-utilitarianism and rule-utilitarianism still stand? It does. There will still be cases of the sort (my second sort) in which, in principle, even quasi-perfect agents will need to have coordinative rules. A number of deviations from the rule at issue in any of these cases would produce a net gain in utility or happiness, but a greater number would have a reverse result, with no means for the time being of coordinating the agents' actions so that the greater number will be avoided. The difference from allowing exceptions to rules of the first sort, not specially prized as coordinative devices, whether the exceptions are known or unanticipated, is clear enough on inspection: the allowed exceptions can be made without limit of number and not affect overall utility and happiness adversely. If it is understood that the discretion to make exceptions is to be used not carelessly but judiciously, either in conformity with the known exceptions or in making unanticipated exceptions that can be justified on similar grounds, with the agents who make the exceptions accepting the burden of proof, the problem about coordination will not arise. In neither case will the abnormal actions aggregate to a net loss of benefits.

Normally, the rule will prevail, even in cases where there is some reason to believe, but not conclusive reason, that an exception should be made. Rules with exceptions, the grounds for exceptions, and the burden of proof are all features of the practice in which any rule is embedded; respect for the rule in this practice as a safeguard against the imperfections of agents in information, freedom from bias, and good will emerges with a strong defence of rule-utilitarianism.

Scanlon's Dilemma for Rule-Utilitarianism Vanishing in the Revisionary Process

The distinction between act-utilitarianism and rule-utilitarianism goes through, with places for the reasoning characteristic of each, whether it is feasible to have flexible rules or whether inflexible rules alone are available. In either case, however, the people who hold this position might seem to face 'the acute dilemma' that T.M. Scanlon has put forward as a 'very serious objection' to rule-utilitarianism when they try to specify the rules that they support.[33] 'If,' Scanlon says, 'it is some sort of ideal rules ... general conformity to which would have the best consequences – then the utilitarian case for a concern with rules, rather than merely with the consequences of isolated acts, appears lost ... For ... the benefits from these rules can be gained only if the rules are in fact generally observed. But if, on the other hand, the rules that are to be applied must be ones that are generally observed, the critical force of the theory seems to be greatly weakened.'[34]

The dilemma vanishes if the relation between the ideal rules and the rules now generally observed takes its due place in the process of generating and revising rules, a process that, especially after its very first phases, is dominated by the Revisionary Process. Scanlon takes a static view of the relation, but a dynamic view is appropriate. (The metaphor from physics, time-worn in manifold careless uses, here for once has a reasonably precise application.) A sensible practical program for rule-utilitarians (for me, anyone who agrees that in some circumstances act-utilitarianism must work indirectly by way of rule-utilitarian reasoning) would be to begin by supporting current rules (like the rules about promising and truth-telling and homicide, for example). The program then goes on to consider modifying them stage by stage in the direction of the ideal rules, in the way that allowing for voluntary euthanasia would improve on the current rule or rules against homicide. Criticism, and reform following criticism, would make much of the discrepancy between the current rules and the ideal ones. There is no dilemma here. With the growth of information and improvements in analysis, the rules identified as ideal in themselves may change, but that, too, will lead not to a dilemma but to renewed efforts of criticism and reform in the Revisionary Process.[35]

2

Does Utilitarianism (Bentham's Master-Idea, Applied as Hedonic Act-Utilitarianism or Otherwise) Require Perfect Information about Consequences, Leaving Coordination Problems Aside? No*

Nietzsche (and, before him, Bishop Butler) argued against consequentialism that people are never in a position to know the whole truth about the consequences of their actions. In personal choices this problem can be avoided by acting according to rules. In choices of social policy, we choose likely improvements on a present policy, not as a once-for-all decision, but in the course of a continuing policy-making process that offers room time and again for revisions that correct for adverse developments.

Nietzsche dismissed utilitarianism (hateful to him anyway as an expression of British commercialism and petty-mindedness), because as he reasonably (but mistakenly) thought, it calls for knowing the truth about all the consequences of any proposed action, which is impossible. Thus, as he too hastily concluded, utilitarianism is a theory with no possibility of application, Bentham's innovating efforts and expectations notwithstanding. In a Note of 1888, published with *The Will to Power*, he says, 'The value of an act must be measured by its consequences, the utilitarians say ... But does one know the consequences?

---

* Based on, and in part reprinted from *A Strategy of Decision: Policy Evaluation as a Social Process* by David Braybrooke and Charles E. Lindblom. Copyright © 1963 by The Free Press; copyright renewed 1991 by David Braybrooke and Charles E. Lindblom. So far as reprinted, reprinted with permission of The Free Press, a Division of Simon & Schuster Trade Publishing Group. (I also have permission from my co-author, Lindblom.) Also based in part and in part reprinted from a review essay by me (on a book by Jennifer Hochschild), 'Scale, Combination, Opposition,' in *Ethics*, 95 (July 1985), 920–33, © 1985 by The University of Chicago. All rights reserved. In respect to any reprinting from the essay, reprinted with the permission of The University of Chicago Press.

Perhaps as far as five steps. Who could say what an act stimulates, excites, provokes against itself? As a stimulus? Perhaps as the ignition spark for an explosive?'[1]

Before utilitarianism was named, which was after Bentham wrote, and before Bentham wrote, Bishop Butler, though he did not go so far as Nietzsche, had taken a sceptical view of consequentialism on similar grounds. In his *Dissertation on the Nature of Virtue*, he says,

> We are constituted so as to condemn falsehood, unprovoked violence, injustice, and to approve of benevolence to some preferably to others, abstracted from all consideration, which conduct is likeliest to produce an overbalance of happiness or misery ... [Moreover] though it is our business and our duty to endeavour, within the bounds of veracity and justice, to contribute to the ease, convenience and even cheerfulness and diversion of our fellow-creatures, it is greatly uncertain, whether this endeavour will in particular instances produce an overbalance of happiness upon the whole; since so many and distant things must come into account. And that which makes it our duty is, that there is some appearance that it will, and no positive appearance sufficient to balance this, on the contrary side; and also, that such benevolent endeavour is a cultivation of that most excellent of all virtuous principles, the active principle of benevolence.[2]

If there is a partial defence of utilitarianism in the latter part of Butler's remarks, it is a very weak one, so weak that it invites the objection about not knowing consequences all over again. It is true that the partial defence harmonizes with the point often made on behalf of utilitarianism that, if we take received moral rules as considerations proven by long experience to be reliable if not infallible guides to the best consequences, we do not have to inquire anew about consequences in the instances to which they apply. As William Shaw reminds us and J.S. Mill said before him,[3] we already know a good deal about the typical consequences for human beings of various actions and what we know is for the most part embodied in familiar moral rules. The rules serve as a remedy for dealing with the difficulties of not knowing consequences.

They thus serve to deal with one of the two distinguishable issues that Nietzsche and Butler bring up, the issue that the recent debate about 'consequentialism' has been preoccupied with. This is whether moral agents, making choices with moral significance in their personal lives, are to take consequences into account. I think they inevitably have to do this, sometimes. However, it is not implausible to hold that normally they do not; normally they can act according to rules, the rules that Mill had in mind, the same rules that figured in my preceding chapter as required by imperfect motivation and imperfect information.

It is utterly implausible to suppose that the problem about consequences can be laid to rest in any such way when social policies – to be chosen by political communities or associations – come up for discussion. This is the second of the two issues brought up by Nietzsche and Butler. What is utilitarianism to do about consequences when it is called upon as a guide to social choices? Sometimes – perhaps often – it will be in order to let received social policies, including rules with moral import, stand and to act socially in accordance with them. But even these choices depend on the consequences' being acceptable. Received rules of central moral importance will sometimes require adjustment: The rule against homicide, even that aspect of it that Butler refers to as leading us to condemn unprovoked violence, may require adjustment, given the prospect of alarming consequences (letting an enemy power prepare the destruction of our country), uncomfortable continuing experience with the exception for self-defence, or arguments for voluntary euthanasia invoking the painful consequences of disallowing it.

The problem of consequences returns whenever new social policies – new rules – come up for discussion or arguably unprecedented public actions have to be taken. I do not mean to suggest that this is something entirely distinct from calling for revision in received rules. Voluntary euthanasia can serve again as an issue requiring an unprecedented public action in favour of a new rule, just because the familiar rules do not seem to fit it. The consequences of adopting a new rule as a social policy will have to be looked into. Conservative moralists might wish to stick with the received rules in unchanging circumstances. Circumstances in the modern world, however, are always changing, as technology changes, population increases, and (in some quarters) religion decays. New rules demand consideration affecting the use of land, the conduct of business, personal vehicles, and all manner of other things. But how will any of the proposed new rules work out? In every case, it will be important to consider consequences; but can we know enough about them to make the consideration worthwhile?

The objection, if it can be sustained, bears upon choices of social policy not in rare, even fantastic, circumstances but in normal circumstances.

There is a deep mistake underlying the objection, however, a mistake about how policy-making is carried on. It is a double mistake: first, of ignoring the possibility, which exists for any approach to policy-making, of revising policies stage by stage after they have been adopted; and, second, a mistake that betrays attachment, more or less conscious, to a conception of policy-making that to its great cost disregards the way in which current processes for evaluating consequences, making decisions about them, and carrying out the decisions have adapted to the possibility of revising them afterwards. It is, again, a relatively static conception, which may embrace changes in policy but does not take into account how the process of policy-making is continuous from before adopting the changes to, endlessly, afterwards. We do not ever know the whole truth about consequences; but, as a fuller understanding of how policy-making is carried on makes clear, we do not have to know the whole truth about consequences to deal with them effectively.

The policy-making process came in for some emphatic attention at the end of the preceding chapter, but for all the fuss made about it in my Introduction, where was it during the body of the chapter? It was there, not fussed about in exactly the same terms as in the Introduction, but visible and important if it was looked for. The argument about the considerations that generate rule-utilitarianism turned on the availability or non-availability, full or intermittent, and if intermittent frequent or infrequent, of a policy-making process. The policy-making process was not perhaps the dominant theme of the chapter. It will be in this chapter, where rule-utilitarianism continues to be the version of utilitarianism normally at stake. The policy-making process will also be a prominent theme in several of the chapters to come.

Infinitely Many Consequences, or At Least Unmanageably Many? Some Logical Features of the Concept of Consequences

If the various distinct consequences of any action were literally infinite, one would certainly have to grant that the consequences could not be known. There are not literally an infinite number of consequences, but the practical difficulty about getting a manageable account of them is almost as bad. One cannot go on counting consequences to infinity, because consequences cannot be counted at all. There is no principle of identity to tell us, given a topic that serves as a source of consequence-statements, when we are dealing with two consequences or with one consequence described in different ways; or whether we should count only general consequences and not partial aspects of them. (Consider, for example, the statements, 'It was a consequence of the mill's closing that a number of men lost their jobs'; 'It was a consequence of the mill's closing that unemployment figures in the town surpassed the worst figures of the Thirties'; 'It was a consequence of the mill's closing that John Weaver lost his job.' Have we two consequences here, or one, or three?) These difficulties afflict attempts to get manageably adequate accounts as much as they do accounts that aim to be complete.

A given issue about what course of action to adopt may raise a number of topics. Can we firmly distinguish between topics? How distinct is the topic of local workers losing their jobs from the topic of the variation over time of local employment? To the extent that topics can be distinguished, we would still have unmanageably many consequences assignable to any given topic. They would form families of consequences, indistinctly bounded to the extent that the topic is indistinctly bounded, and none of them susceptible of complete enumeration. Further consequences will come up without any easily specifiable limit of time and in respect to multiple formulation. One event is a consequence of another; it, in turn, has later, multiply formulated consequences of its own; and so on without limit. Yet there is no criterion in ordinary language, much less any unique system for categorization, that allows us to judge events not to be consequences because they are too remote in time.

Some philosophers (e.g., J.J.C. Smart) have thought that the influence of a present event becomes negligible over time, considering the many events with causal influence that may intervene. They were thinking, I expect, of personal actions rather than social policies like the migration of a whole population to another continent. Even so, they would not seem to have taken sufficiently into account the large consequences for the world climate that chaos theory is ready to trace to a tiny event – a butterfly flapping its wings in Mexico.

The *jeu d'esprit* that people sometimes play with historical consequences (like tracing the discovery of America under Spanish auspices to the attractions that Cleopatra offered Caesar and Antony – think of her pretty nose!) gives results that would not be amusing if they were not felt to be far-fetched. They would not be amusing, however, if they were senseless results, whether or not we bring in chaos theory. None of the concepts employed is used inconsistently or incoherently. If they push too far, they do not push over any exact boundary.

Not only are the formulas attributing consequences to a given action liable to unlimited multiplication; there is considerable incentive to multiply the formulas, since a further one may always serve the turn of someone advocating any course of action or resisting it. If this is sometimes an abuse, it is one that cannot be stopped without a good impartial reason for cutting short the account of consequences. So the abuse hardly aggravates matters; the good impartial reason is absent when there are no abuses; abuses or not, there are unmanageably many consequences to consider. One might always cut off the account just at the point in time or in breadth of investigation at which over-whelmingly injurious consequences began emerging.

The (Misguided) Synoptic Conception of Policy-Making

The embarrassment of being unable to obtain complete and accurate accounts of consequences afflicts with particular intensity the synoptic conception of evaluation and policy-making, though the conception is insensitive to the embarrassment. The synoptic conception falters in any attempt to apply it, so only by taking some licence with language can it be called an approach to policy-making, much less a procedure for policy-making. In the book that C.E. Lindblom and I wrote together attacking the synoptic conception, *A Strategy of Decision: Policy Evaluation as a Social Process,*[4] we cite as one champion of the conception the distinguished Dutch economist Jan Tinbergen. In his book, *Economic Policy: Principles and Design,*[5] Tinbergen ascribes to an ideal policy-making process the following features. (1) The policy-maker should work with an agreed-upon set of values; (2) he should clearly formulate the aims to be pursued in advance of choosing among alternative policies; (3) he should undertake a comprehensive overview of policy problems and of alternative policies; (4) he should accept the responsibility for coordinating the policy to be chosen with other policies; (5) as an economist he should undertake to take a comprehensive view of economic values and variables. What could seem more sensible?

The conception attracts professional students of public administration as well as economists. Lindblom and I cite Marshall Dimock as saying, 'First, there are always the problem and the issues. Second, there are the facts and analysis that need to be applied to the issues. Third, there is the setting forth of alternatives and the pros and cons applicable to each possible solution – all this in the light of larger institutional goals and objections. Fourth, there is the decision proper, which depends upon choosing among alternatives.'[6] We need not wonder at finding Dimock adopting the synoptic conception. It figures in the common understanding of rationality, whether or not this is elaborated as in the economist's theory of rational choice for a consumer or an entrepreneur. Harold Lasswell says, without questioning the propriety, so far as they go, of such theories, 'Rational theories typically assume that the chooser is able to specify his preferred events under all the contingencies that would occur in an exhaustive map of expectation.'[7]

One unsophisticated argument for attempting to apply the synoptic conception as an approach to policy-making is an argument seductive even to people who have some idea of the difficulties of working out adequate accounts of consequences. The argument is that the policy that we have decided upon will turn out to be a mistaken one if it has intolerable consequences that we omitted to consider, a worse mistake if we passed over more eligible alternatives that had been open to us. So must we not consider all consequences beforehand?

There is another idea that heightens the attractions of the synoptic conception: the logical or mathematical elegance of a rational-deductive system for choice, like the multi-dimensional preference map attributed to an ideal consumer or, at the social level, a complete social welfare function. The solutions deduced from a rational-deductive system will be untrustworthy, by the very assumptions of those methods, if they are not comprehensive solutions, as will the solutions that might be sought for with a Benthamite calculus. How can they be comprehensive if they leave any consequences out? It is no good (given the synoptic conception) suggesting that one can make do with reasonably reliable approximations. No approximations can be relied on to take into account every crucial factor; the solution may fail to be comprehensive not only on minor points but on the very points that lead to disaster.

One way of trying to save the synoptic conception from the embarrassment of consequences would be to ignore themes of value that require consequences to be considered. That would be preposterous; for it would mean omitting to consider health, happiness, welfare, cultural progress – the themes most prominent in utilitarian thinking, theoretical and applied, as in the thinking of the general public; it would mean setting aside even the future performance of duties and the future respect for rights, two concerns prominent with anti-utilitarian thinkers. For these, too, figure in the consequences of actions and policies. Even if questions about what are duties and rights now could be resolved without considering consequences, the resolution would not eliminate all grounds for considering them among the consequences of present decisions.

Another way of trying to save the synoptic approach would be to allow that consequences are to be considered, but to assume, first, that all the consequences that need to be identified can be inferred from the theories of social science that happen to be on hand; second, that the time at which the world or at least human history will come to an end is known; and, third, that there is (at least in the mind of anyone adopting the synoptic approach to evaluation) a complete system of values that will not change. No consequences that seem intolerable now will turn out to be tolerable in the future; or vice versa. These assumptions are equally fantastic.

For the synoptic conception to be of any use at all, short of being fully realized, there must at least be a criterion for judging an account of consequences entirely sufficient even though incomplete. Is a criterion to be supplied by stipulation? However, stipulation will not eliminate the consequences that are to be disregarded. It will just sideline them. In general, such a stipulation would have the effect simply of giving arbitrary sanction to an arbitrary limitation, but this is bankruptcy for the synoptic conception, which calls for being not arbitrary but complete.

H.L.A. Hart and A.M. Honoré, in *Causation in the Law*,[8] describe certain restrictions that commonly govern the ascription of consequences to given actions. For example, consequences will not be traced back beyond certain sorts of intervening actions. If one man drops a match, but the ensuing fire would have gone out if a second man had not fanned it back into life, then subsequent damage would be a consequence of the second man's action, but not of the first's. Restrictions of this kind do not dispose of the problem of consequences. It does not follow, from the application of the cited restriction, that only a manageably small number will be left to evaluate. Moreover, the restriction can be applied only retrospectively. It is no actual help to agents or policy-makers trying to evaluate actions and policies beforehand.

In general, one cannot assume beforehand that the chain of consequences will be broken, at a specifiable time, by an intervening action on someone else's part.

After shifting to a view of policy-making that is serial and revisionary and thus in accord with real current processes, there are at least two things that have to be done for utilitarianism in answer to the objection about unmanageably many consequences. First, it must be shown that utilitarianism can be associated with reasonably specific ways of selecting the consequences that are to be considered in evaluating actions and policies. Second, it must be shown that utilitarianism deals as prudently as possible with the inevitable danger that some important consequences may be overlooked (partly because not all the consequences will have been identified). Synoptic use of the felicific calculus is of no help to utilitarianism in either connection. The strategy of disjointed incrementalism, which I am about to describe, provides as much help as, in the nature of things, can he hoped for.

The Strategy of Disjointed Incrementalism

To the 'synoptic' conception of policy-making, which formally requires taking into account all the consequences beforehand, Lindblom and I (with Lindblom taking the lead) have opposed the strategy of disjointed incrementalism, which makes full use of the Revisionary Process touched on at the end of the last chapter. The strategy rejects the synoptic approach to take into account the serial nature of policy-making, which allows for repeated revisions in various stages after the initial adoption of a policy. It also aligns the theory of policy-making, as the synoptic conception does not, with current policy-making processes in which stage-by-stage revisions prominently figure. I shall combine an incrementalism having these features with utilitarianism, treating the strategy as the vehicle for applying utilitarianism and, in particular, for dealing with the problem about not knowing all consequences.

To begin, I shall have in mind circumstances in which the virtues of the strategy manifest themselves, and I shall be giving little or no attention to other circumstances in which the strategy does not work well. For the time being, I shall give little or no attention, either, to other approaches to policy-making that may displace the strategy there, and sometimes even, misguidedly, in circumstances suited to the strategy. The synoptic conception will never replace the strategy, because it is wholly impractical – a fantasy. The strategy shines by contrast.

However, it must be borne in mind that there is the other contrast to draw, not just between theories but in practice, when one feature or another of the strategy is misused, or has to be modified or set aside because the circumstances call for another approach. I shall get around to discussing these qualifications in due time.

The inadequacy of the synoptic conception in the face of the general problem about consequences is no accident. It ignores the intractable multiplicity of the values that may bear upon the choice of policies or actions – and hence upon the greatest happiness – the conflicts among these values, their lack of exact formulation, and their liability to change with new experience and new information. The synoptic conception is not adapted to the limited problem-solving capacities of human beings any more than it is to the inadequacy of the information with which these capacities are fated to deal – an inadequacy hard to improve on because getting more information is generally expensive. The synoptic conception is not adapted to the diverse and complex forms in which problems about the choice of actions and policies often present themselves. It gives no help, furthermore, with the question of how its failures can be overcome by limited practical remedies arrived at by suitably cautious procedures. It is not useful, invoking the ideal, to suggest, 'Come as close as you can!' How could we tell how close we have come? (There is also a technical reason, put forward in 'the general theory of the second best,'[9] arguing that we may go far astray from the optimum in trying to settle for second best.) These are the grounds for saying that the synoptic approach does not even offer a useful ideal.

By contrast, the strategy of disjointed incrementalism, whether or not under that name, is in familiar use. (Indeed, so much in use that it is hard to find instances of non-incremental policies that are not imaginary, like collectivizing agriculture in Canada from sea to sea – or instances, in the Soviet Union, China, or Cambodia, of revolutionary excess.) Consider its application to the agonizing problem created for urban amenities by traffic congestion. (Traffic congestion looks like something very distant from the moral issues raised by justice, promises on desert islands, deathbed undertakings, or euthanasia, but it is characteristic of utilitarianism to take matters like traffic congestion seriously. It not only affects urban amenities – by making the air that city-dwellers must breathe unpleasant to smell and dangerous to inhale, or by making it impossible to carry on a conversation in a normal tone of voice on the sidewalk [a criterion for assessing congestion proposed by the British urban planner Sir Colin Buchanan]. The polluted air also endangers their health in various serious ways, as does the nervous strain and frustration of getting about in congested areas. And these are only the beginnings of the evils that have to be considered.)[10]

Were someone using the strategy to take present problems about automobile traffic in a central city as a point of departure, she would ask how the congestion could be reduced, or how at least the growth in congestion could be reduced.[11] The strategy calls for identifying – and making, since it is a strategy not only for evaluation, but also for choice – marginal, incremental improvements. What is 'incremental?' *A Strategy of Decision* defines the term as 'a change in a relatively unimportant variable or [a] relatively unimportant change in an important variable' (64). For 'variable,' we can read 'feature' and thus move away from consciously scientific theses about society to theses that people in general may be expected to share with social scientists. People in general know that changing from an absolute monarchy to a democratic parliamentary system is a change in an important feature; legislating to celebrate national holidays on the nearest Monday to anniversary dates is something that people in general will recognize as an incremental change. To extend the area of the central city subject to metered parking is incremental; to do away with private automobiles overnight is not. The definition, inevitably loose, works well enough, though it will have to be qualified later in this discussion as relative to a given jurisdiction, large or small. I shall also offer an alternative definition, in which to be incremental is to leave in force institutional insurance that can compensate for untoward consequences.

The strategy has further features. It is, as in the example just given, remedial in orientation. A difficulty about social activity or the environment invites attention; maybe it persists long enough to compel attention. Thus, the Revisionary Process is engaged, first, in contemplating revision of present policy, but then in following up the revisions introduced, to revise during further rounds of discussion as called for. Here, the strategy works serially, to follow up one improvement with another, extending the area already subject to metered parking, but also to revise or even revoke improvements that turn out to be questionable. It will cease to demand that new office buildings incorporate garages, since the result will be to bring yet more traffic into the central city.

The strategy considers only a limited number of alternatives (strictly speaking, a limited number of alternative formulations of consequences)

– charging a price to motorists for using streets in the central city; staggering working hours; extending metered parking – and a limited number of consequences for each. The number is, to be sure, always expansible, though not randomly or idly, instead in a typical case (when the process is working well) only for pressing reasons. Since many people and groups may participate, alternatives left out of account by some participants will often be explored by other participants, typically by the very people and groups most concerned to get attention for those alternatives.[12] Those same people and groups will have an incentive to support, even invent, redesigned alternatives and on occasion bring in further values that will supersede the ones originally motivating the choice of policies.

The strategy may move, not always from objectives (remedial, incremental improvements) to identifying alternative means, but sometimes from means in hand to objectives (other, perhaps more eligible improvements) that could be pursued with them. Metered parking was introduced to benefit motorists by making sure that lots of people got a chance to park; it was discovered that metered parking effectively deterred people from commuting by car to the central city in the expectation they could leave their cars parked along the streets all day. Supposing that a reduction in traffic congestion (or a check to its growth) answers to utilitarian prescriptions for happier city life, this becomes the utilitarian choice of policy. The value of making things easier for motorists wanting to park in the central city gives way to the superseding value of checking congestion.

Operations under the strategy are not neatly systematic, or even coordinated. That is why Lindblom insisted on calling the strategy 'disjointed.' If it leads to various participants' acting at cross-purposes with one another on a given issue, that presents (along with the value of having multiple views) a particular problem about coordination to be solved, perhaps ad hoc, with little or no thought of setting a precedent, though there may be a call for adopting a precautionary procedure specific to issues of the sort in question.

How the Strategy Works on Consequences Beforehand: Precautionary Virtues of the Strategy

For my purposes in the present book, the strategy of disjointed incrementalism makes its most significant contribution to the defence of utilitarianism by dealing with things as they stand after actions have been taken and after policies have been given effect, successful or unsuccessful. However, the features of the strategy may also be looked upon as precautionary virtues that do something to reduce alarm beforehand about possible consequences; and I shall first treat the features as precautionary virtues. William Shaw says that utilitarians expect agents to make decisions on the basis not of actual outcomes, but of expected outcomes, and on this basis are held responsible.[13] This is partly right: agents can have beforehand only information about expected outcomes. But of course it is the actual outcomes that count in the end; the problem for the agents beforehand is to deal with expected outcomes in a way that, so far as possible, will avoid untoward actual outcomes and make it possible to cope with them when they occur, expected or not. This requires not just assembling a judiciously selected body of information about expected outcomes; it also requires dealing with the inevitable incompleteness of information in a suitably cautious way. Decisions must therefore be made in a way that keeps in mind a more complex relation between expected outcomes and actual outcomes than is implied by simply directing attention to expected outcomes.

Evaluations by a Single Policy-Making Agent

The strength of the strategy lies to a great extent in its use in a social process. Yet a number of its features can be heeded in practice (though perhaps not so fully) by single agents acting, not on choices in their personal lives, but in a policy-making capacity – single voters perhaps, empowered officials, advisers to government, independent critics – and it clarifies the theory of these matters to bring in the social process later. For the time being, I shall proceed on the assumption that we have in view a single agent evaluating the consequences of alternative social policies (maybe proceeding to a choice of policy following the evaluation).

PEREMPTORY VALUES

Does the untidiness of real processes of policy evaluation and policy-making mean that anything goes? Far from it. The process may be governed – it typically is governed – in orientation and specific operations by ethical values. It is a way to apply utilitarianism, and though such an application makes the pursuit of meliorative values central (the Greatest Happiness itself; many intermediate considerations instrumental to the Greatest Happiness), the pursuit of them may be constrained in practice by a number of peremptory values. People involved in the policy-making (not all of them necessarily utilitarians) will insist upon such constraints.

A meliorative value is one that presents itself in different strengths for different alternatives. It calls for comparing alternatives, in respect to its strength for each, before passing judgments on alternative actions or policies. Alternatives, for example, may contribute more strongly or less strongly to the general happiness. (Utilitarian values – the Greatest Happiness itself; and intermediate instrumental values – are both meliorative and distributive: it matters what proportion of the affected population shares in their realization and to what degree.) A peremptory value is one that does not wait upon comparing alternatives; it can be invoked to endorse out of hand, peremptorily, actions or policies that have certain compelling features, for example, divine prescription. Other peremptory values can be used to dismiss out of hand actions or policies that have certain intolerable features, for example, putting an innocent person to death. Somewhat less poignantly, a peremptory value placed on privacy might forestall monitoring cars and drivers so closely in the course of controlling traffic congestion that the drivers can no longer carry on complicated private lives.[14]

Peremptory values have often figured in objections to utilitarianism; they figure in some of the objections taken up in separate chapters of the present book. Utilitarianism can fend off the objections, and that is the general line that I take with them. Alternatively, utilitarian doctrine may be modified to accommodate the objections by constraining the sets of alternatives and consequences to suit, though the more peremptory values that are accepted from the objections and accommodated, the more one may wonder whether the theory is still utilitarianism. True, one may define utilitarianism as any ethical doctrine that has a place in the last resort, after the operation of various constraints, for having decisions turn on variations in such a meliorative value as human welfare or happiness. Then very few ethical doctrines will not be versions of utilitarianism, though there will be some – the Ten Commandments or the Book of Leviticus – presented on the theory that what God demands suffices to constitute the content of ethics.

An intermediate position offers itself visibly short of this extreme. Some peremptory values (as we shall see in the next two chapters) figure explicitly or implicitly in how utilitarianism is defined for application. They are operating features of the theory. Other peremptory values (as shown in the previous chapter) can be supported as implications of utilitarianism – embodied in rules that utilitarianism argues for. Our concern here is not with any permanent modification of utilitarianism as a theory, but with temporary, ad hoc uses of peremptory values to assist with the consideration of consequences by putting some consequences out of consideration beforehand, before a given choice of actions or policies is made. These ad hoc uses may represent so many present pressures on policy-makers, who, utilitarian though they may be in conviction, must accept it that the best that they can do for the moment is adapt themselves to the pressures and compromise to get something of what they want done. For example, they will be able to establish family-planning clinics with public funds, but not have them give advice about abortion. This adaptation will at least have the advantage of making the set of consequences to be considered limited in certain ways and hence more manageable.

Peremptory values may come into discussion as themes, without being exactly defined and without being associated with specific rules. It is convenient for my purposes, however, to suppose that, after they have been brought in, rules – at least tentative and temporary ones – are the vehicles that carry them to application. Such rules, which may range from not sacrificing innocent lives to not increasing the tax burden on the elderly or on disabled veterans, help define the perspective in which for the time being policy problems are approached and within which the strategy – or utilitarianism-with-the-strategy – operates. Policies that run counter to peremptory prohibitions will be ruled out of discussion, regardless of any meliorative case that may be built up for them by the operation of the strategy. Policies that, alone of the suggested alternatives, are favoured by a peremptory prescription (like that of keeping the promises entailed by a contributory public pension plan) will be adopted without further ado.

People who use the strategy can have no complaints about this procedure unless they happen to reject the peremptory themes that the rest of the community finds decisive. They themselves, we may presume, are attached to peremptory themes of their own. This attachment, as Butler held, is a normal characteristic of human beings. It may also be, in effect, an indispensable device for limiting and focusing comparisons as the strategy requires, though we have supposed that other factors have a part in determining perspectives – habit and tradition, for example, and the scope of received social science.

When it is allied with the strategy of disjointed incrementalism, utilitarianism thus accepts, in practice and at least ex tempore, some peremptory moral judgments that have been made objections to it. This is not to say that the judgments will always guide the strategy to good results. If the strategy is lucky in application, there may be enough agreement on an array of peremptory values for them to serve as shared rebuttable presumptions,[15] and there may be results both unambiguous and generally accepted as good. If the strategy is not lucky, however, the peremptory values advanced by various parties active in the policy-making process may create deadlock.[16] Equally bad, if not worse, compromising with the peremptory values urged upon it in a given practical context, utilitarianism may sacrifice too much in its own basic concerns, and the values may lead policy-making astray in other ways (e.g., by giving disproportionate weight to objections mistaken about the facts).

REMEDIAL ORIENTATION

The remedial orientation of the strategy may be adopted by a single policy-making agent as well as in a social process. The orientation helps to save utilitarianism from many conflicts with peremptory rules (in addition to those already accepted as constraints) by insisting on having remedies when the rules have been violated – especially, as it may turn out, systematically violated – which may suggest defects in the rules, and by concentrating upon remedies in other connections. The sting in many objections to utilitarianism lies in the supposition that utilitarianism would override important moral considerations – peremptory rules about justice, for example – in order to achieve benefits to some extent gratuitous – to increase, for example, the happiness of people who are already happy. If what is in view, however, are, besides violations of peremptory rules, impairments to the well-being of various members of the population – contamination of their water supply; failures of the schools in teaching literacy; and, yes, growing traffic congestion – gratuitous benefits are not in question. The remedial orientation does not entirely exclude objectionable sacrifices, since some remedies may entail sacrificing some people's happiness (or even their lives) to that of other people. (This issue will be dealt with in the two chapters following.) The remedial orientation has a further effect upon the survey of alternative actions and policies beforehand, together with their expectable consequences. The synoptic approach encourages people to cast about, it may be in flights of fancy, for what may be imagined to be optimal alternatives well beyond the bounds of present policies. Besides complicating policy-making in other ways, casting about so widely inevitably increases the number and variety of alternatives to be considered. Confining the alternatives to remedies for a specific current problem puts many alternatives and many consequences aside. It is not an optimizing approach, but a satisficing one, which stops (at least for the time being) with adequate remedies.[17]

REDESIGNING (THE REVISIONARY PROCESS BEFOREHAND); SUPERSESSION

The redesigning and superseding features of the strategy can be heeded by a single policy-making agent, though not generally with the variety of ideas that may be generated in an active social process when it is working at its best. For a single agent can perceive that a policy not at first contemplated would do better on one or more scores than the policies that she first considered, or, whether or not it does better on each of these scores, that it will still offer a combination of benefits in which it excels the other proposals and embodies an attractive compromise. For example, the agent hits upon the idea that it will be more efficient – fewer missed renewals, less need for reminders – to have drivers' licences renewed on their birthdays than on the anniversaries of the days on which the licences first were taken out. Or the agent may see that a compromise policy, not hitherto considered, will preserve the most important historic amenities of the city and at the same time allow for considerable new development and the construction jobs that the development will generate.

In these cases none of the values at stake drops out of consideration and no new ones may be brought in. But there may also be supersession of values: to cite again a humble case, the objective of reducing the amount of traffic in the central city supersedes the value of giving motorists a better chance to park there.

Supersession, as I am thinking of it here, means that themes originally thought to call for concentrated attention are superseded by others, which may sometimes be more general ones, though still only instrumental to the Greatest Happiness (the health of children being superseded by the health of the community), sometimes quite different ones (no longer how metered parking can serve motorists, but how it can be used to deter them from commuting into the central city). Supersession, in effect, establishes an ad hoc order of priority among different values. Under the strategy, and likewise for the single decision-maker, the order of priority adopted in a given dispute is determined, moreover, if it has to be determined at all, ad hoc (and probably not in ways that are easily isolated from the ways in which the dispute as a whole converges on a solution). Often, however, the question of priority can be entirely evaded by the Revisionary Process as it operates before deciding upon an action or policy. Within the limits of their opportunities, people using the strategy will seek, for political reasons, to redesign policy alternatives so that all the values that have been invoked in discussion favour the policies that are finally advocated. It is often perfectly possible in practice to find the various compensating features needed, regardless of the difficulties of formulating a general solution to the problem of combining values.

INCREMENTAL ALTERNATIVES

A single agent can act as the strategy calls for in limiting the set of alternatives that he considers to incremental ones. The agent will not spend any time working out the advantages and disadvantages of abolishing private automobiles or of collectivizing agriculture in Canada from sea to sea. He will look at measures that would reduce traffic congestion in the central cities to some significant degree, or at least check its growth. If he is dealing with the problems of farmers, he will look at measures that would encourage them to form cooperatives for purchasing equipment and supplies or for marketing their products.

The predictions on which the agent will be relying in contemplating remedial, incremental solutions for current problems will be, ceteris paribus, predictions of the ordinary kind, subject to ordinary kinds of failure. By favouring limited, incremental departures in policy, the strategy does, however, improve the chances that the predictions will be reliable. The changes contemplated under the strategy are not only relatively less drastic; they also take place within a range of moves for which there is usually a concentration of information in the community.

Those using the strategy, or operating as single agents in its spirit, endeavour to preserve the known benefits of present policies while eliminating some at least of the known disadvantages. They will want to have the central city go on being accessible to commuters from every direction but get rid of the traffic jams on the most crowded routes into the city. Because the discussion is focused in this way, the advantages and disadvantages of all the alternatives brought up can be considered more systematically. The deliberation, by single agents or in a social process, will thus have something like a defined agenda. Alternatives, with their consequences, will be discussed extensively, but not aimlessly. Whatever information is mobilized will run less risk of being lost from sight because of wild fluctuations in the terms of discussion, a point that no one will undervalue who has ever sat in a committee.

INSTITUTIONAL INSURANCE

A single policy-making agent, though she cannot by herself be expected to supply institutional insurance, can be mindful, when she decides upon what actions and policies to favour, of the need to make reasonably sure that they do not outrun the capacity of current institutions to correct for mistakes. What is required in the real world, instead of vain endeavours to identify and evaluate all the consequences of given actions or policies, is to make sure (as sure as reasonable prudence requires) that when unforeseen consequences do appear, they will be manageable ones. They will be manageable if they fall within the capacity of continuing institutions to undo or to remedy.

Among the institutions important in this connection, which a policy-making agent should avoid impairing, are the central features of popular government: periodic elections and regular sessions of the legislature, both of which guarantee periodic opportunities for the Revisionary Process to operate as policies are reviewed, though they cannot guarantee that the opportunities will be used or wisely used. Again, however, groups alert to their own interests will make themselves heard. A policy-making agent should not think of removing their opportunities to do so; in effect, she should respect the social process in which the strategy can fully operate. Other institutions provide ways of suspending the operation of policies until they can be submitted for legislative review; and ways, either automatic or discretionary, of relieving immediate suffering, pending the reaction of other agencies. There are courts to which injured persons can resort for redress of grievances. There are various welfare schemes for making sure that people are extricated from floods, resettled, given unemployment benefits, supplied with food and medical care. There are discretionary funds and emergency powers in the hands of officials with various responsibilities in and above the public bureaucracies, and there are ways of creating temporary new agencies, public or private, to deal with crises. When a policy goes wrong, there is usually a way of immediately remedying its most urgent disadvantages. The capacity to supply such remedies is one of the tests of an adequate political organization – indeed, of an adequate social organization of any kind. (Of course, a given society may fail the test, in various ways: by not having appropriate agencies; or by having the agencies, but agencies too inefficient or corrupt to do the job.[18])

The presence and relevance of these institutions is so obvious that it may be asked why they need to be mentioned at all – or at the very least, why so much should be made of the obvious and commonplace. Yet, as is often the case in philosophy, the obvious and commonplace have to be brought back into view to check the operation of seductive but misguided ideas, in this case the ideas that encourage people to adopt the synoptic conception and delude themselves that it can be applied.

Further light can now be cast on the significance of insisting on limited, incremental departures. Limited departures are, in general, better insured, as single agents can recognize. They are safer because they leave so much more room, in the way of other factors that can be adjusted, for remedying unforeseen consequences. In particular, the inclination of the strategy – the virtue of incrementalism – is to shun any policies whose scope is such that if they miscarry, the evils will exceed the remedial powers of existing institutions. This inclination does not rule out innovations, even far-reaching innovations, but it does require that insurance be in force for each step. Conceivably, agriculture in Canada could be collectivized, step by step, from sea to sea, within twenty, even ten, years if the consequences at each stage were favourable or could be made so by remedies.

What I have just said may be regarded as making (or hypothesizing) an empirical connection between incrementalism, defined in terms of the contrast between important and unimportant features of a society, and having effective institutional insurance. But the connection may be converted into a definitional one: an incremental policy is one that leaves effective institutional insurance in force; a policy that leaves effective institutional insurance in place is an incremental one. For a change, great or little, in an unimportant feature of society will fall within the institutional insurance in force, as will a minor change in an important feature, and vice versa.

The Strategy Fully Realized, Not with a Single Policy-Making Agent, but in a Social Process

All the virtues of the strategy discussed so far amplify and strengthen, as a matter of probable empirical fact, when we apply them, not to decision-making by a single policy-making agent, but to a suitable social process of discussion, evaluation, and choice. This shift of focus removes the problem about consequences from its usual locus in ethical theory, which is the single agent. Indeed, the upshot of the shift is a focus twice removed from the usual one: first, from the single agent engaged in personal choices; second, from the single agent concerned with choices of social policy. The shift transforms the problem, in a way already foreshadowed in treating, as I just did, a single policy-making agent as being mindful of the capacity of social institutions to manage mistakes.

Concentrating attention on the responsibility of a single moral agent incites exaggerated fears about overlooked consequences in personal choices, a fear that reappears with choices of social policy. The institutional environment in which any given agent acts is left unspecified; at most, it figures among the passive data of his problems. He is considered as acting upon his environment. Possibly it responds to his actions, but it does not participate in making decisions. He is all alone so far as his decisions are concerned. It is not contemplated that there is some way in which he can parcel out parts of his problem-solving task to the agents and institutions surrounding him. Moreover, for some philosophers, his task is not only lonely: it is fateful in the highest degree. Each agent acts irrevocably, once and for all. Each in acting assumes responsibility for the whole of the future so far as it will be affected by his present action.

The fears generated by this view can be avoided by recognizing it for what it is – a fantasy induced by excessive abstraction. Agents in the real world, even if they are acting under assignments of responsibility for social policy, do not assume responsibility for the whole of the future. It would not be ethical perfection for them to assume such responsibility; it would be madness, as it would be in personal choices. Nor do agents in the real world usually act irrevocably. Why should they be supposed to forget, in ordinary moral situations, that they will have future opportunities for intervening, singly or in combination with other agents, opportunities that they may watch for and use? Even if each agent were acting entirely by himself – in social policy, an autocrat – he could place some reliance on his capacity to steer away from dangers when he came upon them.

Moreover, he is not acting alone. The most important fact about responsibility in the real world is that it is defined and limited by a person's social role. There are institutions surrounding him that may be called upon to assist in dealing with unexpected and untoward consequences. The overall task of anticipating and dealing with consequences is parcelled out among different people and different institutions. If one considers the implications of these forms of assistance being available, the moral problem about unforeseen consequences takes on an entirely different aspect. There may be no way of foreseeing all the consequences of an action or policy. There are ways of taking precautions, exceeding the powers of any single agent, when the consequences are troublesome in ways unforeseen.

The strategy of disjointed incrementalism allows for – indeed, capitalizes upon – a variety of personal tastes, interests, attachments, and obligations, and it envisages the mutual accommodation through free discussion of persons and groups with different standpoints. A single policy-making agent, as I have noted, could try to anticipate what a discussion would bring up; but a real discussion is often more reliable in activating different standpoints and inciting a variety of proposals and arguments. Even a splendid success in evaluation by a single, policy-oriented agent is likely to reflect the real presence of a variety of other agents and investigators with whom he is in communication.

A case in point is the evaluation under a social policy orientation by David Ehrenfeld of the use of rBGH (recombinant bovine growth hormone) to increase milk yield in cows.[19] (Milk yield in cows? Some strong moral implications will quickly surface.) From initial questions about whether there is a difference in the milk harmful to the humans who drink the milk and whether there is a difference harmful to the health of the cows, on both of which points there is some evidence for harm, short of being conclusive evidence, Ehrenfeld moves to a broader view (leaving behind the values of human health and animal health considered separately) in which he considers how these values might interact. The admitted increased incidence of mastitis in the cows requires treatment by antibiotics, which find their way into milk that evades preventive controls and also bring into human consumption strains of bacteria resistant to antibiotics, with a resulting tendency to reduce the effectiveness of antibiotics in treating human diseases. Here the value of human health comes back, but in a different, roundabout connection. It comes back again in the next stage of Ehrenfeld's evaluation of rBGH technology: to support their increased milk yield the cows treated have to have more food, in particular, more protein. The most convenient way of providing this is in the form of food supplements derived from the carcasses of dead animals, including sheep, horses, and other cows. This, of course, is the very practice that has been incriminated in mad cow disease and in Creutzfeldt-Jakob disease in human beings, both instances of spongiform encephalopathy.

Next, Ehrenfeld brings up again the value of animal health in the specific form of the value of having them lead normal lives. He reports that rBGH technology may dramatically shorten the treated cows' working – lactating – lives, from twelve to fifteen years without treatment to two to three years with it. (One presumes that the cows' lives overall, their working lives taken together with their lives before and after, will diminish by at least the same amount.)

The issue broadens further when Ehrenfeld reaches out to include the impact of the technology on the welfare and rights of dairy farmers and, he says, on 'the welfare of the communities and larger societies in which they live.' The impact crowds out small dairy farmers who cannot afford the rBGH technology in favour of large industrial farms that can afford it only by becoming entirely dependent on the technology, carrying a large debt load, and inviting organization by a few conglomerates. Furthermore, abandoning the practice on the small farms of keeping up wet grazing areas as well as upland pastures leads to abandoning the role of the cows in eating and controlling exotic species that displace the received flora and fauna of the wetlands. So Ehrenfeld in the end brings in values at stake with a diversified organization of agriculture, among them an explicitly environmental value.

Ehrenfeld has carried out the evaluation of rBGH technology with such a rich appreciation of the variety of its consequences, some of them unexpectedly far-reaching, that his performance may seem to check any inclination to think that a social process will at its best do better in this regard than a single agent. Of course, we are dealing in this case with an outstandingly effective single agent. However, we are not dealing with him alone. He explicitly draws from point to point on the work of others, including medical scientists and rural sociologists. So his evaluation, impressive as it is, is as much a report on a variety of contributions by different agents and organizations to the discussion of rBGH technology as it is the work of a single agent.

PARTISANSHIP AND FRAGMENTATION

The strategy of disjointed incrementalism, at work in a context with multiple agents, converts into an advantage for deliberation what at first sight seems an obstacle: the presence of many partisan groups, which tend to ignore each other when they are not consciously at odds. Hence, the body politic is fragmented rather than coherent. This has obvious disadvantages in respect to reaching an adequate view beforehand of the consequences to be expected from given actions and policies. If there is a problem of assembling information even for an individual investigator, the problem is considerably larger when one turns to coordinating the information communicated by a number of disputing parties. The strategy raises the need for coordination to special prominence, because it depends on fragmentation and division of labour in evaluation. So it does not merely accept the fragmentation (as how could it not?); it may seem to aggravate the disadvantages.

Yet the strategy actually benefits from fragmentation. To discover how the community will be affected by the alternative policies proposed, it holds, in effect, multiple hearings beforehand. It makes room for each group alert enough to make its interest felt to evaluate the advantages and disadvantages of the various policies from its own point of view. The list of meliorative themes associated directly or indirectly with the Greatest Happiness need not be fixed either as to the number of possible items or as to the priority with which the items are to be treated. By allowing for a range of possible tests – for example, statistics on different topics – the strategy meets, in part, the standard objection to utilitarianism about different pleasures having higher or lower places in happiness. Part of the point of this objection is to call attention to the multiplicity of meliorative themes and to the necessity of accommodating them consistently (to the extent that consistency is needed). The accommodation, however, may not be once for all, but relative to any particular policy that deals with more than one of them. The strategy accommodates multiplicity in two ways: by operating in the Revisionary Process to redesign policies so that, as far as possible, they satisfy multiple demands; and by supersession.

Instead of discouraging partisanship, for fear that it will distort the information presented, the strategy is ready (with certain qualifications) to welcome it, because partisanship for one's own group's interest is a dependable motivation for investigating consequences with some zeal. The findings, when they are interjected into the discussion, may be exaggerated, but it is better to have prospective benefits and injuries (especially injuries) exaggerated than never to hear of them at all. This is an important consideration in evaluating the strategy. An article in *The New Yorker* recalls Harold Wilensky's praise for the 'constructive rivalry' fostered by Franklin D. Roosevelt in the organization of his administration. Roosevelt, according to Wilensky, would 'use one anonymous informant's information to challenge and check another's, putting both on their toes.' He also 'recruited strong personalities and structured their work so that clashes would be certain ... In foreign affairs, he gave Moley and Welles tasks that overlapped those of Secretary of State Hull; in conservation and power, he gave Ickes and Wallace identical missions; in welfare, confusing both functions and initials, he assigned PWA to Ickes, WPA to Hopkins; in politics, Farley found himself competing with other political advisers for control over patronage.'[20] The strategy of disjointed incrementalism works with a generalized version of this constructive rivalry. (It must be said that the generalized version is to be invoked with some caution: fragmentation may get out of hand and lead not through disputation to nuanced, constructive results, but to confusion, partisan deadlock, or even an outbreak of violence.)

It is, of course, one of the tasks of joint discussion, which the strategy favours holding, to compare and correct partisan pictures, though it will not usually be felt necessary to correct them beyond the point at which a reasonably harmonious decision on policy becomes possible. (To do so may even be counter-productive so far as resolving conflict goes.) Biased though they may be, however, they provide the community with information about those hazards and benefits of policy that the different groups belonging to the community most fear and most desire (allowing that there are some fears and desires that it would be impolitic for a group to disclose). The expectations with which different groups greet policy proposals are, as I have implied, not always well founded. Nor do the expectations of every group, much less of every group that there might be grounds for forming, get a hearing. Some groups remain latent. Some groups are not well enough organized or well enough led to make themselves heard – a familiar and important defect of the interest-group process. However, at least those fears and desires about consequences that are expressed must be confronted if the community is to be satisfied that the consequences of the various policies proposed have been sufficiently considered.

I have been minimizing the dangers of partisanship and fragmentation in order to show how the strategy of disjointed incrementalism can take advantage of contentious discussion. It must be borne in mind, however, that the dangers are very real. Sometimes partisan distortions get out of hand and, in effect, go uncorrected (that has been the fate of proposals to have something like the Canadian health care system in the United States). Sometimes the contention becomes so fierce and bitter that no agreement on even the most promising incremental policies (steps, perhaps, toward instituting something like the Canadian health care system in the United States) can be obtained. This may happen even if the discussion clarifies the issues; but the contention may be so great and so confused that the issues become less generally understood as the discussion proceeds (maybe something like this has happened with gun control or the 'War on Drugs' in the United States). Dealing with partisanship, as in other connections, incrementalism will not always work well. The case for it is that it works well in reasonably settled circumstances, while other approaches generally do not.

Fixing Jurisdictions

In the discussion up to this point, I have been presupposing that whatever questions about jurisdiction might have arisen have been settled for every issue brought up. Moreover, how they have been settled has been easily imagined: if the issue is fluoridating a town's water supply, the jurisdiction is the town; if the issue is traffic congestion in a central city, the jurisdiction is the city, or perhaps a regional government (in the British case, the national government in Westminster and Whitehall). The question of jurisdiction, however, demands explicit attention. What jurisdiction is to be assumed may often be a matter of controversy in practice and a matter of controversy perennially in theory. When, however – as in practice is usually the case – it is not actually controverted, fixed jurisdictions may be looked to for substantial help in managing the problem of consequences.

Let us use 'jurisdiction' widely, to include not only constitutionally recognized fields of action for public governments and agencies, but also the fields of action for all sorts of private groups with some degree of self-governance in their own affairs – among them, families, ecclesiastical bodies, business corporations, national fraternities, charitable organizations. The jurisdictions are nested, the public ones typically under a relatively neat plan, the private ones somewhat untidily under the legal powers of one or another public jurisdiction. (Thus, in the United States charitable organizations must answer in public jurisdictions, within states to state governments, questions about the integrity of their fund-raising activities and the use in promised ways of the funds that they collect.)

Issues requiring attention to consequences may arise in any of these jurisdictions. In each of them, the field of action of the jurisdiction establishes a perspective that accepts some consequences as relevant for consideration and rules out others. Policy-makers in the jurisdiction, for example, do not have to consider what would be done about the given issue in another jurisdiction. If the jurisdiction, as is often the case, deals with issues of the same sort time and again, it will accumulate experience and knowledge useful to its decision-making. The strategy of disjointed incrementalism, in part for this reason, finds it congenial to work within received jurisdictions; in its tendency to avoid grand questions and in its provision for fragmentation, it makes the best of multiple jurisdictions. The presence of myriad quasi-autonomous groups – so many jurisdictions, in addition to the multiplicity of public ones – is the precondition of fragmentation: of having a general social policy evaluated by many different groups, each from its own perspective. It is also a precondition of effective delegation, of having policies determinately tested and chosen, part by part, by the groups with both the means and the concern to test them. If it makes sense to hold that the weights of various utilitarian considerations are to be settled ad hoc and therefore settled differently on different occasions, then it makes sense to hold that the power to settle them should be pluralistically distributed to match the distribution of information about effects on specific groups and persons.

Are the received jurisdictions not open to challenge, however, as being sometimes too small and narrow, sometimes too big and broad, to treat given issues effectively? This is indeed so, and sometimes persistence with received jurisdictions will lead to bad policies: a city alone cannot control the air pollution created in the region; not even the state or province can do so. The variety of ills uncovered in Ehrenfeld's account of rBGH technology figures in many different jurisdictions, some of them in many different ones at the same time. Will jurisdictions not sometimes be challenged in fact? They will be challenged in these cases, and challenged, moreover, by people using the strategy of disjointed incrementalism. The response of other people using the strategy of disjointed incrementalism is likely, characteristically, to be to demand that some reason be given for shifting to another jurisdiction – an issue said to be too big to be handled effectively within a given narrow jurisdiction; or an issue too narrow, better handled, like recreation for teen-agers, in towns and neighbourhoods than at the state and provincial level. Moreover, people using the strategy will demand that the people calling for the shift accept the burden of proof that the shift will be advantageous.

If there were occasion – practical pressure – for frequently resorting to these considerations, the strategy, and utilitarianism associated with the strategy, might take on an objectionably partisan and conservative cast. In fact, in many long-organized political societies, challenges to jurisdictions arise relatively seldom. There is, in a broad sense that is in keeping with the broad sense of 'jurisdictions,' a sort of constitutional stability in jurisdictions that is a great aid to focused policy-making. Families are left to themselves to make decisions about cuisine, housing, clothing, and support for the education of their children; there is general respect for the decisions that a fraternal organization like the Shriners makes about the initiation of members, honours, dues, and support for charitable causes.

Is stability in jurisdictions in keeping with the basic principle of utilitarianism that 'all those whose interest is in question,' that is to say, all those who are liable to be affected, pleasantly or unpleasantly, should be taken into account in actions and policies? It is always in place to ask whether a given jurisdiction is doing so, or is even capable of doing so. John Stuart Mill was inclined to hold that the Greatest Happiness Principle was indeed best promoted within traditional received jurisdictions like families and neighbourhoods.[21] Against this, however, one must consider how often narrow, small jurisdictions like families and neighbourhoods use up in relatively frivolous expenses resources desperately needed by people outside the jurisdictions.

This is a problem at the heart of ethics, and I think it is not a problem that can be disposed of neatly, certainly not by invoking traditional constitutional and quasi-constitutional systems of jurisdictions. ('Quasi-constitutional' covers the network of non-governmental associations.) The best that I can do about the problem is something that I shall do in the last chapter of this book, after I have dislodged utility from the Greatest Happiness Principle and brought in the concept of needs to take its place for the most fundamental questions of social policy. For now, however, I wish only to note that question-begging as reliance on the traditional constitutional system of jurisdictions may be, it still gives practical help in limiting the number and kinds of consequences that have to be considered.

What the Precautions Accomplish

The objection that it is impossible to identify all consequences before-hand and hence that some very untoward consequences may escape attention retains a good deal of its logical force even when all the precautions that I survey have been taken, and taken as they expect-ably can be, more fully in a social process than in decision-making by an individual person charged with making policy for the community.

'A good deal of its logical force.' This is a tricky issue. The conse-quences that call for consideration after all these precautions are taken may still be too many to take into account. In that sense, the logical force of the objection remains in full force. On the other hand, we may legitimately think that we need to worry about it less because in one way or another the precautions that we have taken beforehand reduce the chances of overlooking a catastrophic consequence. We shall have some inductive experience to support us in this thought. Perhaps, we can even say, the more catastrophic, the less the likelihood of our overlooking a catastrophic consequence. This is not a likelihood that we can pin down as a numerical probability, but it has some weight notwithstanding.

Lessons for Personal Moral Choice

Can some lessons be drawn from the preceding discussion for agents making choices of actions in their personal lives? Most of the time, very likely, they will not reopen moral issues to survey the conse-quences to be expected from their actions. They will act by moral rules, which consorts with one side of the debate about consequent-ialism. Sometimes, however, they will have to consider consequences: Are they to uproot their families and emigrate? Shall they attempt to hold the family farm for the children? Moreover, they should be ready to receive objections to following the rules in given instances where unexpectedly they work out very badly. Then, too, they must reason consequentially. They will do well to heed precautions like those that the strategy of disjointed incrementalism embodies for choices of so-cial policy. If they have time and the opportunity, they should solicit a variety of opinions within the family and outside – from *Landsmänner* who have already settled in the country to which they propose to emigrate; from agricultural economists who can say something about the prospects of family farming in Saskatchewan during the next quarter-century. Above all, if they can, they should avoid committing such a large proportion of their resources that they will have little available to cope with unexpected consequences: coming back if they find the chances of practising their profession in the new country unfavourable; leaving some resources available for children who do not wish to go on farming.

In short, they should preserve as much as possible in resources and freedom of action to deal with consequences after they act. This is what communities and agents acting for communities should do, too.

The Strategy Dealing with Consequences Afterwards

The precautions do more than justifiably reduce alarm beforehand about overlooked consequences. They increase the safety of policy-making by enabling the overlooked consequences to be dealt with more easily when they come up afterwards. Indeed, the essential clue to dealing with consequences afterwards is to deal with them (in thoughtful precautions) prudently beforehand. Hence, having postponed showing how the strategy of disjointed incrementalism deals with consequences after actions are taken and policies adopted, I face a paradox, or at least an ironic anticlimax. Has not what I have to say already been said in showing how the strategy operates beforehand? This is largely true, but not quite so. Consequences, both untoward and unmanageable, may still, in spite of all the precautions of the strategy, arise afterwards. They have to be dealt with, and the main point of the objection about unmanageable consequences is that they may turn out, afterwards, to be unmanageable. The principal idea of the strategy of disjointed incrementalism, coming into play with utilitarianism afterwards, is that consequences are not likely to be unmanageable if the changes brought in by the actions and policies decided upon are incremental ones. However, not only does this not cover all cases (as I shall acknowledge in the last section of this chapter); it will transpire, once we turn to examples, that what is incremental for one jurisdiction – a larger jurisdiction – may be catastrophically non-incremental for a smaller one.

All the features of the strategy canvassed in the survey of precautions come back to count in dealing with consequences afterwards. If the actions or policies have been taken under a remedial orientation, and the remedy adopted turns out to be ineffective or even counter-productive, there will generally be alternative remedies on hand – on hand still, even if rejected beforehand as not so promising – to turn to now, and the information mobilized in the course of considering beforehand the failing remedy will be useful again, perhaps now better understood. The Revisionary Process can be set in motion again, focusing on what turned out to be weaknesses in the action or policy adopted – a remedy itself standing in need of remedying. Supersession of values on the line adopted beforehand can be undone or carried further, or a new value can be seized upon, in a new view of what can be done to make the best of the situation. In some situations the untoward consequences can be dealt with by shifting jurisdictions (e.g., moving to a group with a larger scope and more resources). The fact that the strategy has relied on a social process in which a fragmented plurality of partisan groups have been active and are ready to be active again helps elicit a new variety of proposals.

Above all, however, the closely linked features of the strategy having to do with incremental alternatives and institutional insurance make it possible to deal with consequences unexpected and untoward in an apt and orderly way when they present themselves. Because the actions or policies now thrown into question were incremental in adoption, they will have made less difference to the institutions that can be turned to. The institutions will therefore have retained more capacity to deal with the consequences.

Let us consider some examples, first, some in which we are clearly dealing with incremental changes even at the lowest levels of policy. Fluoridating a town's drinking water is a policy that can easily be reversed afterwards; the infusion of fluoride can be stopped at once should it prove unexpectedly harmful. In the town's arrangements for police service, changing from foot patrols to squad cars is, again, a reversible policy, though if the observed consequences of changing to squad cars are unacceptable, going back to foot patrols may be accompanied by special provisions not formerly present for community policing. In the town's brothels, the prostitutes have some protection from violence: bouncers are on hand to eject unruly customers. Closing down the brothels may expose the women, as it turns out, to so much violence that policy will change: either the brothels will be allowed to reopen or some other way will be sought to protect the women. To look again for a moment at traffic congestion: building more roads and requiring new office buildings to incorporate garages may lead in both cases not to decreases in traffic but to increases. Even local authorities will retain the power to cancel the policy of requiring new garages and to close down the existing ones. They will also have the power to carry out various alternatives to building new roads: setting up light railways; designating special lanes for cars carrying three or four commuters; imposing special charges for bringing cars into the central city (full road pricing); improving bus service; even making bus service free for all riders. In all these cases, the unexpected adverse consequences are well within the capacity of the continuing institutions to remedy by other measures.

A more spectacular example, perhaps, has been the failure of dedicated high-rise buildings for public housing. Did anyone realize beforehand that if they were to contain large, concentrated populations of idle people, they would be trashed by their occupants and become breeding grounds for crime? In some instances, the buildings eventually were razed. In any case, new provisions for housing took other forms. It was also realized in some quarters that finding reasonably satisfactory employment for the people in the housing along with engrossing community-building activities was essential to having liveable, safe accommodations. The realization may not have elicited the energetic commitment of politicians necessary to making something substantial – and substantially better – of it. Nevertheless, setting up high-rise public housing in the first place was an incremental policy, and when it failed, institutions were left on every level of government with the capacity to cope with the failure.

The Fallibility of Incrementalism

I have been making a case for (disjointed) incrementalism, thinking particularly, but not exclusively, of its use combined with utilitarianism. First, we bring into view policy-making as a process in which different considerations may come up at different stages; second, we concentrate upon changes of policy that at each stage make only an incremental departure from the status quo; third, we deal with incremental changes that purport to improve things in accordance with the Principle of Utility (and sometimes do so). I have been letting the second and third points coalesce in the course of treating incrementalism in what utilitarianism must regard as a favourable light. I think that it deserves that favourable light, because it is a better approach to policy-making than alternative approaches and, in particular, a better approach for utilitarianism. It must not be thought, however, that incrementalism will always lead utilitarianism or any other ethics to success. There are a number of ways in which it can fail, or at least fail to be useful:

1 At times incremental policies are not an option (e.g., when the whole country must be mobilized to deal with an external threat).
2 At times there may be so much social conflict or so much disorder as to block effective agreement on incremental policies (or any others).
3 Sometimes an incremental departure may (unexpectedly) turn out to be a provocation that (to recall Nietzsche's language), like a spark, ignites an explosive.
4 The incremental policies chosen may depart in what in time (but only in time) will be realized to be the wrong direction (meanwhile a succession of incremental policies just aggravate the difficulty to be remedied).
5 In some cases, what is incremental for a larger jurisdiction may be non-incremental (and disastrous) for a subjurisdiction.
6 In some cases, it may be hard to tell, even when the jurisdiction has been fixed, whether a change is incremental or non-incremental (thus it will be hard to tell how to apply the strategy in the first place; and if the policy adopted leads to disaster, hard to tell whether it was because the policy was non-incremental).
7 In some cases, though incremental policies are available, a given jurisdiction does better by choosing a non-incremental policy.

All of these points are consistent with incrementalism – indeed, disjointed incrementalism – being normally the best way to proceed, but they need attention if what is being claimed in the thesis, that it is the best way to proceed, is to be fully appreciated. I shall be concerned mainly to discuss (5), (6), and (7), but I shall give some examples of the other points.

(1) Incremental policies not an option. The external threat may be military force or natural emergencies like floods, droughts, crop-failures, epidemics. The English in 1066 had to stake everything on the battle at Hastings; so did Israel when in the Six-Day War it struck first at the surrounding Arab countries. Whole peoples have had to move when crops have failed in their traditional lands. (2) Unfavourable circumstances for discussion. Partisanship on the part of conflicting groups can be, as I have said, a strength in policy-making, but partisanship carried too far may lead to having every policy blocked.

(3) Assassinations have figured in history as changes that were in themselves incremental (the prince or politician could easily be replaced) but that were nevertheless sparks that set off wars or, short of wars, sweeping changes in government. Even the mutilation of a national in a foreign country might be such a spark: England went to war with Spain in 1739 because of public clamour about Jenkins's ear, cut off by Spanish coast guards and brought back by Jenkins to show the House of Commons. (4) Incremental changes may go in the wrong direction and a succession of further incremental changes may sink deeper and deeper into trouble. The Vietnam War is a spectacular example, and also one that shows how the fallacy of 'sunk costs' may sometimes afflict incrementalism: in the late stages of going in the wrong direction policy-makers may hold that all their previous efforts will have been in vain unless one more effort is made. This is an insidious fallacy, because sometimes one more effort may lead to success, though not, of course, because one more effort is ever justified simply by the failed previous efforts.

I turn now to the cases (5) in which what is incremental for a larger jurisdiction may be non-incremental (and disastrous) for a subjurisdiction. When the Newfoundland government closed down outports and resettled their inhabitants in locations more accessible to modern social services, it adopted what was for it an incremental policy, since if things turned out badly, it had the resources to send the people uprooted back to the outports or, more likely, to make special efforts in counselling, vocational retraining, and job creation to convince the people that resettlement was best for them. But the case is to a degree ambiguous: in the view of the people taken from the outports, resettlement could not have been an incremental change; it was a revolution in their way of life. The younger people in the outports may have welcomed the change notwithstanding: the inshore fishery, on which the outports depended for a rather miserable livelihood, was played out, and the younger people were eager to share in the amenities of the outside world. (In some of the outports, it has been said, the sole means of entertainment was a single jukebox.) For the older people and for some not so old, who did not readily find employment after resettlement, there were unhappy consequences for their morale and happiness, which could be explained, at least in part, simply because the change was so thoroughgoing for them. Moreover, the fact that the Newfoundland government could ride out the ill consequences does not imply that it could undo those consequences.[22]

The difficulties of Canadian policy in dealing with the First Nations – the aboriginal peoples – have been even more poignant and, as an example, even more interesting, partly because of the same sort of ambiguity. For the federal government of Canada, an earlier policy (followed from the 1830s to the 1950s) aimed at assimilating the Native peoples into the larger population, by converting them from hunter-gatherers to settled farmers and by setting up schools for Native children. The schools were boarding schools, in which the children were deliberately separated from their families. On both points, farming and schooling, the policy was incremental for the government of Canada and would have been so even if the government had attempted to accomplish both points at once. So was the abandonment of this policy, gradually (though over a much shorter period than 120 years) substituting a new policy emphasizing self-government for the First Nations on the reserves and some degree of cultural independence, though the success of the new policy has been doubtful. For the Native peoples in each case both policies were more than incremental, the earlier one because of the thoroughgoing disruption of Native cultures that it threatened (and that in various degrees the First Nations steadily resisted generation after generation), the later one because it swept aside a comprehensive policy pursued for generations. The example seems to tell simultaneously for the relative ease (for the government of Canada) of reversing an incremental policy and for the difficulty (for the First Nations, a catastrophe perhaps without remedy) of coping with a non-incremental one, always resisting but never getting things right overall.[23]

An example of the sort of overall ambiguity mentioned under (6) in the list of ways to fail is Prohibition in the United States. Did its nationwide scope under an amendment to the constitution and its interference with immemorial personal habits make it a non-incremental policy? Then the widespread defiance of it and the spectacular increase in organized crime that rose up to exploit the defiance demonstrate the unwisdom of proceeding non-incrementally. Or does the ease with which Prohibition was repealed, without any effective demonstrations against repeal and the continued functioning of governmental and non-governmental institutions at all levels, show that Prohibition was incremental after all, well within the institutional insurance available? Even so, there may be an uncomfortable doubt about whether a non-incremental change in the level of organized crime did not remain an untoward consequence of Prohibition. It is worth noting that, incremental or not, Prohibition had incremental alternatives, among them the Swedish policy, which as I understand worked quite well for several generations in reducing drunkenness, of requiring that drink be served in public places only as something accompanying a regular meal.

Such incremental alternatives were not pursued; Prohibition was utterly abandoned. This is one way of dealing with untoward consequences. It is also illustrated, even more neatly, as a possibility in the fluoridation case. The more typical response, however, is to turn to a new policy, either a policy that seeks to remedy the difficulties of the remedy adopted in the first instance or a policy that supplants that remedy with what is from scratch a new one. The prostitution case, if the brothels remain closed and other means of protecting the women from violence are taken up, illustrates the first possibility; so does closing down the outports if they remain closed and counselling along with other measures are used to deal with the unhappiness of the resettled population. Ceasing to build new high-rise public housing and razing the old, while turning to other provisions for housing, illustrate the second possibility, as would going back to foot patrols with added efforts in community policing. So does the abolition of Native boarding schools in favour of a policy of cultural independence in the reservations. If more roads will still be built, though the policy on garages is reversed, and other measures (including the humble one of extending the area of metered parking) are taken to control traffic, the traffic case illustrates the two possibilities simultaneously.

Manifold instances of the success of the strategy of disjointed incrementalism in dealing with consequences unexpected and untoward thus do not demonstrate that it will always succeed. Moreover, the incremental actions and policies that it favours are not always better, in a given jurisdiction, than non-incremental ones, even when both sorts are feasible.

This brings us to point (7). In some situations, in some jurisdictions, actions and policies that defy one or another feature of disjointed incrementalism may succeed better than actions and policies that conform to the strategy in all its features. A clear and telling example is described by Jennifer Hochschild in respect to school desegregation in the United States.[24] If a city tries to introduce desegregation gradually, school by school, white resistance has time to build up, aggravated it may be by mixing too many poorly trained students with others in the schools to which they are transferred. If, instead, the city introduces desegregation all at once over the whole city, it can distribute the poorly trained students so widely that classroom standards can be maintained, since students working up to such standards predominate in every classroom. So it can demonstrate success for desegregation early, before white resistance, aggravated by local failures, has a chance to build up.

The main thing to say about such cases, I think, is again that the policies, non-incremental (and non-serial) though they are in a given jurisdiction (one city among others), may still be incremental in a larger jurisdiction embracing that one. If there is rioting and violence in the smaller jurisdiction, the larger jurisdiction can intervene and restore order. To be sure, if all the other smaller jurisdictions – the other cities – are trying to introduce desegregation in all their schools at once, rioting and violence may be so widespread as to strain the resources of the larger jurisdiction. But then the change, in the perspective of the larger jurisdiction, will be far from incremental. The smaller jurisdiction will also be forfeiting the chance of one smaller jurisdiction's being able to learn from the experience of another, which is another argument for incremental policies.

Will this provision always vindicate the possibility of an incremental approach to action or policy? Unfortunately not. Internal dangers – an epidemic or crop failure – or external threats – another country moving to extinguish or subjugate one's own country – may leave no room for anything but a non-incremental action or policy. The national government may have to enforce rigid measures of quarantine or even organize a movement of the entire population to some other region. Or it may have to mobilize all its people of military age and commit them to a battle in which the prospects of victory are vanishingly small. Moreover, a subset of such desperate situations may be situations that arise as unexpected consequences of incremental actions or policies taken in quieter times. Perhaps it looked safe enough to import a few seed potatoes from a new source, but they turned out to carry a virus that spread to potato patches throughout the country and wiped out an essential source of food.

Do the difficulties illustrated in these cases discredit the strategy of disjointed incrementalism? Some critics might seize upon the cases in which pursuing an incremental policy in given jurisdictions creates non-incremental disasters for subjurisdictions. But these cases do not discredit incrementalism, any more than do cases in which a succession of incremental policies lead ever more disastrously in the wrong direction. Some of them are cases in which the incrementalism has been used without due care for utilitarian considerations, or cases in which the drawbacks of particular incremental policies have not been fully appreciated beforehand or even – for a while – afterwards. Sometimes this is so because there is not enough unambiguous information to show what the drawbacks amount to; then it is not incrementalism that is at fault, but a lack of information.

It may be suggested, as a philosophical criticism, that in every case a non-incremental policy may be made to look incremental by shifting the jurisdiction (and hence the perspective in which it is seen), or, vice versa, that an incremental policy may be made to look non-incremental by such a shift.[25] Then, no incremental policy could be firmly identified as such, and it therefore would not be intelligible to call for adopting one. But this is not so; the criticism is over-ingenious. Fix the jurisdiction and – not always, but often enough – what are important and what are unimportant changes can be distinguished, and the latter can be seen to fall within the institutional insurance present in the jurisdiction. Moreover, what is incremental in one jurisdiction does not always turn into something non-incremental in a smaller one. Extending the area of metered parking is incremental for Greater London, but it is incremental, too, in its impact on a given neighbourhood in Chelsea, should that neighbourhood fall within the extension. Even if a meter is installed in the street before a house, preventing the occupant from freely parking there and forcing him to rent a space in a public garage nearby, that will not make a big change in his life.

Incrementalism may be frequently applicable and also the best way that utilitarianism has of dealing with consequences, and yet fail to save us from disasters or, at any rate, from having to make desperate choices. What, however, in such situations would save us? It suffices – it must suffice to defend utilitarianism on the point of being able to take adequate measures to deal with consequences that incrementalism ordinarily works. That defence is made by invoking the features of practical policy-making that the strategy of disjointed incrementalism highlights.

3

Does Utilitarianism (Bentham's Master-Idea, Applied – If It Is Applied as Hedonic Act-Utilitarianism, Only with Qualifications That May Be Ascribed to Him) Ever Endorse Sacrificing Someone's Life to Make Other People Happy? No*

A statistical presupposition inseparable from taking overall account of evidence about the consequences for all the people in a group precludes sacrificing, in order to get a higher aggregate score, the life of any member of the group whose collective position in respect to utility (or any other personal benefit) is to be improved.

The objection about sacrificing someone's life simply to obtain a higher aggregate happiness score is the most electrifying familiar objection to utilitarianism. It has obtained vivid expression in the notorious case of organ transfer – medical cannibalization, which I take from the Afterword to the collection of Judith Jarvis Thomson's essays *Rights, Restitution, and Risk*:[1] 'A surgeon has five patients who will die unless they are provided with certain essential bodily parts. A young man has just come in for his yearly check-up, and his parts will do: the surgeon can cut him up and transplant his parts among the five who need them. The surgeon asks the young man if he is willing to volunteer his parts, and thus his life; the young man says, "Sorry, I deeply sympathize with your five patients but no." Would it be morally permissible for the surgeon to proceed anyway? Hardly!' Commenting on the case, Thomson contends that 'Hedonic Act-Utilitarianism' (HAU) if it does not come to the wrong conclusion about the example, will be embarrassed to say why the right conclusion is to spare the young

* Based on and in part reprinted from my article 'Liberalism, Statistics, and the Presuppositions of Utilitarianism,' which first appeared in David Braybrooke, *Moral Objectives, Rules, and the Forms of Social Change* (Toronto: University of Toronto Press, 1998). So far as reprinted, © 1998 by University of Toronto Press Incorporated and reprinted with its permission.

man's life. (Thus we return temporarily to act-utilitarianism, though rules, both rules for assessing utility and rules, backed by utility-assessments, for other conduct will again be on the scene before the chapter winds up.) The best that HAU can do, she thinks, is argue that, if the cannibalization goes through, relations between doctors and patients would be so unsettled that more happiness on balance will be produced by refraining from it. The surgeon's being able to proceed in secret would require HAU to produce another argument. Thomson does not press home the attack with this variation of the example, since she thinks it is embarrassment enough for HAU to be found arguing, with the example unvaried, against proceeding merely from the overall balance of happiness. 'That,' she says, 'locates the moral source of the prohibition on proceeding in the wrong place.'

In another famous life-sacrificing case, Bernard Williams's military brute in the tropics – an army captain, whom I shall call El Capitan Sanguinario – threatens to kill twenty Indian prisoners unless you do him (and nineteen of them) the favour of killing the twentieth. Williams might tell you that you would be right to go ahead; but he considers it an unsettling objection to utilitarianism that it would tell you so without further ado.[2] If utilitarianism should advise going ahead with medical cannibalization, would he not think utilitarianism entirely outrageous?

Prescriptions of Life-Sacrifices?

It is possible to invent a doctrine called 'Hedonic Act-Utilitarianism' with a feature that implies such advice; or tends to imply it (which is as far as Thomson carries the charge). Indeed, it is common practice to assume as I myself in effect have been assuming in the last two chapters that utilitarianism is just such a doctrine. One may doubt, however, whether the historic doctrine set forth by Bentham, Mill, Edgeworth, and Sidgwick has such a feature.[3] One way of making this point would be to say only that the historic doctrine – which I shall call Benthamite Utilitarianism (BU) – does not tell us what to do when we do not have the scores that it calls for and hence does not tell us to sacrifice the life of the twentieth prisoner or to cut up the young man for his parts. Another way, which gives us a deeper answer for some cases, equally well supported by history, is to say that BU, as its historic champions understood it, tells us not to monkey with the scores by sacrificing anybody's life. Hence, it tells us not to go in for medical cannibalization in the case arising. Whether, when it is applied to the other example, it not only does not tell us to sacrifice the twentieth prisoner but actually tells us not to sacrifice her is more difficult to say, as I shall explain.

Not one of the historic champions of utilitarianism mentioned treats a case like either of the two before us, though Mill and Sidgwick do mention with approval voluntary sacrifices designed to safeguard or promote the happiness of others.[4] None of them treat any case that allows us more of a ground for inferring prescriptions to take innocent lives than the omission of an explicit block to such an inference. It is fair game, of course, to deduce from a principle, as put forward, untoward consequences that show the principle to have been inadequately formulated, and the authors in question certainly did not adequately formulate the principle that they were advocating. (Understanding counter-examples like those cited as directed against the inadequacy of the formulas, I take them to be perfectly relevant and quite telling.) Given the silence of the historic authors mentioned on the topic, however, may it not be gratuitous to suppose that what they had in mind was a principle with a feature ready to sacrifice innocent lives?

Moreover, it is not just silence that we have to go on; it is silence with a direction. Edgeworth, the most enthusiastic champion of the felicific calculus, marches right up to the point where life-sacrifices might be contemplated – and stops short. To give more means of happiness to people with larger capacities, Edgeworth is willing, in principle, to have those less favoured in capacity driven below the point of zero happiness, but he thinks it an empirical certainty that well before the less capacious are pushed to the point of starving, 'the pleasures of the most favoured could not weigh much against the privations of the least favoured.'[5] Thus, he did not contemplate the privations' being carried so far as to endanger the lives of the least favoured.[6] Moreover, Edgeworth contemplates 'mitigating' the condition of the least favoured class by having them emigrate.[7] No lives are sacrificed; the emigrants are happier than they were, or at least as happy; and, if the home population is happier in the absence of their infelicible former neighbours and companions, the score for the whole group, divided, will be greater than the score for the whole group undivided.

There is a second argument, besides this directed silence, for thinking that BU did not contemplate taking innocent lives. We have from Mill's hand a systematic review of what he considered the serious objections to utilitarianism. The review does not mention the possibility of imposing life-sacrifices just to increase the happiness of other people.[8] Nor, in a later review of the objections, does Sidgwick mention this possibility.[9]

Were they unaware of this objection? Or, if aware of it, did they choose to ignore it as too wide of the mark to be worth answering? If they had read Francis Hutcheson – and it is hard to believe that they had not – they could have encountered, endorsed there, policies that might invite the objection.[10] They might have taken a passage in Godwin's *Political Justice* as endorsing such a policy. Godwin says, 'If the extraordinary case should occur in which I can promote the general good by my death more than by my life, justice requires that I should be content to die.' If they had read on, however, they would have found this endorsement considerably qualified by Godwin's strong aversion to applying coercion contrary to any man's private judgment as to his duty, an aversion in the general case not subject to the presumably rare exception that he allows of using coercion 'to prevent the inroad of universal violence and tumult.'[11] Taking these passages together, Godwin might have seemed to them to be doing no more in effect than allowing for the voluntary sacrifices that they themselves approve but treat as supererogatory.[12] It would not have been possible to dismiss in this way the objection to involuntary sacrifices that they would have found starkly posed in the writings of Hazlitt, whom J.B. Schneewind cites as declaring that Bentham's calculus 'would warrant killing people to provide cadavers for medical students.'[13] They would not have read Sydney Smith, writing in a personal letter to a lady who had published a discourse on education, 'Education has many honest enemies; and many honestly doubt and demur, who do not speak out for fear of being assassinated by Benthamites, who might think it, upon the whole, more useful that such men should die than live.'[14]

Did they not read Hazlitt on this point, or did they forget what they had read? Their omitting to consider the objection is strong evidence that they were not thinking of the objection at the time of writing the systematic reviews – or, less plausibly, evidence that if they did think of it, they thought it so absurd, compared with the objections that they did consider, as not to be worth bothering with. Unless one is ready to believe that both Mill and Sidgwick thought about the objection at the time of writing their reviews, but decided to suppress it as too embarrassing to their cherished views to circulate further, we may reasonably conclude that neither Bentham nor Mill, nor Sidgwick and Edgeworth either, thought of the Greatest Happiness Principle as having a feature that led to the unwelcome possibility of imposing the objectionable sacrifices. Omission from the reviews of objections, taken together with the directed silence noted above, should deter us from ascribing to BU the life-sacrificing implications of HAU unqualified. But if we ask what can explain the curious omission of imposed life-sacrifices from Mill's systematic review, a third argument arises, more illuminating than the two just canvassed. It supports the suggestion that not only did BU not prescribe that lives be taken whenever doing so promotes group happiness; BU came, as its champions understood it, with a logical barrier to so prescribing.

Let us suppose that all four champions rely on the felicific calculus to obtain and add up people's net scores of utility or happiness and that they understand BU to prescribe one action or policy rather than another if and only if the action or policy has a higher total or average score (which give the same results in prescriptions for a fixed population).[15] I suggest – better, given the degree of inconclusiveness in the evidence, I dare to hypothesize – that what best explains Mill's and Sidgwick's omission to treat objectionable life-sacrifices is that however inadequate, even indeterminate, may have been the conception of the Greatest Happiness Principle held by the champions mentioned, so far as they had a common conception, it carried over to the felicific calculus from familiar practice in making comparisons between groups a feature of what I shall call Standard Group Scoring for Individual Traits (SGSIT). A basic feature of SGSIT is that it precludes sacrificing the lives of members of the groups in question (or otherwise discarding them from the scoring) in order to obtain a higher group score. SGSIT applies to comparisons of groups of people, and this is what I am concerned with, but it also applies to certain comparisons of groups of other things. If you are comparing shipments of pigs or potatoes with a view to establishing how close to the market value of a shipment with no defective members the present shipments are, you will not be able to drown the pigs that have not yet attained market weight or throw out the potatoes that are still green, just to be able to claim a higher market value for one shipment of pigs or potatoes than another.

Suppose you have charge of an orphanage inhabited by some thirty boys between ten and fourteen years of age. Perhaps there is some question about their nutrition and physical fitness; this question would serve my purposes. Suppose, however, the most urgent task before you is to have the boys taught a trade, so that they can leave the orphanage and relieve the parish of the burden of sheltering and feeding them. It is decided that the boys will be taught the weaver's trade; at the end of a year they will be tested to see how much cloth they can weave in an hour.

Would you not try to have all the boys learn to weave well enough to support themselves? One way of applying SGSIT in this case would be to give a higher group score the higher the proportion of the boys who at the end of the year weave this well; in other cases, SGSIT might offer the alternative of raising the median score. (I shall not try to define SGSIT further except to say it accommodates this alternative, too. Further features – so many further rules for carrying out the assessments that utilitarianism calls for – may well include such things as not changing the measures used as one moves from scoring one person to scoring another and not combining the scores from one time for some people with the scores from another time for others. However, since we are dealing with a standard – a complex of rules – that we may suppose was at the beginning intuitive, perhaps entirely intuitive, rather than explicitly set forth, it seems historically appropriate to leave SGSIT largely undefined; anyway, for my present purposes I need make explicit only the features that I have mentioned.)

Now, one way of getting a higher proportion of skillful weavers among the boys tested at the end of the year would be for you to kill the slower learners before the test. Would you expect full credit for the higher proportion in that case? Would an advocate of enhancing the skills of orphans, or of youth in general, have to spell out the point that the population to be tested, under SGSIT, is to be the same in composition as the population that you started out with?

Under SGSIT, it would not be an appropriate measure of improvement in individual traits to take the total quantity of cloth woven by all the boys during the hour of testing. The subject under test, one might say, would then shift from how skillful the boys had become as weavers to how much cloth they could weave all told. Bentham's felicific calculus, without, I think, Bentham's noticing, makes a similar change in subject, from making people happy (the people in a given group) to creating the greatest total happiness in a group, which was not then, any more than it is now, even a notion, like the total amount of cloth, with a clear and familiar use.[16] So, in respect to established usage, there is nothing like the conceptual opportunity offered by the notion of the total quantity of cloth. The calculus notwithstanding takes one step (as we shall see in a moment, Sidgwick took another) toward detaching the happiness to be sought from the happiness of the individual members of the group. Is it, however, a step that commits BU to imposing life-sacrifice on any members of the group just to improve the total score? The feature of SGSIT that stands in the way of such sacrifices may still be in force.

Once we have SGSIT in mind, can we ignore it when we read (for example) Bentham's words: 'the balance ... on the side of pleasure' or 'pain' is to be taken to find 'the general good tendency of the act, with respect to the total number or community of individuals concerned'; or 'the general evil tendency, with respect to the same community'?[17] If even one of the total number is disposed of to improve the score, it is reasonable to say that we do not have the sort of score called for; we do not have a score for the same community. Moreover, we have monkeyed with the score in a way that frustrates the objective of improving the traits of all the people who are to be tested.

Would it be a score for the same community in cases of voluntary life-sacrifice? It might be so conceived. We might conceive of the volunteer putting herself aside and comparing the group scores for the rest of the population, first with her apart but not sacrificed, then apart again, supposing the sacrifice has occurred. The instructor in weaving does not count himself among the boys to be taught the trade. Why did volunteering make a moral difference to these authors? And why did they not apprehend that scoring on this basis opened the way to taking innocent lives? The operation, noticed or unnoticed, of SGSIT in the conception of scoring helps answer both questions: involuntary sacrifices were no trouble, because SGSIT gave no scores supporting them; and the volunteer was investing herself with a responsibility setting her (like the instructor) apart from the rest, a complication in the rules of assessment to be associated with SGSIT. It was a complication that left the effects on the rest open for scoring under SGSIT.

Late in *Principles of Morals and Legislation* Bentham touches briefly on capital punishment and allows grudgingly for occasional use of it. Capital punishment is, among other drawbacks, so 'unfrugal' – so apt to cause pointless pain – that it will be justified only in 'very extraordinary cases.'[18] That the allowance is minimal is another argument for thinking that no notion of freely taking lives to improve group happiness scores was in Bentham's mind. Does the allowance accord with

SGSIT? He hardly reveals enough of his reasoning to tell. But it fits what he says to have, following conviction, any prisoner in question set aside before taking the scores for the group (the community): first, the score given the deterrent effect of the other most efficacious punishment; then, the score given the deterrent effect of capital punishment.[19] The comparison of these scores accords with SGSIT. Now the prisoner's scores are considered; and if the net increase in the score for the group (leaving him aside) does not more than offset any net loss of happiness on his part, capital punishment is ruled out. The effect in the end is the same as abandoning SGSIT to include the prisoner's scores in the scores for the group. The approach, however, is very different. To reason by way of an assumption about conviction, hence about punishment being due, then putting the prisoner aside so that SGSIT still operates when the scores for the group are compared, is to reason in a way not easily generalized to taking innocent lives.

Does it accord with history to ascribe to Bentham some familiarity with SGSIT? Sidgwick and Edgeworth, even Mill, were writing after the Victorians had brought in periodic inspection of performances in schools, along with systematic measures of public health; so it is at least not anachronistic to ascribe to them familiarity not just with received informal practice in making comparisons between groups, but also with something like formal procedures (rules of assessment) for testing groups in respect to the traits of their members. With Bentham we face the difficulty that the felicific calculus may have been more of an innovation than it is nowadays taken for – not just a novel application of the idea of systematic testing of groups for improvement in individual traits, but an innovation that introduced the very idea.[20] Yet Bentham did have before him some examples to the point. He was familiar with schools as well as prisons and would have known that a schoolmaster's job (a duty defined by a number of moral rules) was, among other things, to teach every pupil in the class to read and write to the best of that pupil's ability. Parents and school governors would not have been pleased with a schoolmaster who ignored the more backward scholars, much less with one who, to produce a higher average performance at the end of the academic year, early in the first term assassinated them. The population to be scored is assumed to be given, as in SGSIT, and to be treated in the same way.[21]

Sidgwick may be reckoned as adding to BU when he takes up the question of whether a future generation should be larger or smaller.

Moreover, he not only adds this question to the field of application; he takes a further step toward detaching the pursuit of total happiness from the endeavour to make the members of the group happy when he maintains that future generations should be increased (despite any decline in average happiness) to the point where there is no longer an opportunity to make a marginal increase in total happiness by adding a further person. Even with this step, however, no occasion appears for imposing life-sacrifices upon some people now (or in any generation) just to raise the total score for the people remaining.[22]

Have I made a sufficient case for the relevance of SGSIT to utilitarianism, and the prime role that should be given it as a presupposition of utilitarian comparisons? I think my examples about learning to weave and learning to read and write are appropriate enough. They have to do, however, with proficiencies; and readers may bring to them ideas about other ways in which groups are compared in respect to proficiencies. For just as, on the one hand, SGSIT applies to certain comparisons of groups not composed of people, so, on the other hand, it gives way, even in comparisons of groups of people, to other procedural rules when the comparisons concern not the condition of the groups taken as a whole but their use for certain extraneous purposes. If we are concerned to select from groups people who attain a certain standard of proficiency – as fighter pilots, for example, submarine commanders, or orchestral musicians – then we shall rate as superior the groups with higher proportions of people who attain this proficiency, and incline to think that they have enjoyed a better training program. We shall not be concerned with the people who do not meet the standard; there is no reason to kill them, but they will be discarded ('scrubbed') when the training program has finished or even before. Again, we might imagine certain games in which the members of each team have a number of turns to try to add to the team's score. Then it would make sense, if the rules allow this, to select the most proficient members and give all the turns to them. Being put up to bat as a pinch-hitter in baseball or being sent in to kick a field goal in football are at least approximate examples. The other members of the team stay on the bench; if it is close to the end of the game, they could even leave the park. Selecting from groups for proficiency in this way and in the other way mentioned is very far away, however, from trying to discover which groups of people, under which social policies, are happier on the whole. There the purpose of the comparison is defeated if a wrong procedure is used in which SGSIT is not applied.

Have I made a sufficient case for thinking that Bentham, Mill, Edgeworth, and Sidgwick had notion enough about SGSIT to make it a ground for rejecting the charge against BU of being ready to sacrifice the lives of some to increase the happiness of others? Enough of a mystery remains about why they did not deal with the charge explicitly to deter me from categorically asserting that they did have notion enough about SGSIT. If they did not, it is at least an open question whether BU – utilitarianism as Bentham understood it and with the felicific calculus attached – should be understood as associated with SGSIT. The argument for its being associated with SGSIT – one way of answering the open question – is that it is both, given familiar practice and current procedures for making comparisons of people in groups, the default case (what we should assume unless explicitly barred from doing so) and also the way to rebut a charge that would not have come home whether or not the utilitarians mentioned gave attention to it.

SGSIT comes up so quickly and obviously when one confronts the question – 'Shall we, aiming to improve the condition of the group, leave one or more members out of comparison to get a better score?' – that one must wonder why it has not been a familiar feature of discussions of life-sacrificing examples. To the original utilitarians, if we picture them as departing from ordinary thinking with the calculus but still heeding ordinary thinking in respect to keeping the group intact under comparisons, SGSIT may simply have been an unquestioned assumption. But why have present-day critics, launching life-saving objections against utilitarianism, not paused to think of it? I speculate that in their conception of utilitarianism they have been too much and without qualification in the thrall of the total or average score criteria to see that even these might be qualified with respect to life-sacrifice. Perhaps, regarding relevant procedures, in effect they have also confused comparisons of groups with respect to happiness with comparisons in which selecting from the groups for proficiency is at issue.[23]

Forced Choices

Can BU deal with medical cannibalization or the army captain's challenge? This is a question that requires a distinction between forced choices and unforced ones. Let us define a forced choice as one in which no matter what we do, given the options before us, and supposing that there are no other options available that would eliminate the difficulty, someone will suffer a severe reduction in the level of her happiness or even lose her life. The case of medical cannibalization, as so far described and treated, may be an unforced choice. There may be many alternative sources of the required bodily parts (perhaps the possibility of taking one part from one person, another part from another, doing mortal damage to no one). By contrast, the case of El Capitan Sanguinario seems a forced choice between shooting the twentieth Indian and letting all twenty die, and Williams intends us to gather that we can only idly imagine a way out by some third option,[24] which, it should be noted, makes it a very special case. We can generally resort to the Revisionary Process to increase at once the options presented to us and the attractions to be ascribed to them. The notion of a forced choice ('We had no choice'; 'We had no option') is easily abused by people too determined for various reasons to do something discreditable or too lazy to look for a more acceptable alternative.

Williams's case, however, has two complications that might distract us from present purposes. First, the twentieth Indian (whoever she turns out to be) is going to die anyway, so her prospects are not going to be impaired by choosing to shoot her. Second, you, the traveller just passing through, if you choose to shoot, will choose which of the twenty will be shot – thus, you have an additional responsibility, which may distract from the main point about sacrificing a life or lives. Instead of Sanguinario I, let us concentrate on a revised case, Sanguinario II. Thinking better of his first proposal El Capitan says, 'Tell you what, amigo, I'll let all twenty of them go if you kill that young fellow among the bystanders, the one in the red hat; I don't like his looks.'

Let every speculation about Sanguinario's reliability and about the possibility of an intervention fall aside as groundless. Sanguinario (or a sinister Rubenario Goldberg) has enticed you into a contraption that will put the youth in the red cap in your gunsight just a moment before the twenty Indian prisoners come into Sanguinario's field of fire. If you shoot the youth, Sanguinario's machine gun will be rendered inoperative; if you do not, he (or somebody) has set it to fire for sure. You are horrified, but even if you are too horrified to act, would you not understand how somebody in your position might reasonably, if agonizingly, decide that he should shoot the youth? (In Sanguinario I, Williams's original case, could you reasonably disregard the plea that each Indian might make[25] to you to give them each a nineteen in twenty chance of surviving? That they would reasonably vote accordingly, expressing their agreement, given a chance to vote, shows that utilitarianism, if it calls upon the traveller to shoot, has here, in doing so, the beginnings of social contract thinking as an ally.) If so, it is not reasoning from BU that persuades you. You are refusing any advice from BU not to kill, because killing would be monkeying with the scores, and you are leaving behind the incapacity of BU to furnish group scores that tell us to kill.

BU could be augmented to cover such cases, though then we should ask if we have before us historic utilitarianism.[26] To cover forced choices, we could augment BU just to accommodate some scores that it does not, as it stands, accept. SGSIT does not apply. We can get group scores of a sort from algebraic sums of the prospective happiness scores (taken first as pluses, then as minuses) for the twenty Indians who will otherwise die taken together with the prospective happiness score (first as a minus, then as a plus) for the youth who will die if you shoot him. They would not be group scores of the sort contemplated by BU or compared as BU intends, but they would be scores from the same interpersonal felicific calculus in an extended application. With such scores, Augmented BU might explain how the decision to shoot is justified.[27]

Augmented BU performs very well in triage, both in simple cases where it is a question of saving more lives rather than fewer and in more complex ones where the question may be one of saving fewer people for healthy lives than of saving a greater number who must all live with grave handicaps.[28] Let a few safely escape from the cave or submarine? Share out the oxygen so that everyone can get to the surface, but only with severely damaged brains? Again, utilitarianism – without, as it happens, having to carry out any exact calculations – might have an ally in contract thinking, since everyone might agree to have a few escape undamaged and do so even if the few to escape were preselected for exceptional robustness. If forced choices like those presented in triage become common, and even if they do not, moral rules – rules that would fall in with rule-utilitarianism – can prescribe what rules or procedures of assessment are to be used in different cases, sometimes, for example, just counting numbers of lives, sometimes taking into account quality of lives and other considerations.

Augmented BU may do better than BU in dealing with life-sacrifices demanded during wars. Mortality among volunteers might be dealt with in the same way as voluntary life-sacrifice was above, setting the volunteers aside and using BU to treat the happiness of the remaining population. Or, if some of the volunteers are going to survive, the prospective happiness of the volunteers might be added on a probabilistic basis to the happiness of the others. Augmented BU could go beyond this to deal with lives lost by conscripts, supposing that going to war could be treated as a forced choice.

If we turn back to medical cannibalization and redescribe the case with certain specifications, however, Augmented BU leads uncomfortably to prescribing the sacrifice of the young man. Suppose that a very rare blood-type makes the young man the only person on earth who can supply any of the organs that the surgeon's five other patients need. Now we have a forced choice: Cannibalization FC. Augmented BU will favour the five other patients if there is no reason to favour the young man in the comparison of life-prospects among the six or in respect to future contributions to the happiness of others. We have not got back to Hedonic Act-Utilitarianism, since Augmented BU (we may suppose) still forestalls imposing life-sacrifices in unforced cases. Thomson, I expect, would still find the upshot outrageous; I do so myself. But would anybody find shooting the twentieth or the twenty-first person in either of the Sanguinario cases outrageous to this degree? Approve or disapprove, maybe going along with the decision in one case and not in the other,[29] we could hardly reject as entirely unreasonable your decision to shoot in either case if that is what you make your mind up to do. What is it about Cannibalization FC that gives such a different impression from Sanguinario I and II and invites such a different result?

Rights, Natural Lifespans, Emergencies

Thomson says, 'One feels intuitively that the surgeon would be violating a right of the young man's, a fundamental right, in fact, and that is why the surgeon must not proceed. I am sure that this must be correct.'[30] (She doubts, however, whether it is illuminating, since 'we do not yet fully understand how the concept "has a right" itself works,' and, as she observed earlier, to speak of a right may be no more than to say that it would be impermissible to do something, without explaining why.[31])

Evidently the young man – the prospective Medical Cannibalee – does have a current legal right not to be cut up without his permission. Precedents set in disposing of one's body and in agreeing to transplants imply that there is a standing social device (a bundle of rules) recognized in law that amount to his having such a right. But this is a contingent matter, as it is with the existence of any right, moral or legal, considered as a social device, including the right to security of life and limb, which also might be drawn on here. Considered as a moral right – a feature of a rule-utilitarianism – whether or not it is favoured by utilitarian considerations is just what is in question here, and even if were favoured by those considerations, it might not be favoured as much as another social device might be. Considered as a legal right, it is something that the legislature and the courts might dismantle in favour of another social device, maybe leaving no social device standing that would give the young man the protection in question. Moreover, the right to security of life and limb seems to bear upon the Sanguinario cases, too, especially upon Sanguinario II. We may be uncertain about what to do, but at least we have to take seriously the possibility that the extra youth's right is justifiably overridden in the Sanguinario cases. Why is it not justifiably overridden in Cannibalization FC?

We might defend the (prospective) Medical Cannibalee in that case by going deeper than a right as a social device to consider the moral respect due him as a person – as a being whose life must be regarded as beyond manipulation (merely as a means to an end!). Thomson treats the original cannibalization case at three different places in the collection of her essays, and in one of them – the earliest written – she makes no mention of rights.[32] Was this the wiser course? At bottom, here, is there perhaps not a right, but a moral consideration more fundamental than any right?[33] If so, however, we have not yet come upon it, since the youth who will be sacrificed in Sanguinario II is just as much an end in himself as the young man who has come, it may be (for him), so unpropitiously into the surgeon's office.

It is relevant, but not decisive, that in Sanguinario (both Sanguinarios) something wrong would occur whatever is chosen, because the captain or Goldberg has done something wrong – flouted a moral rule, like a rule against bringing innocent lives into jeopardy – in setting the choice up. Hence, to apply a distinction of St Thomas's, we find ourselves, not surprisingly, facing a choice between evils, a quandary *perplexus secundum quid*, which could have been avoided if it had not been preceded by a moral lapse.[34] By contrast, in the cannibalization case, original or revised, we might want to say: nothing wrong is going to occur if the young man survives and the five others die; it is not wrong for people to die. This point is relevant because it reflects the view of received morality; it also accords with Hume's confident assertion, once itself a received view, that though we can be mutilated, what we lose in bodily parts cannot be of use to anybody else.[35] It is not decisive because, first, natural emergencies as well as moral lapses might set up a forced choice between sacrificing one person and sacrificing others; second, because progress in medical technology has made Hume's assertion obsolete.

Yet on at least two points there does seem to be a morally significant difference between Sanguinario II and Cannibalization FC. In Cannibalization FC (as in the original version) the natural lifespan of the young man would be cut short in order to extend the lifespans of the others beyond what nature has allotted them. In Sanguinario II we may suppose that only natural assignments of lifespans for everyone concerned are at issue; the captain's interference is threatening to bring the lifespans to a premature end. In choices forced by natural emergencies, the assignments of lifespans come into question only because of an act of Nature itself. But this reflection brings to light the second significant difference between Sanguinario II and Cannibalization FC. Sanguinario II (likewise Sanguinario I) belongs to a family of cases in which emergencies, contrived by men or caused by Nature, but improbable either way, have to be dealt with in forced choices. Cannibalization FC, by contrast, falls in with systematic planning to sacrifice lives whenever such sacrifices can be made useful in prolonging other lives.

Might not the prospective Medical Cannibalee well ask, 'When did I sign up for any such plan?' In agreeing to be a member of a given society, he might have reasonably agreed that in emergencies, natural or contrived, he would run a risk of being sacrificed in a forced choice. But he might reasonably expect that emergency-forced choices would be quite rare. He could reckon them to be rare, even in an army in wartime, and with that expectation flock, along with others, to the colours. Agreeing to join a society in which there is systematic planning for life-sacrifices in medical connections and perhaps very frequent occasions calling for the sacrifices would be a different matter. Here, as things stand in the world, people will have little or no compelling experience to go on in assessing the risk, though they might suspect that if medical researchers are going to be freely licensed to do such things, the risk might be quite high. Moreover, the risk is one that can be both created and entirely precluded by social policy – by having a rule forbidding the planning in question. That there be such a policy is something that prudent persons could insist upon as being a feature of any society that they would be ready to join.

In Sanguinario I and II, such a policy is not even hypothetically relevant. What Williams has done with Sanguinario is produce an example that no going ethics can deal with comfortably. It will do the Indian victim no good to appeal outside utilitarianism – to contractarianism, say, or to natural law theory. In mentioning what the Indians might vote for, I have touched on contractarian reasoning: it supports the killing. So would natural law theory or Kantian ethics deployed with any care for plausibility. Williams's example bursts, with the brutal captain, out of the range of any established ethics.

Utilitarianism, in the original BU version, which does not allow for comparisons in which the population at issue changes in composition (except, perhaps, under an extension to accommodate increases by births and decreases by natural deaths), supports just such a policy without mentioning or entailing a right. Prudent persons given a choice of joining a society might demand no more than that the BU version of utilitarianism prevail there, except in forced choices. Important measures of justice are accomplished by BU in respect to taking everyone into account, scoring people on the same basis, and forestalling involuntary life-sacrifices.[36]

Augmented BU, which does allow for such comparisons and thus can formally accommodate life-sacrifices, invites a constraint, which might be expressed in a right, on social planning. The notion of a right is undeniably attractive in this connection, even if it (like the notion of a social contract) is here as much as anything else a metaphor for expressing something that we want to say about consent: social contract theory would license our speaking either of a natural right, emergencies apart, to at least one's natural lifespan, which the contracting agents bring to their deliberations; or of such a right created by the original contract. We would thus project the idea of a social device back upon an idealized hypothetical beginning, holding that it is a feature of any society organized on justifiable terms. But in this case it is a familiar projection, already present in a natural right to security of life and limb, and it is a projection with a firm footing in existing social devices.

Ending up with a right protecting the young man from cannibalization is, of course, to come out of the discussion at a familiar place. However, we did encounter some new things to observe on our way through the discussion: first, that BU can be understood as not entailing involuntary life-sacrifices; second, that the subsequent trouble with utilitarianism on this point – the trouble in our time – comes from BU's having been augmented, I expect typically by critics determined to see the worst in utilitarianism, in a way that belies the intentions and preoccupations of the original advocates of the doctrine; third, that the right, insofar as it is compelling, comes up on one side of a distinction between forced choices that cannot be eliminated by social policy and forced choices that social policy can entirely rule out. The right comes up with the latter sort of forced choices. Moreover, I would point out, the right was arrived at only as an option that standing on a principle of moral respect for persons might render redundant.

Let me reiterate the point that BU, unaugmented, forestalls having to resort either to the right or to the principle to save the prospective Medical Cannibalee in the doctor's office. We can preclude having to face the forced choice that comes up in one version of the cannibalization case by adhering to a combination of BU and good statistical method and with this method adhering to the feature of SGSIT that has been crucial to my argument. Following good statistical method and heeding its results for comparisons of happiness or welfare offers an alternative to granting rights – an alternative that may sometimes afford more efficient protection. Consider the presupposition of BU that everyone is to be counted. Should this presupposition lead to a right to be counted? We may well hesitate to accept such a right, important as it is to make as sure as possible that everyone is counted. For, on the one hand, to set up a right and thus give every person who might claim to be a member of the population a basis for insisting upon being counted may entail costs in litigation, administrative distraction, and hard feeling that actually obstruct the community from taking a timely and thorough census. But a census may not be so efficient as a sample survey anyway. Certainly, as the population becomes very large and carefully controlled sample surveys become more accurate than complete censuses,[37] we would do best to rely on samples. Now someone omitted from a sample survey, if the sample had not been suitably randomized, might have grounds for complaining that the sampling had not given her or people like her a due chance of appearing in the sample. But would it make sense to give her to begin with a right to insist on being taken into the sample? Would this not be obstructive – not just a distraction, but something that threatened to bias the sample? Her being counted is sufficiently assured, for purposes of comparing the happiness or welfare of the population under different policies, by general principles of statistical method, which, along with SGSIT, rule out eliminating anyone from the population before the sample is drawn and prescribe giving every member of the population an equal chance of figuring in the sample.

I stress the generality of the principles:[38] with very large populations, leaving this or that person out of the population will not significantly affect characteristics of the sample; nevertheless, if the principles are to be general enough to cover all populations, they will require leaving the population unchanged when sampling from it. (Certainly this stipulation will apply when we draw in what turns out to be for BU as well as for statistical method the limiting case, a sample coextensive with the whole population, something feasible for small populations, something even requisite for accuracy.)

Setting aside for other treatment forced choices of the sort that social policy is powerless to eliminate, the populations and samples that call for comparison under the combination of BU with good statistical method will automatically assure the young man in the surgeon's office of being considered with as much weight and accuracy as is feasible. The combination will also assure him of retaining his place in the population, hence his life. The question of cannibalizing his body for the benefit of other members of the population would never arise. Cannibalization is not a suggestion that BU, properly associated with good statistical method, would ever bring up.

One might object that it is a weakness of BU that it has no stronger ground for rejecting the suggestion, should it come up, than its not being in accordance with the program of policy evaluation and choice that BU has adopted. BU has been saved by insisting on SGSIT as a built-in limit to its application. But is this insistence any embarrassment? Where does the suggestion of cannibalization come from, and with what colour of reason? BU needs no defence against the charge that it makes the suggestion; the suggestion is not one of its embarrassments.

Moreover, the ground for rejection in which SGSIT figures is not mere proceduralism. SGSIT brings to bear a fundamental received feature of ordinary comparisons of groups with respect to properties ascribed to the members of the groups. Utilitarianism in some versions (especially versions laid out by its critics) does not honour this feature or argue why it should not be honoured.[39] The project set up under Bentham's Master-Idea by BU is to take everyone's happiness into account. When Bentham writes in chapter I of the *Principles* of 'sums' and 'sum totals' he inclines toward the interpersonal felicific calculus before he actually introduces it; but even there he may be ambiguous to a degree. The following chapter begins with a treatment of asceticism, the counterpart and opposite of the Greatest Happiness Principle, and Bentham does not write there of increasing the sum of pain for the community; he focuses steadily on the pain of individual persons.[40] To make anyone unhappy does not fit easily with the project of the Master-Idea given a thoroughgoing concern with individual persons. To do away with someone in order to increase the overall happiness score sits even less easily with it. It is absurd to claim, directly or by implication, that you are promoting someone's happiness when you take away any chance of his having any.

I referred earlier to social contract thinking as something that may develop from the idea that no one could reasonably be expected to agree to join a society in which there is systematic planning for life-sacrifices whenever they are useful in prolonging other people's lives (much less, simply in making them happier). Now I think of the argument of this chapter as restoring to view features of utilitarianism that have been present from the beginning, though what I have done may also be reckoned as a repair, insofar as it makes explicit what the classical utilitarians failed to make explicit. This point about agreement, like the point about statistical thinking, was present from the beginning. It can be found in Bentham's claim that the Greatest Happiness Principle was the only principle that could be recommended by a person addressing the public, which we may take to be the people affected or liable to be affected.[41] If this is so, the opposition between contractarianism and utilitarianism is not thoroughgoing. It is true, the opposition might be said to be greater if the contractarian feature of utilitarianism, as Bentham contemplated it, is not internal but external. It could be suggested that having arrived at his stand on the Greatest Happiness Principle without any thought of its being designed to win general agreement, he discovered that in addition to other merits it had this winning feature. This suggestion does not seem plausible, however, given Bentham's procedure of beginning with the aim of individual persons to enjoy a positive net sum of pleasures and pains and then proceeding to a principle intended to accommodate these aims on the part of all concerned. An element of social contract thinking, vital to dealing with the objection about life-sacrifices and with other things, is internal to utilitarianism, though it is generally left understressed.

Beyond Social Contract Thinking

The element of social contract thinking may belong to utilitarianism, but the use of it may press up against the limit of utilitarian reasoning. There are two ways of approaching the making of social policies with the effects of policies upon happiness or other variable features of the individual persons belonging to a population in mind. One way, which is characteristic of utilitarianism, is to concentrate upon the population affected. The other, which is a fundamental feature of social contract thinking, is to concentrate on how the population that will create the effects is to be organized, considering it, at least to begin with, as also the population affected. Social contract thinking treats the problem of organization as a problem of obtaining mutual consent – given your consent, I consent, too, to the authority that will adopt social policies. The beginnings of social contract thinking called upon to help rescue the Medical Cannibalee straddles the line drawn by the distinction between approaches. The Medical Cannibalee is asking whether he ever consented to a certain social policy or even to belonging to a society in which such a policy might be expected to be adopted.

A deeper point that can be made in defence of sparing the young man – the prospective Cannibalee – in the doctor's office carries us well beyond the limit of utilitarian reasoning, past social contract theory, into the central region of natural law theory.[42] The normal context for natural law theory, which historically has been all too often the normal context for calling upon people to sacrifice their lives, is the context of an established community in which common purposes are pursued as aspects of its Common Good. This consists basically of a number of public goods (like peace, order, security, the diffusion of information, the institutional conditions for prosperity) that every member of the community enjoys without precluding other members from enjoying them to the same extent. These public goods, however, have enough to do with private goods to support arrangements for the members of the community to obtain them.

'Mutual concern that members have enough in private goods to meet their needs,' moreover, 'will be one expression of the members' mutual commitment and ... friendship.' Concern about decent conditions for earning entitlements to private goods will be another.

In these two concerns, taken together, the members discover another public good – the community as an instrument for fulfilling humane purposes respecting needs, work, and entitlements. As such, it is an aspect of the Common Good for those who are in need and helped; it is so, too, for those who want the help to occur though they are not in need themselves. Here, full attachment to the Common Good rises far above self-interest. People fully attached rejoice to have laws and institutions that meet the needs of their fellow citizens. They rejoice, too, in the attachment of other citizens to the Common Good, and not merely because it is useful to themselves to have those others so attached. They value the attainment through that attachment at once of happiness and virtue by others. They rejoice in living in a community that thrives by their sharing commitment, attachment, and rejoicing with other members.[43]

Time and practice over some decades, maybe some centuries – in other words, a history of community – must go into achieving the Common Good so conceived. No social contract, however elaborate and however illuminating in theory about various features of a successful going community, can create the Common Good so conceived by reasoning about immediate circumstances and the prospects of co-operation. Hence, no social contract goes deep enough into social relations as they exist and may be in prospect to supply the normal context for calling upon members of the community to sacrifice their lives for a common purpose that falls in with the Common Good. Such a context is absent in both our families of examples, more starkly in Sanguinario.

It may be said that the context assumed, not present in our examples, is one in which the community might well be able to rely on voluntary sacrifices. Indeed, a community, like the United Kingdom in 1914, that falls far short of achieving the Common Good may be able to put substantial reliance on voluntary sacrifice; the British raised a million volunteers or more for wartime service in 1914–16.[44] However, letting people stand by, ready to benefit, while others make the sacrifices is bound to create some uneasiness about the justice of relying solely on volunteers. So the community may move to compelling some of its members to serve. In the normal context, this compulsion is likely to be accepted by many as a reasonable imposition. The normal context in this respect is very far away from the doctor's office and the miscellaneous assortment of people found there.[45]

Part Two

A Restoration That, Accommodating Utility Still,
Replaces the Calculus with the Census-Notion

4

Does Utilitarianism (Bentham's Master-Idea, Applied Not as Hedonic Act-Utilitarianism, but in Association with the Census-Notion Rather Than the Calculus) Ever Require Substantial Gratuitous Sacrifices of Happiness on the Part of Some People to Make Other People Happier? No*

At this point, the calculus may be replaced by the notion of a before-and-after census, which conforms to the same statistical presupposition precluding life-sacrifices, has immemorially familiar uses and gives effective results (which the calculus, still a project, does not). The census-notion formally resists relegating some people to a lower category while others rise to a higher one. In resisting, it invites renewed use of the policy-making process in its Revisionary mode; and directs the course of revision.

The preceding chapter exculpated Bentham's Master-Idea and with it utilitarianism as Bentham thought of it from the charge that it permitted, even prescribed, sacrificing on occasion the life of one person (reducing anyone's own natural lifespan) in order just to promote the happiness (increase the natural lifespan) of others. The statistical principle that I mainly relied on for this purpose does not, unfortunately, preclude sacrifices short of life, even sacrifices that make the rest of the lives of those who make them utterly miserable. For that principle basically requires only that the population whose happiness is at issue not be reduced in number simply to increase the overall happiness score. To have someone still present who is now miserable does not violate the principle.

---

* In this chapter I draw upon my book *Meeting Needs* (Copyright © 1987 by Princeton University Press, Princeton, New Jersey) and on my essay 'The Concept of Needs, with a Heartwarming Offer of Aid to Utilitarianism,' in Gillian Brock, ed., *Necessary Goods* [Copyright Rowman & Littlefield, Latham, Md, 1998]). I have permission from both publishers to reprint what I require for the chapter, but in the end I have reprinted very little. Ideas and the nomenclature carry over, but the exposition runs in somewhat different terms, with different examples, and comes closer in hardly any passages than a loose paraphrase would.

The sacrifice will be especially galling, to make or to contemplate, to those who feel this generalized objection to sacrifice if making it does no more than make some people happier who are already happy. Why, however, it might be asked by people who are not immediately moved by the generalized objection, is the objection felt at all? Are there grounds for it that utilitarianism cannot ignore?[1] I think a number of grounds can be found, all of which would have some weight with people who would press the objection. People may feel more sympathy for the victims of the sacrifice than they do for the beneficiaries, because they will think that (in the general case) the victims did not deserve their fate. They will also think, more coolly, that utilitarianism will attract fewer adherents if it does not meet the objection; and this will give it less chance of functioning as a social ethics in practical use. Moreover, they will think that were utilitarianism to have social application in the way that the generalized objection has in view, there will be people – the victims – who are being treated not as ends in themselves but as mere means to the ends of others. I echo Kant's language, but the point is commonly raised in terms of 'being used,' as a disappointed woman may say in protest to her lover.

One philosopher who gives great weight to the generalized objection about sacrifice is John Rawls, who charges that the Principle of Utility asks that 'even when we are less fortunate, we are to accept the greater advantages of others as a sufficient reason for lower expectations over the whole course of our life.' This demand, he thinks, amounts to treating people as means rather than ends, and no one could consent to being treated so without losing some self-esteem.[2]

How much help with sacrifices short of life will be another idea, the idea with an affinity to social contract thinking, that I deployed in the last chapter? That idea surfaces again in the position that I have just cited from Rawls: people should not be subjected to policies adopted under a principle that they could not be reasonably expected to agree to.[3] It remains to be seen how much help the idea will be here. Conceivably, it might be argued that one could reasonably agree to a principle according to which, given a substantial chance to benefit oneself, some sacrifices would be made to increase the overall group happiness score. One might, not unreasonably, just hope not to suffer personally. This argument, moreover, might cover substantial sacrifices.

Likewise, it remains to be seen what use is to be made in this connection of the further consideration that any sacrifices must be justified by their benefit to the whole community of which the people called upon for sacrifice are members – normally themselves beneficiaries of belonging to the community – and even in sacrifices supporters. Again, this point connects closely with social contract thinking, though it is a more telling consideration within natural law theory. Members might reconcile themselves to sacrifices because of the contribution the sacrifices make to a community purpose. Again there is an argument that might cover substantial sacrifices, though it would not be plausibly applied when the sacrifices were substantial and the contribution to the community purpose was trivial.

To meet the objection about sacrifices short of life-sacrifices I shall go beyond all of these previous arguments. I shall have in mind mainly rule-utilitarianism, in the sense that I shall be preoccupied with the comparisons of policies defined by different rules – though act-utilitarianism comes into the choice between the rules. I shall make a radical departure from utilitarianism as traditionally conceived by substituting for the felicific calculus the notion of a comparative census, to be understood, as I shall emphasize again and again, as a notion operating in conjunction with the Revisionary Process. The census will heed, just as much as the calculus, the statistical principle of leaving intact the population whose condition under one policy is to be compared with its condition under another. Moreover, the census can be associated, like the calculus, with measurements of utility, though the utility no longer has to be interpersonally comparable in a controversial sense. However, during the greater part of the course of the exposition in this chapter I shall shift away from utility to happiness as ordinarily understood. In the next chapter I shall shift from utility and happiness to needs, in the practical experience of policy-making a more effective and compelling idea, though it does not have the scope, embracing all the values that bear upon the choice of policies, that utility has been intended to have.

(Am I repairing, restoring, or renovating? Since the idea of a comparative census can be held to have been embedded in ordinary discourse about social policy before the idea of a calculus came up, and persisted in that discourse side by side with the calculus, especially as regards evidence about providing for various needs, taken as surrogates for utility, there is a case for calling the census a restoration.

However, it is not clearly a better case than the case for thinking of it as a repair so far-reaching as to rank as a renovation.)

The Census-Notion in a Variety of Applications

If we use the census-notion to compare the consequences of two policies, each embodied in a different social rule, we shall be interested in how many people fit into the categories of the census under one policy as against the other. The following form of comparison is suitable in the most straightforward cases:

	Policy A	Policy B
Top Category	40	70
Bottom Category	60	30

Let the numbers be proportions in a given population – if we have a population of 100, not only proportions, but also the very numbers in each category. Policy A might be related to Policy B in various ways; both policies might be new ones, neither of which has yet been adopted. However, I shall generally work with the assumption that Policy A is the point of departure or the policy of the status quo; the point of comparing it with Policy B is to see whether Policy B would be an improvement. Other things being equal (a condition that I shall in a moment particularize, at least in part), with the table of results given, Policy B is superior to Policy A.

For example, consider a comparison that has to do with 100 soldiers who belong to a company of infantry in the reserve and who turn out for six weeks' training every summer. How many of them, it is asked, are capable after one or another of two different six-week programs of exercise and training to run a mile in ten minutes[4] carrying a full backpack and an assault rifle? Policy A is last summer's program; Policy B is this summer's. Here, the census-notion has the firmest of applications: Physical tests at the beginning of each summer program show that the soldiers are in the same general physical condition in both years; whatever strength they acquired during the first summer has been lost in the fleshpots of civilian life during the time since. The distance over the course to be run, which is the same for everybody, is exactly measurable, as is the period of time; there are no borderline cases. We may suppose that the full backpack has an exactly specified weight, and the rifle is the same in each case. There are no borderline cases here either. Interpersonal comparisons have to be made, but they do not require imposing an interpersonal measurement weighting people's preferences on a continuous scale. The comparisons do no more than classify the soldiers as belonging to one or another of the given categories. As such, they rest on unambiguous public evidence about which of the two categories – 'runs the mile in ten minutes or less' – one person fits into as against another. The result of the comparison is useful and compelling: the six weeks of exercise and training under Policy or Program B are significantly more effective in increasing the proportion of the soldiers who can meet the given test of fitness.

A complication may occur: some of the soldiers may have benefited from the exercise and training under Policy or Program B, while others benefit under the other program and actually deteriorate under the special strains of B. So, some of the forty people who passed the mile-run test beforehand may now fall, not passing, into the Bottom Category. I call this 'a change of persons,' which may be present, as in this case, even if all the proportions change favourably.[5] This does not prevent us from inferring from the evidence that the exercise and training under Policy B increases the proportion of soldiers passing, but it does require that we qualify the evidence in a certain way. It raises the question – a challenge to the Revisionary Process – whether Program A of exercise and training might be modified, perhaps tailored more closely to individual soldiers, so that everybody affected by the program would benefit.

Another comparison under the census-notion – a second application – might have to do with the health of people in a given population. Let everybody in the population have a thorough medical check-up, just before a change in health care policy. Interpersonal comparisons have to be made again, but they rest on the evidence of the medical check-ups, and these have exact measurements of vital signs as important components. Then the Top Category would embrace vigorous people free of any life-threatening disease, and the Bottom Category would embrace people who have a life-threatening disease. Perhaps some plausible threshold must be defined for 'life-threatening.' It would exclude, one would think, tumours that might turn cancerous if left untreated, at any rate when treatment was at hand. Even so, some people surveyed might have little vigour and frequent mild illnesses. It might be best to classify them as in neither good nor bad personal health, just so-so; into this category might also be put people, if there are any, about whose health, whether good or poor, the medical examiners cannot agree. Thus, a Middle Category opens up in the underlying form of the census comparison, with results like the following:

	Policy A	Policy B
Top Category (Vigorous Good Health)	20	40
Middle Category (Health So-So)	20	30
Bottom Category (Poor Health)	60	30

Again, we may have a change of persons to deal with. Though the same number of people or more fall into the two higher categories as beforehand, some people in one or the other of the two higher categories beforehand may now, after the change in policy, fall into a lower category. This result would qualify in a certain sense the otherwise unambiguous evidence that the health of people in the population had improved under Policy B and start up in the Revisionary Process questions aimed at discovering a third policy, under which there would be no change of persons.

An even more undermining qualification, and a more telling challenge for the Revisionary Process, would arise if the overall change was a mixed one: if under Policy B, for example, there were more people in the Top Category (say, 30), but also more people in the Bottom Category (say, 65). Then not only would there be a change of persons. There would be, in spite of the fall in the number of people in the Middle Category, in proportion a worse result in the Bottom Category. Would the improvement in the results for the Top Category offset this deterioration? This is a complication that could not arise with a two-category census, but to return to one of those might well lead to arbitrary judgments that would simply mask the problem. By contrast with the change first mentioned, where the evidence still has a favourable implication (even in the presence of a change of persons) as regards the proportions of people healthy rather than not, with this mixed change that implication fails. Again, it is to be expected that there would be a call for finding some way of revising Policy B so that it affected everybody favourably whom it affected at all. The census results incite research and revision, and we are to think of the census as being used normally in conjunction with a Revisionary Process.

For a third application of the census-notion, let us go back to Bentham's Master-Idea and its connection with happiness. Instead of rushing on to utility in the felicific calculus, however, we move, as

Bentham might have moved, more slowly.[6] We are going to use statistical evidence about the happiness of the people affected to decide upon one or another of several proposed policies. We might ask, 'Will any of the policies make the group affected happier?' But we shall easily go wrong with that question, since it tends to focus attention on the group rather than on the people who compose the group. The history of the concept of utility following Bentham has undermined any resistance that our intuitions might have raised against the tendency. It has not entirely brought resistance to an end. We can ask, resisting, 'Will any of the policies make the people in the group affected happier?' We know how to go about answering that question. We observe whether this person and that person are happy and unhappy, and we count heads in the whole population.

Admittedly, happiness is a subject less firm – less determinable, and in particular less firm in interpersonal comparisons – than health, not to speak of running a mile in ten minutes. There may be different varieties of happiness.[7] Some people may be happy about having an unending course of pleasure; others may be happy because they are absorbed in activities deeply satisfying to them – sometimes, in very fortunate cases, in their work – and there may be other varieties. We could take this into account by stipulating that anyone who was happy in at least one of the ways recognized should be classified as 'Happy,' while anyone who was unhappy in all of the ways should be classified as 'Unhappy.' Yet all of these ways might be to such a degree infirm as to leave a populous Middle Category consisting of people who cannot be unambiguously classified as 'Happy' or 'Unhappy' on any basis.

I shall not try to give a sophisticated account of happiness. The points that I want to make are, first, that the census-notion is flexible enough to accommodate various accounts, some more sophisticated than others; but, second, that the concept of happiness that we use in everyday life, unsophisticated though it may be, suffices for an intelligible and even reliable use of the census-notion. The issue is to find out who in the group is happy and who is unhappy. The individual judgments are such as we frequently are ready to make, judgments from observation of members of our family and of our friends. We find that one person has never been really happy since he lost his job; instead of his former cheerfulness, he goes about with a hangdog look and speaks very little. Another person is happy, indeed from time to time elated, because she has had one success after another in her business and profession. She now shrugs off minor setbacks; she is always responsive and helpful in her dealings with her family. These are judgments about happiness sustained over reasonably long periods of time – months, years, even lifetimes. There is certainly such a thing as being happy for a moment, but it would not be plausible to take that up (by itself) as an objective of social policy.

How reliable could a comparative census of happiness be? If we go about making and collecting the observations with due care, I think sometimes there will be evidence about happiness that deserves a reasonable amount of confidence. Suppose that we form teams of three observers (census-takers, censors), people known to be unusually perceptive of other people's feelings and outlooks. They are to ask about the people surveyed whether those people are happy (in any of the recognized ways) about their present lives or situations in life, taking their situations as wholes and considering the behaviour that they typically exhibit over periods of (say) one month. The testimony of the people surveyed will figure in the evidence, but not alone and not always decisively. (Someone says that she is happy, but she is frequently found weeping in a corner.)

One team or another (to check reliability, sometimes more than one team) visits every person in the population, and every team gives every person sustained observation in a variety of situations for several days at least, distributed over several weeks. It is true, people vary so much in what they reveal of their inner life that even close observers who spend some time with them are not always going to be able to tell whether this person or that person is happy or just keeping up appearances. So, again, a number of people will be put in the Middle Category, this time of people not intermediate in happiness, but undetermined to be one or the other.

This approach makes sure that the discriminating observers on which it relies have had the time and opportunity to make informed observations. It also builds in checks on their performance. I think we could say that the results will be pretty reliable, compared with information developed on other subjects by survey research in the social sciences.

Thus, we might have results like these, from a census of happiness (a felicific census, if we are contemplating a choice between two policies and want to know which will make people happier), respecting, for example, policies (some, but not all of them, moral rules) that differ in respect to hours of work, safety at work, and other conditions:

	Policy A	Policy B
Top Category (Happy)	20	40
Middle Category (In-Between)	20	30
Bottom Category (Unhappy)	60	30

Again, we might have had, not results like these, but a mixed change, under which more people became happy, but more people became unhappy, too. There would have been a change of persons besides, at least with respect to the people formerly not unhappy who have now become so. But even with the present results, there may have a change of persons: some of the people unhappy under Policy B may have been happy under Policy A. Nor is that the only objection that might arise about the present figures (or the figures about health in the earlier example). The thirty people left behind under Policy B may all belong to a racial or religious group for which this would be just one more instance of discrimination.[8] This, too, would call for the operation of the Revisionary Process. Like a change of persons, it raises an issue about justice, and both may require adding constraints on the interpretation of census results to the constraints, answering to aspects of justice, already noted in dealing with the calculus (counting everybody; giving everybody's being happy or unhappy the same weight; discarding nobody from the group to get a better score).

Calling for constraints in all these connections is not in any of the connections an objection peculiar to the census-notion, since the same difficulties about mixed changes, changes of persons, and discriminatory changes arise with the calculus, too. Nor is it an objection to utilitarianism, except in a form that shunned all constraints, ignoring the fact that some constraints must figure in the procedures for collecting evidence about policies if any effective procedures are to be had. The presence of the constraints mentioned forestalls various objections by showing that a number of points of justice are anticipated in the procedures.

There are alternatives for utilitarianism to relying on happiness as the subject of censuses, and I shall present the cases for some alternative subjects later. Yet happiness is not a subject to be dismissed lightly. It has an important place in the history of utilitarianism, and it is important, accordingly, to recognize that it can be made a tolerably effective notion resting on observations collected under the census-notion.

Resistance in Censuses of Happiness to Victimization; the Gains-Preservation Principle

The census-notion, applied to happiness, suffices to lay to rest some of the objections to utilitarianism that the calculus generates. Application of the census shares with the application of the calculus the statistical principle requiring that the population remain the same on both sides of a comparison. But the census-notion goes further than blocking life-sacrifices. It resists sacrifices in which as a consequence of moving away from the status quo some people are relegated to a lower category in respect to happiness while other people – even perhaps a lot of other people – are elevated to a now more populous higher one. Such a change of persons may be involved in an overall change that might be mixed or unmixed. When it is a mixed change, an obstacle to treating the change as a favourable one is immediately visible in the results of a comparative census. If it is an unmixed change, the obstacle to treating it as a favourable one surfaces as soon as we identify the people affected on both sides of the change. The change is not an unambiguous advance in either case, and to endorse it one must override just the objections about sacrifice. Why would one do this, with the Revisionary Process at hand and time to resort to it?

In an unmixed change of proportions, as the number of people by which the Bottom Category decreases by comparison with the number of people by which the Top Category increases, the temptation to endorse the change regardless of the change of persons will strengthen. Much better working conditions for most people may be obtained by having a few relegated to dangerous jobs that can be done only by specialists, seamen, or miners performing indispensable services. Would we really forgo a chance of elevating all the people now in the Middle Category (maybe a lot of people) to the Top Category just because doing so would assign somebody to the Bottom Category who was not there before? We might even be tempted to go along with a mixed change if the increase in the number of people in the Bottom Category amounts to only a few persons, maybe one. These are limiting cases, but the objection to treating them as cases of acceptable improvement still seems strong. The objection will insist that, other things being equal (like the absence of some overall emergency forcing a choice), the sacrifice that the one person or the few must make is not justified and hence argues against moving to the policy in question. Having a Revisionary Process at hand, furthermore, enormously strengthens the argument for resistance; if only a few people, perhaps only one, are being asked to make a sacrifice, it should be easier to accommodate them with a revision (at least, the sort of revision that offers them compensation in amount and kind that no person could reasonably refuse).

I have been steadily assuming that we are dealing with cases in which the distribution of happiness under one policy, in the status quo ante, is being compared with the distribution of happiness under an alternative policy, to which the community concerned has changed or is contemplating changing. These are the cases that are crucial for dealing with the objection about personal sacrifices. Yet we might look for a moment at cases of policies that are rivals for being chosen from the start, without any reference to an established status quo.

Mixed changes (hypothetical changes from one policy to another) will still block unqualified endorsement and still call for inquiries that start up the Revisionary Process. Until a revision has removed the obstacle that making more people happy will (hypothetically) come about at the cost of making more people unhappy, the comparison of the two policies will give no guidance as to which to choose. What about changes of persons when the overall changes in proportions are not mixed? Some of the people who would be happy under the future Policy A will be unhappy under the future Policy B even if Policy B makes a greater number of people happy. Assume that in moving away from the status quo ante we are not carrying forward any information about special entitlements that the people affected adversely could claim. Should the people who will be unhappy stand in the way of the larger number (perhaps the very much larger number) who will be happy? An uncomfortable question, but all that may be required to deal with it is, first, that everybody be given an equal chance to be happy under one policy or the other – then anyone who is unhappy when she could have been happy is making no more than a virtual sacrifice. But even a virtual sacrifice should not be lightly accepted; so, second, vigorous inquiries should be pressed in the Revisionary Process to revise one or the other policy so that there is no one unhappy under the policy finally favoured who is happy under the other policy.

Matters fall out very differently when what is in question is moving from the status quo in Policy A to a Policy B in which there is an unmixed overall change for the better but a real personal sacrifice for some people happy under Policy A who will be made unhappy under

Policy B.[9] Some people are drafted to go down into the mines. If the overall change is a mixed one, more people will be going down into the mines, even though more have pleasant white-collar work.

The census-notion, applied in comparative censuses of happiness, does not suffice to block such a sacrifice (or remove the objection that utilitarianism may demand it). The sacrifices create a problem – a problem, people will feel, about justice – that will have to be dealt with politically if the people involved are free to complain and agitate. It is a recurrent sort of problem, which demands a standing form of answer; and the answer lies in a supplementary feature, namely, what in the spirit of Bentham's nomenclature I shall call the Gains-Preservation Principle.[10] This arises quite naturally in answer to the problem as a further directive to the Revisionary Process. In general, if Policy A is the status quo, it can be thought of as typically representing gains in happiness over earlier policies. The Gains-Preservation Principle endorses only those advances in happiness that let people keep these gains in category even if they are not fortunate enough to move higher now. Under this principle (as in a similar, but not quite matching way, under the Pareto Principle), no one is going to be cast aside to get better overall results, and no one is going to be lowered out of the happiness class in order to raise other people up.[11]

This is a very conservative principle in two respects (though it is to be remembered that the Revisionary Principle is at hand to find improvements that the conservatism will not block).

First, it allows people to keep their present positions when keeping them obstructs making substantial improvements for other people. Moreover, people may not deserve their present privileges. The principle does not leave any room for correcting the injustices of the past that have led some people to be in the 'Happy' Category under Policy A. Some will think that the injustices may have arisen by violating some principle of justice arising independently of utilitarianism.[12] Some will think it has arisen because a contra-utilitarian policy was adopted or allowed to persist in the past. In either case, this is a complication that may lead to suspending the Gains-Preservation Principle until the injustice has been corrected. Yet even in correcting the injustice, something like the principle may be invoked to minimize, perhaps by the use of measures of partial compensation, the damage done to anyone's happiness by the correction.

The second respect in which the Gains-Preservation Principle is very conservative is that applied literally it would preclude diminishing any single person's present happiness, even in a trivial way, when someone else's happiness could be greatly increased as an offset. All that some people might be required to sacrifice is having a third colourful Japanese teapot available for making breakfast or having the mail delivered half an hour earlier in the morning. One might deal with any difficulty so trivial by asking people if they will consent to the reduction. Or one might offer reasonable compensation, perhaps after arbitration. The stakes are small enough for the challenge to the Revisionary Process to be easy to deal with, though sensitive policy-making will recognize that what is trivial to one person is not trivial to another.

Awkward to a degree as both these difficulties may be, they hardly are so serious (especially with improvements that can be reached through the Revisionary Process) as to discredit the combination of the census-notion and the Gains-Preservation Principle and what the combination accomplishes, applied to meet the objection about personal sacrifice over its whole range. That range includes painful and prolonged deprivations as well as sacrifices of life itself. In other words, it includes occasions on which the problem of motivating utilitarianism is at its acutest. But the combination pretty much solves the problem of motivation, since under it the sacrifices that make some results from the calculus most objectionable do not arise. The combination guarantees everyone against a loss of position when on the whole, and for other people, an improvement is in prospect. Overall, everyone could expect to gain something or at least lose nothing from social improvements governed by the combination. Some people might still be ready to gain at the expense of others, but they would have a hard time defending their motives.

Nor are the difficulties cited of a magnitude that matches the advantage of the combination of the census-notion and the Gains-Preservation Principle in relation to the two considerations brought up in the preceding chapter to rescue utilitarianism from the objection about life-sacrifices. The combination, which respects the statistical principle of not reducing the population under comparison to get a better result, also provides for the idea from social contract thinking that policies should be adopted only under a principle or principles to which everyone affected can reasonably be expected to agree. Who could reasonably be expected to agree to a principle that would require a big personal sacrifice in some situations just to benefit a random set of other people? But the combination also meets the deeper condition underlying this one: that people are normally bound to obey, especially when sacrifices are required of them, only policies adopted by a community to which they belong and adopted by that community to advance a common purpose, that is to say, something that falls under one feature or another of its Common Good. (Some provisions might be included, without which the community would have reason to think worse of itself, for aid to strangers.) So I shall stand by the combination of the Gains-Preservation Principle with the census-notion as an appropriate feature of a renovated utilitarianism.

If we insist upon the condition of not making anyone now happy unhappy (or undetermined, neither happy nor unhappy), blocking any endorsement of policies that fail this condition, have we fallen under the spell, so limiting for welfare economics, of the Pareto Principle? We have not fallen there. The Gains-Preservation Principle was something that I originally introduced in the context of public concern about meeting needs. There it clearly leaves open the possibility of transferring resources from people who have more than enough to meet their needs to people who have too little. That goes beyond the Pareto Principle, since the people giving up the resources may prefer to keep them. In application to happiness, the Gains-Preservation Principle is somewhat more conservative, since even if people could be happy with some other combination of resources, in some respects more modest, than they now have, giving up some of the resources may still be painful. But even here the Gains-Preservation Principle is not the Pareto Principle. It leaves open the possibility that resources can be transferred even contrary to their preferences from people now happy, without making them unhappy, even for the moment (which might be only transient) in which having to forgo a third Mercedes SUV is vividly present to their minds. Moreover, whether or not people prefer to stay in their present positions, if they would still fall in the same happiness category after a change of policy, the Gains-Preservation Principle does not stand in the way (as the Pareto Principle would) of transferring resources from them.

Is the Resistance to Victimization Categorical?

Does the combination of the census-notion with the Gains-Preservation Principle lay to rest the objection about imposing sacrifices of happiness short of life-sacrifices? I think the combination, taken together with constraints against discrimination, does just about as much to eliminate, or at least minimize, the sacrifices as can reasonably be expected. It also has, I shall show, as an uncategorical answer, the appropriate character, to many philosophers perhaps surprising, that the best possible answer will have. Nevertheless it is an answer that does not quite suffice to lay the objection to rest.

Let us go back to the census results (given above, p. 111) that show thirty people remaining in the Unhappy Category even under the policy more attractive on the point of happiness. If their being in the category is an effect of discrimination, the constraint bearing upon discrimination blocks us from deeming the policy entirely acceptable and incites us to turn to the Revisionary Process to find a policy that escapes the effects of discrimination. However, can we really count on finding one? Moreover, without discrimination's playing any part, the best policy that we hit upon may leave some people unhappy (indeed, in all realism, it is likely to do so).

Rawls's objection seems to arise again.[13] Even if no one in the Unhappy Category is being used in any plausible sense (a whipping boy; a servant; a double in dangerous situations) as a means to procure 'the greater advantages' of people kept in the Happy Category or promoted to it, still the otherwise favoured policy assigns people (say, the thirty people of our original example) to 'lower expectations.' By itself, however, this does not invite Rawls's objection. That objection concerns being assigned to lower expectations 'over the whole course of our life.'

The logical possibility of making a choice of policy once and for all, to hold over 'the whole course of our life' cannot be extinguished, and Rawls's objection would apply were such a choice ever to come up. To return to a theme prominent in earlier chapters, however, policy-making choices are not usually of this sort (to understate matters). They are made serially, in a process where later rounds can be expected to afford opportunities to remedy difficulties left over in policies chosen now.

How long will the people left behind have to wait for remedies? By hypothesis they are not going to be given relief in the present round of policy-making, which for many possible reasons will have to conclude before remedies have been found. But it cannot be guaranteed that the remedies will be found in the next round either, even if they are diligently looked for – and so on, in further rounds. It cannot even be guaranteed that the difficulties that beset the people left behind and cause them to remain unhappy will be identified on an early round.

Even when they have been identified and remedies for them have been found, the remedies may take a long time to operate with full effect. This has been the case with familiar and visible difficulties like discrimination on the basis of race and gender, and might well be the case with difficulties that are present without discrimination. One might hope for a watershed – a tipping point – after which the difficulties to be remedied fade out slowly, perhaps, but surely. But this cannot be guaranteed either.

Can we count on the remedies being (sooner or later) successful and thoroughgoing? No. Yet this is not because the project, first, of promoting all unhappy people to one or another of the categories above and, second, of promoting all people in the In-Between Category (neither happy nor unhappy) is entirely hopeless. It is reasonable to expect to make some headway with both stages of this project – to be able to move some people at least out of the Bottom Category and out of the In-Between Category as well; and why should we believe that the remedies used to make headway will surely give out short of the goal? Furthermore, what looks like a fantastically ambitious project if it is taken up for a national population of hundreds of millions or even (as in Canada) of some 30 million does not look so fantastic if we consider a family living in one household. Could not the obstacles facing any member of the family be identified and with some serious effort be removed? But if a serious effort succeeds in this way in one household, why not in many? Why not, in the end, in all?

Suppose, however, that it is conceded that with any large population we cannot reasonably expect in practice to make everybody happy, no matter how many rounds of the Revisionary Process are allowed for the efforts. Then, the practical position that utilitarianism is led to is nevertheless one that relies on the prospect of continuing efforts to make as many people as happy as possible. In present circumstances, when the time has come for a choice, the policy to be chosen is the one that, subject to the Gains-Preservation Principle and to constraints against discrimination, does best, among the necessarily limited number of options considered, on the comparative application of the census-notion. But that policy is chosen, in keeping with utilitarianism, only subject to the proviso that efforts continue in the Revisionary Process (as long as the problem remains) to increase the number of people in the Happy Category by reducing the number in the two categories below.[14]

Thus, in a way characteristic of the spirit of this book and reflecting (as so characteristic) some of its distinctive themes, the objection about sacrifices of happiness short of life-sacrifices is answered by invoking, first, a continuing process, serial and remedial, of policy-making, in which the Revisionary Process will figure vigorously if conscientious utilitarians have their way; second, the commitment to carry on in that process, without flagging, the project of increasing the proportion of the population (and the successor population) that are happy rather than unhappy; third, the use of the census-notion in combination with the Gains-Preservation Principle with constraints against discrimination. That is not a categorical answer. It leaves open the possibility of contravening Rawls's objection in a logically possible once-and-for-all choice. It leaves open the possibility, logical again but more realistic, that the number of people in the Unhappy Category will never be brought down to zero. Yet I think it is a powerful answer, nevertheless, and I think that a better answer suited to the serial and remedial nature of the policy-making process will not be forthcoming.[15]

Prospects of Decline Rather Than Prospects of Improvement

The discussion so far has had in view choices of policy in which prospects of improvements are at issue. The improvements may not extend to everyone, but at least under the conditions stipulated for the use of the census-notion they will be undertaken only if no one loses out personally when they are brought in. Something should be said about choices in which the prospects, whatever is done, are prospects of worsening conditions. I shall distinguish two possibilities: first, situations in which the worsening is not inevitably imposed on some specific subgroups in the population; second, situations in which such impositions will occur.

Worsening Shared Out

Suppose the resources of the community have shrunk, because of drought or pestilence or war. One way of dealing with the diminished prospects for the community might be to focus on the remaining resources and try to make sure that they are distributed in a way that does as little damage as possible to people's positions respecting resources. Redistribution on the basis of a proportional or perhaps a progressive tax might be the way to do this. I shall discuss this possibility further in the next chapter, when I concentrate on surrogates for utility or happiness, especially provisions for needs. Here, I consider another approach, which focuses on the present achieved status of people – the happiness of some, the unhappiness of others, the intermediate status of people neither clearly one nor clearly the other.

The Gains-Preservation Principle can no longer apply if (as I shall assume) the resources available to the community have shrunk to the extent of making it impossible to retain the present position of everyone involved. But the spirit of the Principle can still operate if the approach that is taken is, first, to minimize (in choosing among the alternatives proposed) the number of people changing from the Intermediate Category to the Unhappy one; second, to minimize the number of people changing from the Happy Category to the Intermediate one; third, to restore the people made unhappy to a higher category on as early a successive round of policy-making as possible. (I shall assume that reducing people from Happy all the way to Unhappy does not come into the picture; the resources, though shrunken, are flexible enough and extensive enough to limit the required changes to those specified.)

This approach extends (hand-in-hand with ideas about justice) the solution of the motivation problem to some of the worsening situations. Again, we could introduce a refinement according to which anyone to be reduced from one category to a lower one would have an equal chance with everyone else in the higher category to escape the reduction. But we might have to deal with complications in some possible cases where giving everyone this equal chance precluded a solution in which fewer people had to change to the lower category. So long as anyone contemplating agreeing to the procedure did not have to fear being singled out for victimization, the overall chances of escaping reduction because the number reduced would be minimized might suffice for motivation.

Consistent with earlier remarks about the policy-making process, we must suppose that minimization goes no further than minimizing reductions in a choice from a finite, indeed rather limited, set of alternative policies. Round after round of revision, however, could be expected to succeed the first choice of policy, with the aim, if the overall situation did not worsen further, of restoring the positions of as many people as possible, thereby in time minimizing the reductions ever further. If the overall situation did worsen, the two stages of minimization would be applied to a limited set of alternatives then available, with the hope that revision could begin again soon afterwards.

Burden of Worsening Imposed on Specifiable Subgroups

Consider, now, worsening situations in which there are subsets on whom the sacrifices must be imposed. The most prominent cases will be men (and women) of military age, who have to be called into dangerous service to defend the community. But other cases can easily be thought of: for example, householders whose homes have to be destroyed to stop the spread of a fire. In some situations, they could be compensated, indeed have new houses built for them. If the resources of the community are too limited to do this, however, or at least too limited to do it right away, the subset would bear something like the full impact of the worsened situation, just as the subset of men and women of military age would bear the full impact of a situation worsened by war or the danger of war.

Would people still be motivated to accept such burdens? The selection of the subgroups who are to shoulder the burdens is not arbitrary; and that is at least a step towards establishing the justice of the selection. Furthermore, without bringing in notions about community, the Common Good, and common purposes, we could still argue that people who consider that they benefit from the procedures followed in the other sorts of situation that I have considered (improvements; worsenings that can be shared by the whole group) could accept the risk that they would have to shoulder such burdens. Certainly the motivation to do so would be more easily forthcoming if there were some prospect of being compensated. Those who return from the war can be given various privileges, like bonus points on civil service examinations; if they return wounded, they can be given medical care and occupational therapy. If the risks of not returning or returning wounded are low, the compensations may be reasonably attractive. Similarly, people who have had to sacrifice their houses, and the part of their happiness bound up with their houses, may in time have new houses given to them and become attached to them. How long this process would take is a question that cannot be given a simple answer, though at least the answer would be easier to come by than it would in large questions about compensating for generations of victimization of the sort experienced by American blacks.[16]

Motivation to accept the sacrifice imposed on a subgroup would be more easily forthcoming also if it were one aspect of being motivated to accept the combined procedures and benefits of living in the community where they operate. If we consider by itself the motivation to accept the dangers, not fully subject to compensation, of military service and other burdens similar to military service in this respect, a direct conflict with self-interest arises, of just the sort that in this connection gave so much trouble to Hobbes.[17] With the combined procedures in view, moreover, we set our feet on a path that leads from utilitarian accommodation for self-interested motivation toward public-spirited motivation, based on habits of cooperation and fellow-feeling, and finally toward attachment to the Common Good.

The Advantages of the Census-Notion over the Calculus; the Greatest Happiness of the Greatest Number

A systematic list of the advantages of the census-notion over the interpersonally additive calculus will include a number of items.

First, the census-notion actually works; it is continually present in the actual practice of policy-making, where utility is never heard of. Even if its guidance were confined to the cases in which the results are unmixed, free of change of persons, and non-discriminatory, it would have more practical scope than the calculus, which does not figure in practical politics at all. But if the census-notion combines, as I am continually presenting it as doing, with the Revisionary Process, then its scope expands to the whole range of policy-making; if it is sometimes even so unable to identify an unambiguously acceptable policy, that is normally only a temporary defeat.

Second, the census-notion does not attempt, like the calculus, to arrive at an overall quantum of utility or anything else. Instead – a third advantage – it can use, not the abstract, puzzling idea of utility, but familiar categories relating to human welfare. Taking these two points together, a fourth advantage can be discerned: The census-notion reflects and represents the language – the ordinary language – of the familiar, customary way of making comparisons respecting the happiness (or any other personal property) of people considered as belonging to groups.

Fifth, the census-notion in application makes mixed changes obtrusive, forcing policy-makers back on the Revisionary Process. A sixth advantage, which cannot be so simply formulated, has to do with changes of persons when these come with unmixed changes. The Gains-Preservation Principle takes care of much of the trouble here, but the Gains-Preservation Principle could logically also be used with the calculus (at some cost to received expectations of how it is to be applied). Yet the Gains-Preservation Principle could be so used only by invoking some features of the census-notion, namely, keeping track of how people, one by one, come to be put in higher or lower categories. On this point, the census-notion is a more direct way to showing what needs to be done.

Finally, seventh, the census-notion makes better sense than the calculus does of the slogan 'The Greatest Happiness of the Greatest Number.' This may be more of a theoretical advantage than a practical one, but it concerns a familiar point of theory, which could hardly be more prominent.

Edgeworth teaches us that the slogan 'the Greatest Happiness of the Greatest Number' breaks down in the company of the calculus.[18] For sometimes the greatest aggregated interpersonal score will demand one policy, and the widest distribution of happiness (in the sense of giving as many people as possible a high score) will demand another policy. The census-notion never gives contradictory results like these; the worst that can be said of it is that sometimes (in cases of mixed change) it may give results that do not admit of a favourable interpretation and in those instances do not give any immediate guidance; even then, resort to the Revisionary Process normally prevents a standstill.

In principle, the Revisionary Process could be used with the calculus, too, but only if the calculus is sacrificing full commitment to 'The Greatest Happiness' or full commitment to 'The Greatest Number' – one or the other. Suppose that the champions of the calculus renounced guidance from any cases in which the policy with the greatest overall utility score was one in which, clearly disfavoured by the census-notion, both the number of people happy was reduced and the number of people unhappy was increased. Would they override the mixed cases in which more people become happy, but more become unhappy, too? If they were sensitive to the fate of the people newly becoming unhappy, perhaps they would renounce guidance in this case, too, again, it might be said, under some pressure from the census-notion. There would remain, in principle, a class of unmixed cases, but among these the calculus would select the policy with the greatest overall utility score – the Greatest Happiness, as champions of the calculus understand it – regardless of whether it was the policy that made the Greatest Number happy. They could select, with the census-notion, the policy (among the alternatives considered) that made the Greatest Number happy only by cutting loose from the Greatest Happiness as they understand it.

Edgeworth gave no more explicit attention to the census-notion than any of the other classical utilitarians. Yet it gives, quite as much as the felicific calculus, a way of realizing Bentham's idea that statistical evidence should count decisively in the choice of social policies. But the census-notion, unlike the calculus, gives the slogan in question a fully coherent sense. Consider again the following comparison:

	Policy A	Policy B
Top Category (Happy)	20	40
Middle Category (In-Between)	20	30
Bottom Category (Unhappy)	60	30

The census-notion applied to happiness calls for pushing on from a census result like this – which favours Policy B in respect to, say, opportunities for a congenial social life – to another under a policy that puts even more people into the Top Category (Happy) and even fewer into the Bottom Category (Unhappy). Thus, the census-notion advances the Greatest Happiness by striving to rise from lower categories to higher ones, and it advances the Greatest Number by striving to increase the number and proportion of people in the higher categories, eventually in the highest category of all. From results accepted for the time being as favourable the march again and again resumes, advancing from one increase in happiness to another as opportunities can be opened up to bring such increases about. To be sure, the march would not be easy all the way or at the end for everybody participating if the Gains-Preservation Principle did not apply all along. But if (as I assume) it does apply, people will not be subjected on the way to unpleasant vicissitudes of rising and falling in personal happiness.

Have we entirely departed from historical utilitarianism with the census-notion?[19] Not only is the census-notion at least another formally acceptable way besides the calculus of marshalling statistical evidence bearing upon happiness. As a familiar and commonplace notion of dealing with changes in the condition of people belonging to groups, may it not have been in the minds of the classical utilitarians at least to the extent that a half-conscious sense of this alternative possibility lay behind their use of the slogan about the Greatest Happiness of the Greatest Number? To make full sense of the slogan, there was no need to resort to a notion more exotic than the census. In some passages, Bentham was not a Greatest Happiness utilitarian, ready to go the distance with the calculus, but a Greatest Number one, receptive to census data.[20]

The slogan, taken in conjunction with the census and thus rendered coherent, embodies the notion of an optimum, though one not likely to be at hand or permanent were it attained. It is not an optimum that choice can wait for, though it may guide choices round by round as a distant prospect. An optimum would be reached when no further move is available that would produce (given the constraints) an advance in the sense of achieving more favourable census results. But reaching it would never be certain. How could there be any certainty, given continuing imperfect information, about the more attractive options not being available? New ideas about the use of present resources and technology may come up, suggesting ways to reach further improvements, which will now figure as possibilities in the policy-making process. New resources and new technologies may appear. Certain or uncertain, again, this is not necessarily a Pareto optimum, since the advances here may have overridden preferences in favour of real results in happiness.

If the optimum associated with censuses of happiness is only a temporary halting place, it may seem that, certain or uncertain, stopping there would be settling for very crude results. No more is demanded, even in the end, than that as many people as possible are observably happy on an overall view. But can we not imagine making people now happy even happier? Here, if Bentham had indeed come down this path and felt the want of some way of comparing greater and lesser degrees of happiness in groups, he might, again, have gone on to sketch the felicific calculus. If only we could have stopped him![21]

There is nothing suspect about the notion of there being greater and lesser degrees of happiness. We could imagine censuses with the Happy Category subdivided into 'Tolerably Happy,' 'Happy without Qualification,' and 'Effervescently Happy'; and we can imagine making sense of comparisons carried out in those terms. However, it is hardly as urgent for social policy to go on to refinements of happiness as it is to make everybody roughly happy in the first place. We would be doing very well, better probably than any social system in history has done, if we could make everybody just happy – put everybody somewhere in the Happy category – and if we become preoccupied with doing so, it is a preoccupation that is going to last a very long time, if not indefinitely. Moreover, it is going to be very much more difficult, compared with establishing that this or that person is just happy, to establish that one happy person is happier than another or even happier than she was, having already been happy. Mary was happy before, in spite of a little uncertainty about whether she would keep her job; now that she no longer needs to worry about that, she is happier than ever. But is that really so? Maybe she will be bored, now that she no longer has anything to worry about, but she can't say that without seeming ungrateful for her good fortune.

The Reintroduction of Utility

I said, when I temporarily put utility aside, that the move from the calculus to the census did not require abandoning utility. Now, after explaining and discussing the operation of the census-notion applied to less artificial themes, I can let utility return to the stage. The categories of the census will now be categories of higher and lower utility,[22] and utility may be conceived in as sophisticated a way as is available. It may rest on a subtle analysis of the gratifications of human life.[23] It may be sophisticated in this way or in other ways, yet not by itself license adding up the utilities of different persons to reach an aggregative score. The system of measurement proposed by John von Neumann and Oskar Morgenstern rests on establishing a scale person by person by discovering, given three goods x, y, and z such that the person in question prefers x to y and y to z, what probability of having x rather than z in a lottery over the two the person accepts as equivalent to having x for sure. It does not by itself offer such a licence.[24] However, if one follows John Harsanyi in joining to it the assumption that we can find a position (behind a veil of ignorance or otherwise) in which people do, in fact, have the same values for x and y and so forth, the combination of this assumption with the von Neumann and Morgenstern system supports interpersonal additions.[25] Another sophisticated approach to measuring utility, that of John Broome, has the same feature.[26] Broome elaborates with great exactness and subtlety a system – the structure of 'good,' he says, for inducing an interpersonally valid scale on personal 'better-than' relations for particular goods. (Broome emphasizes an 'interpersonal addition theorem' that rests on three premisses: that every person at issue has a coherent 'betterness' relation, that is to say, one that conforms to the axioms of expected utility theory; that the betterness relation for the group to which the persons belong is also coherent; that 'there can be no increase in general good without an increase in some individual's good.' The theorem is not an argument for interpersonal comparisons. By assuming that the general betterness relation is coherent, which includes its being complete, Broome acknowledges, that he is assuming that interpersonal comparisons are possible.[27])

Even if the system of measurement permits interpersonal additions of utility, the census-notion makes no use of such additions. Indeed, the cautions built into the census-notion itself and in its supplementation by the Gains-Preservation Principle require in effect that interpersonal additions be renounced even if they are feasible. For it is the census-notion with its cautions that must govern, not any reversion to the calculus.

In one rather astonishing passage,[28] in which he discusses an example that cries out for connection with the objections about sacrifice and victimization, Broome treats interpersonal additions as governing, blithely ignoring the objections.[29] Two people are compared, having in the one case, £100 in a first distribution and £20 in the second, while the other person, who has £200 in the first distribution gets £320 in the second. Once, we have the two persons' utility functions, Broome holds, we can infer that the better distribution in the general betterness relation is the one that gives the greater total of utility. But the two utility functions may be such that both persons get the same undiminished utility for pounds within the range of £20 to £320. Then, by Broome's approach, the second distribution is better than the first, the victimization of one person to favour another notwithstanding.

The pounds sterling are just a stand-in for a plausible specification of the goods for persons and groups. Broome, preoccupied with structural considerations that in his view would apply to any of a variety of specifications, leaves the choice of specification open. But even if in his example we substitute for pounds sterling something more plausible as a specification, say, life-situations (including chances to change them for the better), the objection about sacrifice and victimization applies. Anyone who takes the objections about sacrifices and victimization seriously, as I and others do, must insist, however, that such additions must be blocked if they run against the constraints regarding changes of persons, even changes of persons with changes of proportions, that I have shown the census-notion to resist. This seems to require throwing away information otherwise relevant to promoting the good of the people in the groups at issue. To some extent, it does require this, but as I shall point out in a moment, the information is not necessarily all lost.

Let us return to the census form of comparison:

	Policy A	Policy B
Top Category	20	40
Middle Category	20	30
Bottom Category	60	30

This time let the categories rest on utility scores given by the approaches referred to or some other approach equally sophisticated. If we identify the Top Category as including only people having a utility score above a certain figure, say, above 700 on a scale of 1000 and the Bottom Category as having a utility score below 300 on the same scale, the table represents Policy A as giving an improvement in utility. We do not add the utility scores between persons, even if the approach that we are adopting licenses this. We go no further in comparing persons than to put them into one or another of the three categories.

How satisfactory a basis for choosing between policies does such a comparison offer, resting as it does on personal utility scores? When we put aside various technical objections,[30] the comparison invites being regarded as a more exact version of a common-sense comparison resting on observations of personal happiness, an elusive subject for ordinary observation. The exactness is in its favour; it would enable us at the very least to reduce the number of cases assigned by ordinary observation to the Middle (undetermined) Category. Moreover, the exactness will lie at least in the neighbourhood of what policies might be aiming at in achieving congenial distributions of personal happiness.

On the other hand, one may expect that, as things stand, it will take an impractical amount of expert attention to carry out the measurements for every person affected; one may expect that it will also demand an impractical amount of time on the part of the persons whose scores are to be measured. Experts and ordinary citizens will have to cooperate in each case to establish a scale of utility and then discover where Policies A and B are on that scale. One improvement in measuring utility to be looked for is having systems of measurement that are easier to use.

More important, the scores, if they are to be taken as letting us make comparisons more exact than ordinary ones, must fall in with ordinary observational assessments of personal happiness, in the sense that they must not rate people happy who are, on those assessments, unhappy or vice versa. There is a problem to be solved about divergence from the ordinary assessments. People do not always have preferences that advance their happiness. It may take them much time and wide experimentation, for which they will have only limited opportunities, to develop preferences that allow them to progress toward happiness. So it may be unsafe to take any measurement founded on present preferences as a substitute for an assessment of personal happiness.

This difficulty undermines any conviction that a census result about the comparison of utilities would otherwise carry. Is it really a compelling consideration in social policy that people should rise from one category to another in their personal utility scores? I do not think that policy-makers will have strong intuitions about the moral significance of utilities; for one thing, utility scores as such have never been objects of consideration in making policy, so that policy-makers have had no practice dealing with them. Stronger intuitions have to do instead with happiness; even stronger ones, which can be translated into explicit standards of provision, have to do with meeting needs.

If a sophisticated system of measuring utilities is adopted and put into practice in such a way that both the rising and falling of people in the census categories are recorded convincingly, some use may be found for aggregative utility scores as well. For people concerned with the objection about personal sacrifices, they will not override the constraints associated with the results from applying the census-notion. If, however, they suggest that some other policy, not favoured by a census-comparison, has more good to offer – for some people, life-situations (including life-chances) better than they would get under the policy favoured by the comparative census – then this will be a fact that can activate the Revisionary Process and incite efforts to revise policies so that one moves closer to the aggregative score and still heeds the constraints associated with the census. (In the next chapter, I shall make use of this possibility in suggesting how to deal with values that go beyond meeting needs.)

The upshot of these reflections is that utility, though it can be applied under the census-notion, may do no better there, as a guide to policy, than happiness; or, if people are attracted by aggregative utility scores away from the constraints against victimization associated with the census-notion, it may do even worse.

Happiness and Alternatives to Happiness

Shall we go back then to happiness? But under the sketch that I have given about how to conduct the observations, evidence about happiness requires procedures that are, if not so elaborate and impractical as the ones currently suggested for arriving at personal utility scores, still elaborate enough to look impractical. Moreover, even with these procedures, happiness remains an elusive and a relatively infirm subject for the application of the census-notion.

Shall we shift then to a firmer subject? Personal health offers itself, firmer than happiness yet akin to it, since happiness and health generally run together. It can indeed serve as a surrogate for happiness or for the satisfactions that utilitarianism has aimed at under utility. Health is a theme that has been developed for use in policy-making in what are known as 'Quality of Life Comparisons,'[31] which consider health over people's whole lives and discount years of being bedridden and invalid in other respects.

As a criterion for the evaluation and choice of policies, health, especially health as a subject developed in some such way, is certainly firm enough and specific enough to serve. Moreover, so developed, it may be applied so as to avoid the temptation, with a measure for health and an aggregative calculus, of ignoring the constraints against sacrifice and victimization that I have been treating in this present chapter. However, health does not give as great a variety of clues to progress in policy as the concept of needs, which can be developed equally well for firm and specific application. 'Equally well' – in one important sense better, since it can be developed without ever outrunning familiar forms of comparison in favour of an index as complicated as Quality of Life becomes under refined attention. Providing for the various needs, moreover, can serve equally with health (indeed, has served) to make them surrogates for health and utility; such surrogates account for whatever reputation utilitarianism has had for being a doctrine with political influence. So I shall shift on from the theme of happiness to the theme of needs as subjects for comparative censuses.

Part Three

A Renovation That Makes Provision for Needs
Prior to Concern with Utility

5

Does Utilitarianism (Bentham's Master-Idea) Fail Because of Problems about the Intelligible Systematic Use of the Concept of Utility? No*

The concept of needs serves better currently than the concept of utility to establish priorities of social policy in the application of Bentham's Master-Idea, and serves better because, among other things, it drastically reduces problems about measurement and interpersonal comparisons. Moreover, real-world applications of Bentham's Master-Idea to date have typically made use of the concept of needs, not the concept of utility. Amartya Sen's 'capabilities' approach, which for part of its way goes hand in hand with the concept of needs, but goes further, might come in to deal with questions remaining after needs have been met; so might utility in some guise, and the pursuit of pleasure.

Bentham's original purpose, to hold actions and social policies accountable to effective evidence of their impacts on human welfare, has proved cogent enough to enable utilitarianism to survive a long-standing embarrassment about the evidence of such impacts, namely, the embarrassment about not being able to make anything effective in practical application of the felicific calculus. Utilitarianism has even survived more recent embarrassments about evidence. One comes from redefining utility as simply a matter of realizing preferences and then in consequence foundering in the renunciations of welfare economics, reduced to silence with the Pareto Welfare Principle whenever a con-

*In this chapter I draw again upon my book *Meeting Needs* (Copyright © 1987 by Princeton University Press, Princeton, N.J.) and on my essay 'The Concept of Needs, with a Heartwarming Offer of Aid to Utilitarianism,' in Gillian Brock, ed., *Necessary Goods* (Copyright Rowman & Littlefield, Latham, Maryland, 1998). I have permission from both publishers to reprint what I require for the chapter, but in the end I have reprinted very little. Ideas and the nomenclature carry over, but the exposition runs in somewhat different terms, with different examples, and comes closer in hardly any passages than a loose paraphrase would.

flict of preferences crops up. Another, arising from the same redefinition, consists in the paradoxes with which social choice theory has beset projects of aggregating personal preferences. Largely as a consequence of not allowing for the Revisionary Process as a way of escaping from impasses, it has appeared that there is no satisfactorily rational way of doing this, that is to say, no way that can meet the apparently very modest demands of Arrow's conditions.[1]

Utilitarianism does not have to accept the Pareto Welfare Principle; and utilitarianism does not come to a stop with Arrow's theorem and social choice theory. Moreover, utilitarianism keeps in view an indispensable project, even when with utility and the calculus it does so in a form not realized and perhaps, for practical purposes, of doubtful realization forever. What alternative is there, in ethics or in ethics applied to politics, to the project of Bentham's Master-Idea, utilitarianism in some sense, broad if not narrow, of according ineluctable importance to the impacts of policies on human welfare? And how (though philosophers and economists have made it a puzzle just how) can such impacts not be considered (whatever else is), sometimes decisively considered, in evaluating social policies?

True, these questions do not seem to be obvious to the point of being rhetorical if they are approached through the recent debate about consequentialism, in which Samuel Scheffler's work has been the centre of attention.[2] But that is because either the debate has been about a different question – as I said at the beginning of chapter 2, not about the evaluation of social policies, but about whether persons should act as moral agents on consequences alone (or at all); or the debate has been carried on without discriminating between this question and the questions about social policy. I think that it is preposterous to suggest that persons (even if they act normally simply to heed moral rules) should not be ready to consider the consequences of the actions that they are choosing; but I concede that it is, by an order of magnitude, not so preposterous as to suggest that consequences can fall out of consideration in the choice of social policies. I have had something to say in preceding chapters about the choices of personal agents, but my main concern throughout the book has been and will continue to be choices of social policies by governments (or other collectivities).

Systematic Construction of a Schema for Needs

If utilitarianism is, right now, to contribute more than an unfinished project to the choice of policies, and, so contributing, to deal with the consequences of those policies, it has to be recast. Looking for evidence about human welfare, it has, at least for the time being, to set aside not only the felicific calculus in favour of the census-notion, but also the notion of utility, given its difficulties and the lack of practice in its use. The most promising way of recasting it is to make use of the concept of needs. This is so in spite of the association of the concept with the tiresome subject of 'neediness,' which many people dislike dealing with, and its association, too, with the indignities, manifesting that dislike, that often accompany measures intended, grudgingly, to help needy people.[3] Needs cannot be disregarded in social policy even if there is currently no neediness. The many, repeated, concrete applications of the concept of needs make it less elusive than happiness, with which, by comparison with needs, practical politics has had relatively little practice; and it ranges over a greater variety of things than health, which in effect has to do with a subset of the things within its range.[4]

To be used without uneasiness, however, the concept of needs has to be, if not recast itself, at least extricated from the incessant confusion with which it is commonly used. Many needs are adventitious, tied to personal goals that come and go with wants or desires that not everybody has. Some of those goals may be mere fantasies. What within human powers (even powers carried as far as we could expect research to go) can give them invisibility without being annihilated, another life, or the power of unaided flight? Not everything that people intensely want apart from fantasies is something that they in every case, or sometimes in any, need even adventitiously, for some goal both optional and feasible. Not everything that people do need to reach adventitious goals is something that they need without qualification. They may need jewellery or a limousine to impress neighbours or customers or a set of golf clubs to play golf; on the other hand, they would cease to need these things if they ceased to pursue the goals at stake. They cannot cease, during the whole course of their lives, to need food, shelter, clothing, safety, companionship; they cannot escape, at times in their lives, the need for education and the need for sexual activity. These are the sorts of subjects that are most assured of coming to bear with moral force upon people moved to safeguard and promote human welfare.

The claims made under the concept of needs, however, often do not in practice heed the cautions implied by distinguishing feasible goals from goals not feasible or, given feasible goals, adventitious needs from needs not adventitious. Just because the concept has so much moral force, people, even small children, seize upon it, in whatever connection it can be deployed, as a vehicle for demanding anything that they strongly want. A four-year old accompanying her mother shopping pressed the demand for a toy by saying, 'I don't just want it; I need it.' The mother, a political philosopher, thought this showed how hopelessly confused is any thought of there being a distinction between needs and wants. But does it not show, on the contrary, that the distinction is so familiar that a four-year-old child can use it, knowing its force?

There is an analogy with what the emotive-imperative position in ethical theory recognizes in the case of the yet more general term 'good'; people appropriate this term for a wide variety of (implicit) 'persuasive definitions'[5] and thus jeopardize its moral force. The way to make sure that the cautions about the concept of needs are heeded – in effect, the way to safeguard the moral force of the concept by limiting its use – is to seize upon certain features of familiar usage. These features can be exhibited in a systematic construction: a schema for the concept of needs. (One or another analogous program can be undertaken to safeguard the moral force of 'good.') The construction is no doubt a technical refinement; the features of familiar usage are not. Coordinated by the construction, they offer a guide to effective application of the concept of needs in evaluating policies. The construction installs the familiar features in the schema and thereby produces a framework that facilitates appropriate discussion (argumentation seeking conviction) and negotiation (bargaining – offering to be more generous on one point if another is treated less generously).

The schema, as constructed, is idealized in at least two respects; first, in aiming to frame an organized view of the use of the term 'needs' that it takes as basic, though it is not (I think) the most frequent use. The organized view is, it is true, something that the construction assumes will be achieved through discussion and negotiation, and the construction allows for these things. However – and this is the second respect in which the construction is idealized – the discussion and negotiation allowed for are assumed to have the schema in view as a project to be filled out point by point. This salience for the project, as I shall explain in due course, is not likely to be found in real-world politics or policy-making. For the time being, however, I put off descending all the way to the real world, and I assume salience.

The construction begins by assuming that there is a Reference Population whose needs are under consideration and a Policy-Making Population,[6] which may not be identical with the Reference Population, whose understanding of the concept of needs will be decisive for the policies adopted for the Reference Population. The most frequent case, however, is one in which the Reference Population is identical with the Policy-Making Population, and that is the case that I shall mainly have in view here. But the case in which the two populations are wholly separate, which I shall come to later in the chapter, is important for policies affecting economic development in the Third World.

The construction would finish up in a schema with a number of dimensions (so many aspects of the concept of needs) in which full agreement would come about in the Policy-Making Population only after protracted discussion and negotiation. This discussion and negotiation, I assume, will be open to general participation. Moreover, the Population will participate in both its Reference and its Policy-Making capacities. In its Reference Population capacity, the Population will testify to the effects of policies upon them. In its Policy-Making capacity, it will decide, among other things, what to make of this testimony.

The Policy-Making Population, let us suppose, has to agree on two things: the needs to be met in that population; then, once that issue has been fully defined and settled, the arrangements, that is to say, the policies, to meet them. The first issue invites philosophical attention. The second issue I shall have to leave, in the main, to social scientists.

What is the issue now about defining needs? It, too, can be taken to have two aspects: first, fixing upon a List of Matters of Need; then, fixing upon the Minimum Standards of Provision for each Matter of Need on the List. The List on which discussion settles may vary; perhaps everyone will agree to have food, shelter, and clothing on the list, but (considering that the List is to guide social policies) not everyone would perhaps agree to have sexual activity on the List, or recreation. In my book *Meeting Needs*,[7] after considering several lists, some of them in official use by policy-making agencies like the UN and the OECD, I put forward a two-part illustrative List, in which all the needs, like those just mentioned, are not adventitious needs but course-of-life needs, which people cannot escape at any time, or at least not escape during some periods of their lives.

A first part, strongly coloured by connections with physical functioning:
1 The need to have a life-supporting relation to the environment (not too hot, not too cold; not too dry, not too wet; breathable air)

2 The need for food and water
3 The need to excrete
4 The need for exercise
5 The need for periodic rest, including sleep
6 The need (beyond what is covered under the preceding needs) for whatever is indispensable to preserving the body intact in important respects (e.g., to be spared blinding light; to be spared the loss of a limb).

A second part of the List goes on to embrace:
7 The need for companionship
8 The need for education
9 The need for social acceptance and recognition
10 The need for sexual activity
11 The need to be free from harassment, including not being continually frightened
12 The need for recreation.

The List is not unique, though some items, I believe, would figure, explicitly or by implication, on any serious list. It is not complete, or, at least in the eyes of some humane and generous people, it would not be accepted as complete; they would like, for instance, there to be some provision for aesthetic development in art, music, and dance. Some items on the List will appear more controversial than others. To some extent, this is because they are not often subjects of official policy, in force or even seriously proposed. Meeting the need for sexual activity hardly seems at first sight anything that anyone would want a government to do; meeting the need for companionship may seem to be in a similar position.

Yet one has only to think of cases in which something puts meeting these needs in jeopardy to see that urgent recourse to official policy may occur. In the past governments have brought ships full of brides to colonies with unduly high proportions of men; even now, in some enlightened countries, they provide for conjugal visits to men (and I suppose, women) in prison. Were some contaminant to appear in the air that threatened to make most men impotent, people (both men and women) would not wait long to call for government action. Again, for the most part, official policy lets people find their own companions. Some concern is often shown for old people living alone, however, and something is done to abate their loneliness. They are visited by social workers; brought 'meals on wheels'; transported to recreational activities with other people.

Still, these things are perhaps not often very visible aspects of government policy and are often left to volunteer helpers insofar as they are not left entirely to people to take care of by themselves. Yet it would be a confusion to deny that they are matters of need just because they do not currently require official attention or even any attention at all by outsiders. However, at some times in some places all the Matters of Need on the List may be left, given provisions for external defence and for maintaining internal order, to private enterprise to meet in the market. Suppose this arrangement is entirely successful. Then there would be no occasion to use the term 'need' in perhaps its most frequent use – its episodic use – to call attention to a shortfall, or prospective shortfall, in provisions for needs in the sense of being Matters of Need on a basic List. (There would be no 'needy' people.) However, it would be a confusion to think for that reason that the items on the List were not needs that have to be met somehow or other; they all (for people who accept the List) will demand urgent attention if, though continually met now, provisions for them begin to fail, so that they go or will go unmet. In other cases, notably the need to excrete, people may not make the connection between certain current government policies, even if the policies are very ambitious and expensive, and the Matter of Need that makes the policies (sewer systems; sewage disposal works) indispensable. It is a Matter of Need nonetheless.

The Minimum Standards of Provision, variable anyway with respect to persons provided for – one person will need more food daily than others; a special diet not including milk or peanut butter; more attention in early education; longer training in special skills – will also vary in respect to generosity of provisions and in respect to differences in culture. Even were the List of Matters of Need – food, clothing, shelter, and other things – to remain the same, variation in the kinds of resources, religion, and other factors would make some provisions ineligible under the conventions of one culture that are perfectly eligible in another. It would not do to offer pork as provisions in an Islamic culture. In this part of the present chapter, to be sure, we are dealing with the simplest case: one population and one culture. However, a lot of the uneasiness about the fluidity of the concept of needs should fade away with the recognition that Matters of Need can remain the same, while provisions, and hence Minimum Standards of Provision, vary with conventions.

Conventional variation does not prevent us from making the definition both of Matters of Need and of Minimum Standards of Provision answer to a Criterion, and once a Criterion has been chosen, what I shall call 'the schema for needs' is complete in named features (except for the inclusion of a Principle of Precedence with which it is to be associated, which may as an option be treated as a feature of the schema itself). Under the names of the features there are details to be specified by discussion and negotiation mindful of the Criterion. Any of a family of Criteria having to do with life and death and, short of these things, with adequate functioning might do. Many people, however, would, I think, find persuasive a Criterion according to which something was a Matter of Need with provisions meeting the Minimum Standards of Provision if and only if without having such provisions the persons in question would no longer be able to carry out fully basic social roles. Provisions for meeting needs are thus indispensable conditions of carrying out the roles. (We could go back to indispensable conditions for life itself, but I think doing so would restrict the use of the concept of needs in this connection in a way that falls far short of what people are currently willing to accept. Just keeping alive may require much less in resources than living with minimum decency.) Four of these social roles may be specified: they are roles as citizens, workers, parents, and householders.[8] It is worth noting that people generally desire to have these roles. The Criterion would work logically to sort out needs from mere preferences if people did not want them, but if they did not, misgivings would start up about paternalism (should people's preferences be overridden to meet their needs?) and about the point of acting in accordance with the Criterion.

Specific though the Criterion may be, some disagreement about what it requires is to be expected, and what provisions are required is something often settled by settling, in accordance with prevailing views, upon minimal packets of provisions, with some ingredients not themselves strictly defensible by the Criterion. However, if the List and the Minimum Standards of Provision become uncomfortably inflated, the schema of the List and the Minimum Standards can always be contracted, and the ingredients of the packets reduced in variety or quantity, until effective agreement is reached. Or the schema can be expanded, on evidence that the ingredients of current packets do not suffice to prevent observable impairment in the functioning of the people provided for. Moreover, if more generous feelings set in, as a result of general prosperity and of confident expectations regarding personal incomes, the Minimum Standards of Provision may invite a more liberal interpretation.

How are policy-makers to tell whether the needs of the population are being met, or met better under one set of policies than under another? The basic form for telling is given by the census-notion, expounded in the chapter just preceding. I shall not here go into the main features of the notion at the length that I did in the preceding chapter. I shall concentrate, instead, on showing in concrete detail how the census-notion works with the concept of needs. The notion is to be understood in this application, insofar as it is looked to for guidance in adopting policies, as something used with a schema sufficiently filled in to have application and in conjunction with several operating principles or conditions besides: a Principle of Precedence, the Revisionary Process, the Gains-Preservation Principle, and certain conditions ruling out invidious discrimination.[9] The Revisionary Process and the Gains-Preservation Principle figured in the preceding chapter; below I shall explain what the Principle of Precedence amounts to. All of these features are more crucial to human thriving and more telling in generating moral force when they are applied in conjunction with the concept of needs than with other subjects, for example, utility or even happiness.

The observations that the census-notion (unlike a calculus of utility) requires are philosophically unproblematic and fall well within the compass of familiar everyday practice. Suppose that inquiry is to be made into the extent to which shelter, as a Matter of Need, has been provided for in the Reference Population. The Minimum Standard of Provision is set after discussion as having a place to sleep that is dry, well ventilated, and in the winter heated to 68 degrees Fahrenheit. Then, after observations have been made everyone in the Population (or everyone in a statistically valid sample) will have been assigned to one category or another in a table like the following, which assumes a Population of 100 or a sample of that size from a larger Population:

| With Shelter | 70 |
| Without Shelter | 30 |

Someone proposes a new policy for shelter, which promises to increase provisions to cover half the number of people now without shelter. A comparative census table taking both the present policy into account and the new policy would take this form:

Status Quo		New Policy	
With Shelter	70	With Shelter	85
Without Shelter	30	Without Shelter	15

Other things being equal, it goes without saying, the new policy would bring in a clear improvement in respect to meeting the need for shelter.

At this point, the Principle of Precedence comes to bear. Moving to the new policy may be possible only if some of the people who have shelter in the status quo give up some goods. This may be so even if the situation does not worsen for the society as a whole. They might, for example, have to give up in part or postpone their plans for remodelling their kitchens. The Principle of Precedence requires them to give up goods that they themselves do not require to meet their needs under the Minimum Standards of Provision applicable, if only in this way can the Minimum Standards of Provision be met for some members of the Reference Population. We may think of the Principle of Precedence as something that members of the Policy-Making Population accept (under the assumed idealization) along with accepting responsibility for meeting the Minimum Standards of Provision for a List of Matters of Need with respect to a certain Reference Population. It is this acceptance that makes various uses of the term 'needs,' backed by the Principle, vehicles for the moral force of the concept of needs. If people do accept these things, and their sacrifices are proved to be indispensable, they will feel that they ought to give up in part or postpone the remodelling and may do so with good grace, or something approximating it.

Other things being equal, the Principle of Precedence, invoked with a rigour that for descriptive purposes I shall relax later, calls here for the new policy to be adopted, even if it reduces for some people (say, 10 of the 70 under the status quo policy) resources over and above what they require to meet their needs. Cherishing their plans for remodelling, they might prefer to keep these provisions, but the Principle of Precedence overrides such preferences (and thus defies the

Pareto Welfare Principle, which licenses only moves that do more to heed some people's preferences without running counter to the preferences of anybody). It also discredits majority rule in some instances. If the 70 per cent of people with shelter in the status quo vote for keeping their surplus resources and using them to improve their own shelters even though this means 15 per cent will go without shelter who might have it under the new policy, they will be defying the Principle of Precedence and with it the moral force of the appeal to needs. They may get away with it; as things stand, they generally do; but that does not, in the perspective of the concept of needs and the Principle of Precedence, make their voting any the less discreditable.

The Principle of Precedence overrides the Gains-Preservation Principle in the matters – outside Matters of Need – not given precedence. The Gains-Preservation Principle applies, however, within the sphere of needs; it will block taking provisions away from some people, to the extent that their corresponding needs are no longer met, to meet the needs of others. On this point, it harmonizes with the Principle of Precedence. The Principle of Precedence does not require people to give up meeting their own needs to meet the needs of others or to give other people's mere preferences more weight than their own preferences, much less their own basic needs.

Unlike the Principle of Utility, understood as associated with the calculus (and also understood as associated with the census-notion), the Principle of Precedence is not an optimizing notion. Like disjointed incrementalism, with which it may be combined, it is a satisficing notion,[10] which falls silent when certain conditions have been satisfied – in this case when the Matters of Need on the List have been provided for in everybody's case according to the Minimum Standards of Provision. Both parts of the List must be provided for, but the Principle does not operate beyond. Any second stage of a comprehensive program for social policy, which would treat matters of preference only, commodious living, and happiness, would not fall under the Principle. Moreover, first-stage satisficing under the Principle of Precedence might happen and still leave room for finding more economical provisions – and room, too, for making the provisions more agreeable. Perhaps both things could be accomplished together: a diet could be found that was as nutritious, more varied as well, and less expensive. A half-dozen varieties of sushi wrapped in nori along with tofu and more seaweed in miso soup might take the place of cheeseburgers, ketchup, fries, and Coca-Cola. The Principle of Precedence does not stand in the way of such improvements, though it does not demand them.

In worsening situations, when the society must retreat from a more comfortable position, the Principle will cut back provisions for matters of preference only and for commodious living to make sure that everybody's needs continue to be met. This goal, of meeting all the needs on the List, is thus treated as a lexicographical priority, strictly speaking, a priority that is lexicographical only up to a satiation limit that is the conjunction of the satiation limits for all the Matters of Need. The goal is the conjunction; the conjuncts are the Minimum Standards of Provision, a range of minima, that is to say, of satiation limits, varying from person to person, for each Matter of Need. In severely worsening situations, the Minimum Standards of Provision may be reviewed and become more narrowly defined (e.g., by reducing by one feature or another the packets of provisions in which barely necessary provisions normally have been included: the oatmeal cookies are left out, though the peanut butter and raisin sandwiches remain). There may even be some reconsideration of the Matters of Need figuring on the basic List. The position of recreation, for example (and not only of this) may become precarious.

'Satiation' is the correct technical term, borrowed from economics; but the technical use clashes incongruously on the present topic with the connotation of its ordinary use. To make the clash unobtrusive, I shall refer to 'SL-lexicographical priority' rather than to 'satiation-limit-lexicographical priority.' With SL-lexicographical priority, until every Minimum Standard of Provision for every person in the Reference Population and every Matter of Need has been reached, matters of preference only, a residual category not associated with Matters of Need on the List, have to wait in everybody's case.

Is this procedure practical? That is to say, does the idealization on this point fall within the bounds of plausible empirical possibility? Waiving for the moment the point that people may not be ready to conform with such rigour to the Principle of Precedence and abstracting from the untidiness of public debate and public policy, it is practical so long as the resources available to the Policy-Making Population, here identical with the Reference Population, allow it under suitable arrangements to meet all Matters of Need at the Minimum Standards of Provision and still leave a surplus, if only a vanishingly little surplus, for other purposes. It might take some time to find the most suitable arrangements; the market may prove effective in some connections and not in others, and arrangements to supplement the market without impairing its effectiveness so far as it is effective are notoriously controversial.

Nonetheless, SL-lexicographical priority for Matters of Need will turn out to be practical if it can be honoured within the limits of the resources available to honour it. Moreover, any worry about having room to work with within such limits may be based on a very farfetched hypothesis: citing in 1996 estimates by the World Bank, Partha Dasgupta says, 'The financial requirement for a broadly based human resource development strategy designed to meet basic needs would total approximately 5.5% of GNP' even in countries in sub-Saharan Africa (where military expenditures have been running at 4.2 per cent of GNP).[11] That would leave a considerable surplus after needs have been met. Unfortunately, this procedure does not guarantee meeting them; more than the surplus may be captured by privileged people and used otherwise.

How often will there be clear improvements in view, straightforwardly satisfying both the Principle of Precedence and the Gains-Preservation Principle? In comparisons confined to one Matter of Need, perhaps quite often. The List of Matters of Need, however, presents more than one Matter of Need to be provided for; and combinations of policies that would bring in clear improvements in respect to one Matter of Need may actually worsen provisions for another, or at least bring the provisions for some people whose needs are now being met below the Minimum Standards of Provision for them. The census-notion, as a basis for guiding policies, might be defeated again and again in this way.

The operation of the Revisionary Process, however, transcends this limitation. In the Process I mean to include suggestions from any source about revisions in existing options, or suggestions of new options that, like the revisions, offer ways of avoiding difficulties with the existing options. Suppose the new policy for providing shelter would make an advance in meeting the need for shelter, but reduce below the Minimum Standards of Provision the provisions for a number of people in respect to education (say, by diverting funds that would have been used to repair schools), or simply leave many people without such provisions (because new schools will not be built). People concerned to apply the Principle of Precedence will turn to the Revisionary Process to find a combination of policies that will increase provisions for shelter without having an adverse effect on provisions for education.

Discussion and Negotiation within the Bounds of the Idealized Project

For all its reliance on familiar ideas and familiar sorts of observation, how realistic would it be to claim that the construction just described could ever be carried out in real-world politics? Some features of the construction are realistic enough. The Criterion, for example, resting as it does on familiar social roles, invites ready assent at least to the most basic items on the List of Matters of Need – food, shelter, clothing, safety. I do not oppose having people entertain other criteria in the family, including criteria that make more (as Gillian Brock and others would make) of personal autonomy.[12] I am so intently concerned, however, to demonstrate what can be made of the concept of needs as a currently practical and effective alternative to anything that has so far been made of the concept of utility that I prefer a Criterion the ingredients of which everyone understands with a minimum of help from philosophical analysis and discussion. (They would also readily understand a criterion in which life itself is at stake, but as I have said, I think this would be a more restrictive criterion than we have to resort to, even with less than generous views about what other people need.)

Moreover, I think that a Criterion resting on familiar social roles will do markedly better than one resting on autonomy in fixing for effective political use ideas about Minimum Standards of Provision. We may expect much more disagreement on the Minimum Standards than on the basic List of Matters of Need. In both cases, however, the basic schema (the List of Matters of Need taken together with Minimum Standards of Provision) will contract or expand according to the extent to which ready agreement on the content to be ascribed to them can be brought about through discussion and negotiation in a given Policy-Making Population. The discussion and negotiation would continually appeal to the Criterion, which anchors the schema in firm, if narrow, ground – matters of fact about the consequences for people's activity and productivity of contraction or expansion. This firmness is also present in the framework of discussion and negotiation that the schema offers even when it is only present in outline, as the project of constructing it goes on.

What extent of agreement should be sought, given the idealization that we are assuming about sustained attention to the project of constructing a schema? It would help to show that the basic schema could be completely fixed for a time for use in a variety of applications. One might argue in this connection that given a contracted schema for this purpose, a consensus embracing pretty much the whole of a Policy- Making Population is not out of reach. Some sort of official body might organize a general discussion, and if, when discussion ends for the time being, a minority of 5 per cent or 10 per cent persist in irreducible disagreement, they could be ignored.

There are real-world instances of promoting general discussion of issues, constitutional and otherwise, that may serve as models for the process of discussion and negotiation that the project of constructing a schema would involve. At the time of writing, the province of British Columbia is organizing a process by which a citizens' assembly chosen in various stages by a random process will consider whether the electoral system of the province will be changed and how. If it decides on change, its proposal for change, unrevised by the government, will be put to the electorate of the province for approval.[13] Similarly, the project of constructing a schema for needs as a sort of constitutional basis for priority in government policy might be publicly organized and carried to the end, navigating all the points to be considered that I have just allowed for in an idealized description of the construction. The model might be taken from British Columbia or from various schemes for involving rank-and-file voters in discussions of policy like James Fishkin's 'deliberative polls,' which have had many successful operations in the United States, the United Kingdom, and other countries.[14]

Arguments aiming at consensus upon the contracted schema might invoke, sardonically, the Matters of Need and the Minimum Standards of Provision that would be appropriate for people being kept in prison. Should not the population out of prison have provisions, too, at least at this level? It might be said that the provisions should not be given them; they should in every case do work to get them; even prisoners are typically made to do work, though hard cases, held in maximum security or solitary confinement, may not be. But this is not a question about what should be on the List and what the Minimum Standards of Provisions should be – in other words, not a question of principle to be settled by fixing the Criterion and appealing to it. Though no doubt people adjust their positions on one to accord with their positions on the other, what is to be in the schema is one issue; what arrangements are to be made to give it effect is another. The best arrangements for giving the schema effect for the population not in prison might be arrangements encouraging self-sufficiency (entailing in some places agrarian reform) among them or arrangements that leave everything to the market.

Discussants with more generous ideas about needs may well be unhappy about settling for a contracted schema and the market. However, they are settling only for the time being. The Revisionary Process will operate. In future rounds of policy-making they will be able to argue for expanding the scheme. Meanwhile, if the settlement reached in discussion and negotiation favours reliance on the market, it may be doubted whether any widespread disinclination to accept the Principle of Precedence would stand in the way of an agreement fixing the schema and guiding its use. The very people who might be most disinclined to make sacrifices to conform to the Principle may be people who think that the sacrifices will never come home to them: the best arrangements for self-sufficiency, in the convenient view of laissez-faire, will make any sacrifices unnecessary.

Much more often than not, what will make it difficult to fix upon one persistent, agreed-on schema is that contracting and expanding it will not go smoothly. Contracting the List, people may differ on which Matters to strike off in which order; they may differ also in being readier to accept more generous Minimum Standards of Provision for some needs than others – for example, some will be more generous respecting provisions for safety (which comes up under several heads on the List), some more generous respecting provisions for education. Moreover, some people may be ready to subscribe to a longer List with less generous Minimum Standards of Provisions for all the Matters on it, while others would be more generous about Minimum Standards of Provision for the Matters, fewer in number, that they would take into account. In the face of considerations like these, advanced by Gillian Brock as criticisms of my account in *Meeting Needs*,[15] I think the best course to take is not to take a stand on the combination of strong conditions that by limiting variations in attitudes in the Policy-Making Population would guarantee smooth contraction or expansion of the schema. The best course is to treat the schema and the other features of the construction as offering so many dimensions in which discussion or negotiation may be called for, before and during the operation of the Revisionary Process. The discussion or negotiation would occur before any comprehensive use of the concept of needs, giving SL-lexicographical priority to all Matters of Need taken together, could be made sure of.

Is this allowance enough for discussion, variation in interpretation, and negotiation? That is to say, again, does it consort in the way of plausible empirical possibility with the amount of idealization that I am, by hypothesis, conceding? It is consistent with the allowance, and indeed it is a point that I would insist upon, that we can predict from the familiar use of the concept of needs that some Matters of Need will be settled upon very quickly, along with some Minimum Standards of Provision below which discussion will not descend without becoming absurd. The moral force depends in part on there being some received agreement, extending across differences in social and economic position as well as in political beliefs, on the dimensions of discussion exhibited in the schema: What Matters of Need are to be on the List? How full will be the Minimum Standards of Provision? The moral force depends also on there being some received agreement, likewise extended, on how to begin filling in the schema. Food will be one of the Matters of Need, and more food than a thimbleful of rice will be required every week by every member of the Reference Population under the Minimum Standards of Provision for food.

Too much fashionable flapdoodle about the politics of interpretation in which the concept is no doubt involved will obscure the possibility of capitalizing on this agreement to bring about at least modest reforms. It will also be to a degree self-defeating. If you wish to convince people that facilities should be provided battered wives, enabling them to live apart from their husbands, should you omit making the point that in their present households their needs for bodily, mental, and emotional security, including freedom from terror, are going starkly unmet? Even someone who would prefer to make the case in terms of rights might think twice about jettisoning the possibility of founding the women's rights on the narrow but firm ground of their minimal needs.

In *Meeting Needs*, when I came to consider what was realistic to expect in the way of application of the concept of needs in the complex democratic politics of a populous industrial society, I moved from SL-lexicographical priority for the Principle of Precedence, which only a thoroughly conscientious Policy-Making Population could be expected to press home with strict final priority, to what I called 'Role-Relative Precautionary Priority.' This allows for people's being more attached to priority for Matters of Need when they are charged with working out policy proposals than they are when as citizens they must choose between the proposals, and more attached in their role as citizens (coming together to make decisions for the Common Good) than they are as consumers. Recognizing how addiction to tobacco runs counter to people's meeting their needs, the proponents of policy may seek to eliminate the tobacco industry. As citizens, however, they will divide on how long elimination should be put off, given the unsettling economic effects that eliminating the industry would have for many people; as consumers (some of them, in their capacities as proponents and citizens, strong adversaries of the tobacco industry), they will go on using tobacco so long as the industry feeds their habit. Yet even in such a situation the concept of needs counts for something. With the Principle of Precedence, it leads to agitation about the tobacco industry and to proposals that sooner or later, bit by bit, curtail its activities.

The Place and Force of Needs in the Rhetoric of Real-World Politics

Lying within the bounds of plausible possibility surrounding an existing political system, which is where I have been carrying on the discussion of the project of constructing a schema for needs, and being a plausible reflection of what actually goes on, there are two different things. I am far from claiming that the process of constructing and settling upon a schema for needs as I have described it, with the aim of showing what, firmly and systematically, can be made of the concept, represents anything that has ever been fully realized in an existing political system. What does go on there in respect to the use of the concept of needs, I hypothesize, falls into the embrace of a rhetoric with a number of distinguishable features – so many different vehicles for the concept of needs. I shall have something to say in a speculative way about how frequently these features present themselves in political discussions, but in the end it will be a matter for empirical accounts of such discussions to establish, first, the actual presence of those features and, second, their comparative frequency.

Many other things besides needs come up for discussion in real-world politics and it must be supposed that there are periods in which needs get only fitful attention there. When they do get attention, attention specifically in association with a use of the term 'needs,' I suppose it is most often the episodic use of the term that crops up, the use in which it is pointed out that the Reference Population or some part of it confronts a shortfall in providing for some specific need. The food banks tell the Policy-Making Population that the resources in money and kind that the food banks have on hand are running short. More people need food from the food banks than the food banks can supply. Or people in the government, in a party in opposition, or in an organization like Habitat declare that there are many more people who need low-cost housing than there is decent low-cost housing to meet the need. Or a number of school boards report that they need more funds to hire specialized teachers and to keep class sizes at reasonable levels.

Occasionally, the non-episodic use of the term 'needs' that comports with the schema will creep in, though the schema itself remains invisible. The non-episodic use has already crept into one of my examples. When it is said, 'There are many more people who need low-cost housing than there is decent low-cost housing to meet the need,' the first use of the term 'need' is episodic, relating to a current shortfall. The second may pass for episodic, too, but it invites an additional interpretation as a non-episodic use, according to which, as in the schema, the need for housing, that is, for shelter, is always present, whether it is met or not, though in this case it happens to be unmet. Indeed, in this case and in the others illustrated, the episodic use gets its force from there being a non-episodic use referring to a persisting need that has to be met, whether it currently is met or not. People understand the episodic use in these cases as something associated with persistent, ineluctable properties of human beings, course-of-life needs like those in the schema.

The non-episodic uses also creep in with comparative statements about needs. The Reference Population needs, right now, more food if it is not to starve, but it also needs shelter, and with its schools ruined or run down, it needs, right now, provisions for education. People in the Policy-Making Population will agree, I suppose, given good evidence, that people in the Reference Population have a current need for all these things. It will be said: they have scant supplies of food, so they need food; they have no shelter or only inadequate provisions for shelter, so they need housing (or, at the very least, a sanitary encampment); their schools are ruined and they are desperately short of teachers, so they need resources for education. They need resources in any of these three connections just as much as they need them in any other. And why is this? The episodic uses of the term 'needs' are comparable, because all are backed by non-episodic uses referring to undeniably persistent course-of-life needs.

Going even this far with the comparison leads to a glimpse of something like the schema. The needs referred to in the non-episodic uses are comparable because they have the same footing, a footing expressed by the phrase 'course-of-life needs,' or expressed more familiarly by saying, 'People can't get along without shelter any more than they can get along without food, can they?' Perhaps there will be momentary resistance to the contention that they cannot get along without education either, but the way to surmount that resistance is to show that the non-episodic use here refers to something that in the long run – indeed, in the not-so-long run – people will be unable to perform basic social roles without education or social training. They will not thrive, and for want of their contributions, their society will not thrive either.

With the same footing, all the needs referred to in the non-episodic uses of the term will make a coordinated demand for resources. But when anything like such a coordinated demand occurs, we come into the presence of the schema on one side at least, a partial view, but already a view in which it can be understood that the appeal to needs will be limited in an important respect: if the needs are to make comparable demands, they will have the same footing. So, though a number of persistent needs must be provided for, whether or not they are provided for currently, no one is being asked to write a blank cheque to deal with an ever-expanding List of Matters of Need. Nor are the Minimum Standards of Provisions associated with the Matters of Need on the List easily expanded beyond current limits; the cheque will be limited in that respect, too. Indeed, if the needs can be met by making sure that the market does all that it can do under laissez-faire, there will be no cheque at all to write.

These limitations, however, may not be enough. They do not allow for the untimeliness, normal to the real-world rhetoric of needs, of bringing in even a partially glimpsed schema, much more bringing in the idea of a complete one. To many people, invoking the schema will be compromised by association with the tiresome subject of 'neediness'; and by the suspicion that in many cases, perhaps in all cases unless shown otherwise, those said to be in need are so through their own improvidence. Such people will not be reassured by showing how the needs brought forward by the episodic use can all be coordinated on the same footing (by the same Criterion) in a comprehensive schema. On the contrary, that will still seem to them a step toward asking for authorizing a cheque, drawn on tax revenues and ultimately on themselves, to cover a great deal more than they are ready to take responsibility for. It will be a cheque that may not cover everything that policy-makers may fancy; but even so, it will cover unpredictably much, and even if it does not do this, it will cover unwarranted outlays.

None of the uses of the term 'needs' that have been mentioned – the episodic use for instances of different needs; the episodic use coordinating instances of different needs with each other and with the underlying needs referred to by non-episodic uses of the term; the non-episodic uses coordinated under a comprehensive schema for needs – may have the moral force for some people of immediate descriptions, from which the term 'needs' is absent, of the desperate conditions of people in the Reference Population. Moreover, to be moving with these people, the immediate descriptions must be accompanied by respect-worthy explanations of how the conditions came about. People are starving because of drought or because they were driven from their farms by civil war; people are homeless because civil war or forest fires or floods have destroyed their homes; people have no schools or teachers because the schools fell into ruin during use as command posts in recent fighting and because the teachers have fled the country if they have not been executed or imprisoned.

What emerges from this survey of possibilities in the real-world rhetoric of needs is what I shall call a 'Multi-Vehicular Pattern of Presentation for Needs.' The vehicles are utterances that consist of so many uses of the term 'needs,' to which I add the paradoxically 'anonymous' use in which an episodic use gives way to immediate description of the condition of being in need. The uses are, to review them,

1 utterances in which the term 'needs' has its episodic use;
2 utterances in which different needs referred to in the episodic uses are compared as on the same footing;
3 utterances in which the footing is found for one or more episodic uses of the term 'needs' in the non-episodic use of the term for persisting course-of-life needs of the sort that may suitably figure in the schema;
4 utterances in which the schema for course-of-life needs are brought, at least in part, into view;
5 the 'anonymous' use, displacing the episodic use in single or multiple instances.

The moral force of the concept of needs comes to bear on different occasions with one or another of these vehicles.

An utterance will have moral force for a given set of human beings if the persons in the set accept it as expressing an emotion in favour (or disfavour) of an action of some sort or a policy and as expressing, besides the emotion, an imperative in accord with it; and if, further, the persons in question, moved by the emotion and the imperative, find them appropriately moving because they can be associated with a convincing moral argument that is itself accepted. When the utterances on the list just given have moral force, all these conditions are fulfilled; in particular, the condition of being associated with a convincing moral argument is fulfilled by being associated with utilitarianism, recast to put needs in the place of utility. Even a glimpse of the schema brings the moral arguments of utilitarianism recast to bear; and the schema with the Principle of Precedence lays out the systematic connections of those arguments.

On a given occasion, one vehicle may hold central attention and bear more force than any other on that occasion. On the given occasion some vehicles might bear vanishingly little moral force and hence do little or nothing to move people to act upon the needs in question. Just how often any of the vehicles are used and with what force in moving people to act requires systematic observation and analysis of actual discussions.[16] I have gone no further here, except for incidental speculative remarks, than to offer, with the Multi-Vehicular Pattern of Presentation for Needs, a hypothesis in plausible reasoning about what different vehicles are to be looked for.

Needs as Surrogates for Utility

Attention to needs can substitute for attention to utility. However unrefined may be our practical ideas about utility or even about the less recherché subject of happiness, we may assume, while we are waiting for the concept of utility to be perfected, that it will favour their happiness to meet the needs that people have for pure water, unpolluted air, heat neither too little nor too much, food, clothing, shelter, education, along with recreation. So we act to meet those needs, perhaps by establishing a truly competitive market, perhaps by setting up, along with the market, arrangements to correct the imperfections of its operations.

Real disputes about policy (where utility is hardly ever, if ever, mentioned) often have to do with needs – with whether a given Matter of Need should be met by government policy, for example, or whether the Minimum Standards of Provision for given Matters of Need are being met for everybody by present policy. People are homeless; people are hungry. Temporary shelters are jammed or dangerous. Ten times as many people are resorting to food banks.

Is the census-notion at work in these examples? Of course it is, though maybe (as must often be the case) without the data's being set forth in a comparative table. The table in each case is easily generated. If the number of homeless people has risen, other things being equal (leaving aside, for example, an increase in population), then the proportion of people whose need for shelter has been met will have fallen. If ten times as many people are resorting to food banks, then (again, leaving aside an increase in population), there are fewer people who are otherwise safe from the danger of going hungry.

	Previous Situation	Current Situation
With Adequate Shelter and Food	99,000	90,000
Without Adequate Shelter and Food	1,000	10,000

To comment on these figures by saying that some action ought to be taken to provide better for the needs in question may seem obvious, indeed banal. Given what is at stake for the people concerned, the data could not be dismissed as trivial. Would sophisticated thinkers opine that it is intellectually trivial to insist on the significance of the data and the application of the census-notion in this instance? But 'banal' and 'intellectually trivial' are epithets that consort well with my contention that the census-notion, especially in application to needs, though not only there, is familiar and commonplace, and even with my contention that the notion is telling and effective in practical politics. Its full effectiveness, to be sure, depends on its being used in conjunction with a vigorously responsive Revisionary Process. But this conjunction is realized often enough to be itself familiar.

What is not banal or intellectually trivial is the amazing disregard of the census-notion during some two and a half centuries by philosophers and economists thinking about utility as a feature of utilitarianism. If a case was to be made for a felicific calculus, a calculus of utility, should it not have been a matter of prime concern for people making the case to show that it was superior to the notion in familiar use for evaluating evidence about the impact of policies on the people belonging to groups at issue? As I have repeatedly contended, however, the calculus is not, or at least not yet, superior. So far as use in practical politics goes, it remains a project. Even were it able to deliver the comprehensive evaluations that it promises, it would invite intractable challenges if it were applied in violation of the constraints about personal sacrifices that the census-notion embodies, on its own and in combination with the precautions that I have discussed earlier.

If needs normally take the stage in real disputes about policy, what does the concept of utility accomplish in them? Nothing, a bold observer might say, unless it is taken as a device for talking about other matters better talked about in a straightforward way. For example, some neoclassical economists late in the nineteenth century and early in the twentieth century made an effort to justify progressive taxation by the hypothesis of interpersonally comparable diminishing marginal utility for income. But this effort had the disadvantage that no conclusive evidence could be produced for the hypothesis. It can be claimed that rich women with sensitive tastes becoming continually more sensitive are getting as much utility out of the marginal dollars that they spend on designer handbags as poor women of uncultivated tastes and phlegmatic disposition do out of marginal dollars spent on the ingredients for apple pie, and that the fashionably rich women would lose more utility if proportionately more dollars were taken from them.

Far better to say, in defence of progressive taxation, that the poor find it difficult to cover their basic needs, while the rich can indulge in the most frivolous preferences. This point can readily be established by a census. If it is agreed that the issue is whether larger incomes leave a larger surplus (supposing any incomes did) over meeting basic needs with standard forms of provision, the census results on this subject will be a foregone conclusion.

How did utilitarianism accomplish anything in real disputes while it relied on the concept of utility? The distance of the concept from practice was present in the theory of Benthamite utilitarianism from the beginning. What saved the doctrine from conflict with ordinary practice in policy-making, and indeed enabled it to have some practical efficacy, was just the assumption that reforms in matters subject to census comparisons – checking crime, building sewers, regulating hours of factory work, and so forth – would bring about gains in utility or happiness, and that such results would be corroborated by the felicific calculus were the calculus ever to be put to use. For, one could assume, as at least in a rough practical way, that providing for this or that Matter of Need would foster utility or happiness. People are not so likely to be happy day by day shivering in the rain or snow or having to do without bread or rice as they would be otherwise. The need for shelter, specified as a need for sanitary housing, met by introducing a modern system of sewers, was an effective, robust, and fully intelligible surrogate for utility or happiness. As the utilitarian and public servant Sir Edwin Chadwick[17] perceived, London tenements with courts ankle-deep in human excrement generated diseases that stood in the way of fulfilling anything like the Principle of Utility, were one to find a way of applying it. Again, the census-notion comes to bear. Chadwick's endeavours would not have been an unqualified success had they created insanitary housing in other places (to which the sewage that he aimed to displace might have been diverted) or an entirely satisfactory success if at the same time, without his doing, an even greater number of people came to be living in insanitary housing as a further consequence of inadequately regulated capitalism. (I did not put the need to excrete on my illustrative List of Matters of Need because I was thinking of Chadwick's endeavours; but his endeavours do give a nice historical confirmation of the claim of excretion to figure on the List.)

Latent in the idea of the felicific calculus, let us recall, is the discrepancy between promoting the greatest happiness and promoting the happiness of the greatest number. But little difficulty could be expected from this discrepancy while the assumption that marginal utility declined with income in an interpersonally comparable way was in force;[18] nor would much difficulty arise about giving people's needs some sort of priority over attending to anyone's preferences. At least given utility functions varying only within the same plausible range, the biggest returns in utility would be found in bettering the condition of the many poor, not in bettering the condition of the few rich. Furthermore, if the poor had the dispositions most essential to their own survival, they could be expected to find big gains in utility in further provisions for what Marx called their 'primary needs' or 'necessary needs'[19] – the Matters of Need on my basic List. If they were not assumed to have such dispositions, argument for any sort of redistribution lost a good deal of its force. What would have been the point, to recall a Tory canard, of giving the poor bathtubs if they were going to store coal in them? Or of letting the poor keep proportionately more money if they (like some of the rich) were going to use it to kill themselves with drink? Yet any absence of difficulty on these points just offers more evidence to back the suggestion that utilitarianism in practical political application depended for its plausibility and effectiveness on the operation of surrogate ideas, in particular, ideas about needs.

Amartya Sen, in *The Standard of Living*, has expressed himself as reluctant (even though tempted) to endorse the concept of needs in the absence, he intimates, of a demonstration that the concept of needs can meet the test of utility, that is to say, among other things, of the expectations of precision associated with utility.[20] I think that here he has got things exactly upside down. The concept of utility is nowhere in direct application in practical discussions of policy-making; and though Sen has a lot to say, all of which I applaud, in objection to relying on the concept of utility for the evaluation of policies, its absence from practical policy discussions is not something that he makes any fuss about or even notes. (This is true even of his later book, *Development as Freedom*.[21]) In sharp contrast to the concept of utility, the concept of needs is in application on every hand (though not always under that name, and in a complex pattern of representation and application that I have hypothesized, above). If utility works out in a way that seems to conflict with the concept of needs, reflective equilibrium is not going to give so much weight to utility as to needs.

Should utilitarianism come clean about the practical difficulties and abandon utility? Given the intellectual investment, ever continuing, in philosophers' and economists' discussions of utility, abandonment will not be easy to bring about. The idea that there can be a felicific calculus founded on convincing interpersonally valid measurements of utility has not died out, though notably an author like Broome carries on with the idea only in disregard of the objections that I treated in the two preceding chapters about imposed personal sacrifices.[22] Furthermore, utility holds a place in the ideal of having a comprehensive measure to which all disputes about moral value can be reduced and settled. It would be a big disappointment to have to abandon this ideal, and philosophers are not lightly going to give it up.

Yet for the time being at least, recognizing the effectiveness of the surrogates, in particular, those embraced by the concept of needs, utilitarianism recast could commit itself to a two-stage program. In the first stage, whatever temporary concessions it would have to make in practice, it would frankly champion SL-lexicographical priority for needs – all the needs on the two-part List of Matters of Need – settled upon with Minimum Standards of Provision after due discussion under the schema for basic needs. The schema would bring to bear upon choices of policy empirical evidence under the census-notion. But any settlement with respect to any Matter of Need or any of the Minimum Standards of Provision would be subject to reopening, so long as a case for reopening it could be made invoking the Criterion. The evidence acted upon in this connection would vary, but activists would go on collecting more evidence as part of the case for reopening. In the second stage of the program would occur the pursuit and mutual accommodation of preferences that do not express needs, but that still must be heeded to have commodious lives and happiness. In both stages the program would have to honour certain constraints about equality and justice, including some that resonate with the concerns of social contract theory.

Should the Concept of Needs Expand to Occupy Utilitarianism Recast in Both Its Stages?

The expansion of needs, whether by adding more Matters of Need to the basic List, or (more likely) by raising the Minimum Standards of Provision for the Matters on the List already, is one way to accommodate matters of preference that lie with commodious living and happiness outside any specified basic List of Matters of Need. If discussion and negotiation have led to a very austere List, moreover, there will be a lot of room for expansion. Later, in favourable circumstances, people will make substantial use of the room: they will be persuaded, for example, that under the need for education children should be given, instruction not only in reading, writing, and arithmetic, but in history, geography, and civics as well, even the cultural frills of dance, art, and music. At the same time, the need for recreation may be added, if it did not figure there before, to the Matters of Need on the List and expand with other Matters to embrace opportunities for self-development, in particular, development of personal talents. The Criterion may be amended to consort better with this expanded use of the concept of needs. A good deal of what utilitarianism has historically been concerned with in the scope of happiness could be reached by expanding needs in this way, indeed, reached by just the expansions described. Perhaps the whole of the concern could be embraced, in sufficiently favourable circumstances, given people deeply concerned with the happiness of others as well as themselves.

There is a danger, however, in expansion, a danger that may be felt even in the early stages of expansion, that the moral force of the concept of needs will weaken as expansion goes on. The force of the concept of needs can be carried beyond the bare minima where the force is strongest and in many cases, I would hope – even in the present circumstances of politics – to more generous standards of provision than are now commonly adhered to. However, I think the concept should not be expanded so far as to obliterate the distinction between the first stage of the program of utilitarianism recast and the second stage or to risk making an approach to meeting needs indistinguishable from an approach to achieving all the good things in life that feminists, environmentalists, and activists for other causes seek, even when it is perfectly reasonable for them to seek these things.

It is one thing to call with alarm for food for the hungry or shelter for the homeless; it is another to call for having every child try out a variety of musical instruments and settle for instruction on the instrument on which she is most apt or experiences most enjoyment. If it is to keep its distinctive force, the concept of needs can go only part of the way to defining the Common Good and making sure of a commodious life, though it is a vital initial part of the way. If you want people to act on hunger and homelessness, perhaps you had better not give people any idea that these things demand attention no more urgent than instruction in music. Tragically, many people, even in rich countries like Canada and the United States, do not benefit from the application of the concept of needs, even in respect to the bare beginnings where the concept is firmest and its force least deniable.

It is not only the concept of needs that risks dwindling moral force as it expands to embrace more topics. The moral force of the concept of happiness risks something of the same sort, though in reverse, losing force, not in second stage but in the first. Happiness brought up too soon can easily seem a sentimental distraction from the serious business with needs of the first stage. Brought up in a distinct second stage of the program of utilitarianism recast, happiness is clearly entirely in place. No longer subject to qualification by more urgent considerations, happiness can command the scene, directing the development of preferences and justifying special provisions for commodious living.

Another danger of expanding the concept of needs, or at least a certain awkwardness, would come from retaining the idea of lexicographical priority (or SL-lexicographical priority) as the expansion continues. Would enough opportunity be left for personal initiatives or experiments? Or even enough room for social ones? At present, a good deal of policy-making takes place in contexts that are not visibly structured or restricted by any sort of schedule of lexicographical priority. Under the thoroughgoing expansion of needs at issue, every policy question would be brought within one schedule and settled on the basis of finding a place there. I am not sure that this is objectionable, but it certainly is untried, indeed, much further away from being tried than a carefully circumscribed schema of basic needs, which itself is (as I have acknowledged) to a degree artificial and ideal.

The Stand on Needs Compared with Amartya Sen's Capabilities Approach[23]

In a number of recent works, two of them cited a few pages above, Amartya Sen has outlined an approach to social policies that, in effect, embraces both stages of the program that I have imputed to utilitarianism recast. Struggling free of his earlier habitual deference to utility, Sen would bypass it in favour of 'capabilities,' and the 'functionings' that with those capabilities people are free to engage in. These range from such things as walking, performing simple physical tasks, through being able to earn a livelihood through some sort of work, skilled or unskilled, to functioning as a concert pianist or as an amateur astrophysicist. The resources on which the capabilities are founded are sometimes material (food, tools), sometimes intellectual (mastery of the mathematics used in land surveying), sometimes social (being treated as an eligible candidate for employment as a teacher of music), sometimes moral and psychological (confident about taking a lead in political protests). Thus, capabilities extend far beyond provisions for basic needs to include having resources to take part in higher cultural activities, indeed, to attaining all aspects of what Hobbes would call 'commodious living.' (Without Sen's perhaps intending this, his 'capabilities' would serve all the functionings that for Karl Marx, young and old, would fall under a rich and expanded sense of 'needs.')[24]

What Sen is doing with the capabilities approach relates to the Criterion in the schema for needs as a multiplication of the functionings already found there. The Criterion already takes into account some important functionings: as householder, parent, citizen, and worker. By multiplying the functionings that capabilities are to serve, Sen is able to bring under capabilities all the provisions for needs at issue in the first stage of the program for utilitarianism recast and, as well, all the provisions for additional (expanded) needs and matters of preference to be dealt with only in the second stage. But Sen's approach does not rely on preferences in either stage or license the frivolous associations of 'matters of preference only.' The three-term relation between resources, capabilities, and functionings is an objective one, which transcends preferences. One will not have the capability to function as a land surveyor if one does not have access to a theodolite or other instruments needed by a surveyor.

Another advantage of the capabilities approach is that it lends itself more obviously and easily to the emphasis that Sen wants to give to treating as agents the people who are to benefit from policies. Their agency is to be strengthened by enabling them to engage in more functionings. Agency is present in the schema for needs: the basic roles that figure in the Criterion are roles for agents, and one of them at least – the role of citizen – connects in an important way with justice and political liberty. Moreover, agency is at work in the discussion and negotiation that occur during the course of settling upon the details of a schema (or of reopening the question of settlements). Yet people often benefit quite passively as recipients of provisions for needs.[25] Focusing on capabilities tacks away from passive recipience.

All these valuable aspects of Sen's approach could be kept in an approach that combines his generalized concern with capabilities and the priority given by the Principle of Precedence to needs as the special concern of the first stage of the program of utilitarianism recast. The most basic capabilities are the capabilities that social policy can make sure of as best it can by meeting needs. Sen himself uses the term 'needs' freely to refer to these basic capabilities.[26] It is natural to do so. It is also advantageous, since though (as I conceded in an earlier section of this chapter) the term, even the concept of needs, does not in every use on every occasion move everyone, it already has a familiar history of moral force, which the term and the concept of capabilities do not have. Moreover, the moral force has some claim to universality, based as it is on universal properties of human beings. No one can thrive without food and freedom from harassment, or even without some provision for companionship and recreation.

By contrast, capabilities in their upper range are very diverse and are not capabilities that everyone has to have or will want to have. Some people will want one capability; other people, another. People who go in for amateur boxing are not likely to be the same people who want to be violin soloists. So the capability approach does not escape the overriding problem of the second stage of a program of evaluation that expands beyond basic needs. It is not plausible to hold that all the diverse capabilities there must taken together be given lexicographical priority over anything else. Needs in the first stage already have that priority, and there is not in the second stage anything else in the way of permissible activity to give priority to. We can avoid expanding the concept of needs to the point of losing its moral force by turning to capabilities that do not correspond to needs, but we cannot avoid dealing with the diversity of capabilities.

Policies Answering to the Second Stage of the Program

Whether or not we adopt Sen's 'capabilities' approach, we must return to the problems of the second stage of the program of utilitarianism recast. This second stage could be carried on under the auspices of the 'capabilities' approach. Alternatively, it could offer a place for measurable utility if the project of measuring it effectively in practice is ever put through, at least a place where it could be invoked under the safeguards of the census-notion and the Gains-Preservation Principle. Here, too, might be a place for sophisticated conceptions of happiness, like Wayne Sumner's, according to which happiness is 'the condition of being satisfied or fulfilled by the circumstances of one's life' when one can 'endorse or affirm' one's life 'in terms of [one's] own priorities,' reviewed without prejudice or contingently reduced expectations.[27]

Provision for matters of preference only, commodious living, and happiness, left for the second stage when the expansion of needs has come to an end (one may hope, a cautious end) can obviously be ampler the more surplus productive capacity the community has available apart from the capacity committed to meeting needs. In any case, however, observing strict final priority for needs will in a sense make it easier to provide for preferences. With strict final priority the tendency is as fully realized as it ever will be to use the concept of needs to collect a number of matters of action and set them apart as decided, with no further collective decision to be made about this status by aggregating personal preferences. Conflicts about the policies to be adopted as means to meeting the needs thus agreed upon may remain, as well as conflicts about matters of preference only, as regards, for example, the form and character of public entertainment. It is settled, however, that as matters of prior importance the agreed-on needs will be met without any permanent diversion of resources to matters of preference only. Not so much hangs upon attention to these matters, therefore, and imperfect measures respecting them will be more tolerable. Will it not be foolish, then, in the absence of any effective rival concept, to belittle needs because they solve only part of our difficulties? They will have solved the most important part.

For the rest, quite straightforward measures, avoiding any attempt to aggregate preferences either by a felicific calculus or by a social choice guaranteed to be rational, might serve well enough, in particular for private goods, like the apples that people eat or the shoes that they wear, consumed by individual persons (or households) to the exclusion of consumption by other people. One such measure would be to distribute in equal packets money income for expenditure on matters of preference only – on commodious living and the pursuit of happiness. Then individual citizens could decide for themselves how much they wanted to spend on more elaborate provisions for meeting their needs than those guaranteed by the Minimum Standards of Provision. Some would pass up the meat loaf that they could have anyway in favour of *pinard*, sashimi, or *Wienerschnitzel*. Individual citizens would simultaneously decide for themselves how much they would spend on goods that did not enter into the Minimum Standards of Provisions for needs: a case of dry *oloroso*, a sports car, a trip to the Caribbean.

Everyone might become better off if, as an alternative measure, the community adopted Rawls's Difference Principle to apply to the sphere of matters of preference only (and thus to commodious living and happiness) through application to the packets of discretionary income made available for expenditure there. Larger packets would be given to some to just the extent that they furnished incentives for greater production and thereby led to those worst off in the Reference Population enjoying, through sharing in the output, a higher standard of living than they would under a regime of equal packets. Thus, those who, being worst off, would be the most urgent cases to check for possible victimization, could in fact freely and rationally consent to an unequal distribution, given safeguards against oppression by the better off. (Their basic needs would have been taken care of by a social minimum fixed directly as the upshot of discussion and negotiation under the schema for needs.[28]) Strictly speaking, some could perhaps argue that they themselves would not be among the worst off under other arrangements, but this argument would lose some force if under the present ones they had had with the Difference Principle a fair opportunity to try out for better paid work. Even if the argument survived, facts about the course of past history and about institutional inertia might persuade the people for whom it survived that it was unrealistic to demand any other arrangements. They might also be persuaded that other arrangements would have equally arbitrary results for other people, and that to make anything of the issue would start up an interminably distracting hunt among speculatively possible arrangements.

Strict literal egalitarians, if they saw some sense in these points about the described application of the Difference Principle, might resist the application notwithstanding. With basic needs taken care of, equality of income would look more attractive and any inequality brought in with the Difference Principle less so. Even if the Difference Principle had operated already to make sure that basic needs were met for everybody, there might be principled resistance to increasing the inequality in the sphere of matters of preference. Marxists might object that the Difference Principle would have attractions only for people whose motivations lay still within 'the narrow horizon of bourgeois right,' not yet generous enough to adhere to the ultimate principle of 'From all according to their ability, to all according to their needs!' Utilitarians could be expected to be more favourable. They might well think that some concession from strict equality was justified, provided that the inequalities were not carried so far as to engender apprehensions about concentrations of power or to begin increasing – for these or other reasons – the number of people unhappy because of the inequalities.

Among the questions that remain are questions about the variety and quantity of public goods (in the technical sense) to be produced. Some public goods already figure in the eclectic ethics that I have outlined in utilitarianism recast and its supplements: justice, in a variety of senses; equality; having a scheme of production under which both private goods and public goods essential to meeting needs are produced in sufficient variety and quantity, among them the public goods involved in public health and medical care. If provisions for external defence are regarded as public goods indispensable to a community wanting to enjoy the other goods mentioned, then external defence, too, would be accommodated in the ethics. Weather forecasts might come in as aids to production, especially of food. Perhaps these things would be enough. Sports facilities and facilities for classical music might be left to voluntary associations, as might parks and forests, following the example of organizations like Nature Conservancy in Canada and the United States.

Thus we come, at least in outline, to an end, with a utilitarianism recast to make sure of meeting needs, including needs expanded with general consent, and to make substantial provision in a superstructure, built upon attention to basic needs, for capabilities transcending needs or matters of preference embracing commodious living along with happiness. Its prescriptions in all things will be governed by considerations of justice and equality incorporated as operational features, accepted as compelling supplementary precautions, or respected as empirical conditions of success. The result is not so tidy, not so comprehensive, and not so thoroughly committed to optimizing as utilitarianism has been historically, or at least has aimed to be. However, one broad conclusion that we should draw from the history of the discussion of utilitarianism may be simply that we should not expect to have anything so tidy, comprehensive, and optimal as utilitarianism aimed to achieve. We should be content to have human welfare attended to in a reasonably generous way, both in meeting needs and in promoting commodious living, without having to violate our intuitions about justice and equality. An eclectic, unfinished ethics is the best that we can do for the time being, and that is a powerful, though contingent, recommendation.

Utilitarianism Recast with Needs in the Space of a Complete Ethics

How does utilitarianism, recast to give priority to meeting needs but committed in the second stage of its program to dealing with other matters, deal with other considerations in ethics and politics that bear on both stages? Democracy is such a consideration. Can utilitarianism recast turn out to be at odds with democracy? Can it fail to achieve justice in every respect? Is it compatible with troubling inequalities? I shall not try to argue that it answers in a satisfactory way to certain topics characteristic of natural law theory, for example, sociability (in a sense that came up in an earlier chapter) and common purpose.

I shall not try, either, to give complete answers to the questions posed by the other topics that I mentioned. Were I to answer them, so far as I go, by constructing an apparatus of further precautions to impose a priori on the operations of utilitarianism recast, I would not be giving all the precautions. I shall take another approach, which I think is more in keeping with the history of utilitarianism: I shall try to show that democracy turns out to be an empirical condition for generating attention to meeting needs in the first instance and maintaining arrangements to meet them in the second. I shall try to show the same thing for the aspects of equality and justice not already incorporated in utilitarianism recast as conditions on the operation of the census-notion. Logically, needs can be met under a variety of arrangements, some of them not democratic, equal, or just; but, empirically, they are not so likely to be met and not so likely to be met securely.

1 On the point of democracy consider two regimes.[29] One is a dictatorship benevolent to a degree under which the most basic needs of the whole population – those in the first part of the List of Matters of Need – are met at tolerably adequate Minimum Standards of Provision. Cuba under Castro may be an example. Under the other regime, of which the United States or Canada may be examples, there is a good deal of political freedom and robust though imperfect democratic practices in politics, but the basic needs of a proportion of the population go unmet (shelter for the homeless in New York City; food for old women living alone in Washington, D.C.) or are met only precariously (various needs, in various degrees, for workers cutting sugar cane in Florida). In Canada, the condition of many of the aboriginal First Nations supplies examples of unmet needs. Does utilitarianism recast favour the first regime?

   This would be a more troubling question if we had to grant that there was no prospect of change in respect to democracy or to meeting needs in either regime. Indeed, in that case, I think it could be answered only by taking the other approach on the present topics that I mentioned, that of adding precautions; and rejecting both regimes as running counter to the precautions. On the approach that I am taking, of treating democracy (as I shall treat equality and justice) as something that belongs to the empirical conditions for meeting needs, futurity and the prospects of change are crucial.

   If the dictatorship has stopped with meeting needs on the first part of the basic List, then utilitarianism recast demands that it go on to meeting needs on the rest of the List. If it has done this (as Cuba, I believe, has done with education and other matters), utilitarianism recast demands that it go on to the second stage of its program: matters of preference only, commodious living, and happiness. Will a dictatorship do this? Empirically, the prospects of change may be better with an imperfect democracy: a dictatorship may not do so well by utilitarianism recast as democracy, in most cases, either in pressing to the end the demands of both stages of the program or in maintaining the arrangements under which the demands are satisfied. Democracy gives the masses an opportunity to demand these things. I do not claim that this is the only advantage of democracy, or the only one from the point of view of utilitarianism recast. It is a substantial one, however, and to it may be joined the empirical advantages of democracy in heeding the demands of equality and justice.

2 Utilitarianism recast captures an important sense of equality directly – equality-in-meeting-needs, which means meeting for every Matter of Need the Minimum Standards of Provision for everybody, allowing (as I have pointed out earlier) for variation between persons. This is an objective implied in the priority that utilitarianism recast gives to meeting needs. Utilitarianism recast also captures, with this sense of equality, a sense of equality according to which if people are not strictly equal in power, they are still not so unequal that some of them can easily arrange to oppress the others – forcing the others into servitude, for example, or making free with the serfs' daughters. If people are assured of the provisions that come to them with equality-in-meeting-needs, they will not be so vulnerable to oppression. A pretty obvious trap, it may be said, lies in the assumption that they will continue to be assured of provisions for their needs. For how can this assurance be obtained except under a government with effective police powers that it is ready to use against would-be oppressors in government or out of it? Democracy comes in again: only a democratic government, it may be argued, will use police powers this way, without repressing liberty on its own behalf. But the points about equality-in-meeting-needs and the approach to equality in power resting on it while it exists are distinct from the point about arrangements to achieve and keep these things.

3 Utilitarianism recast, let us recall, captures in the conditions of its very operations a number of aspects of justice that have come up in the preceding discussions. Like utilitarianism without recasting, utilitarianism recast requires that everybody be considered in

gathering the statistical evidence about the impact of policies, and it requires that no one be eliminated in a shift (or hypothetical shift) from one policy to another simply to make the evidence more compelling in the way of a statistical comparison. But utilitarianism recast goes further. With the census-notion as a feature, it resists not only sacrifices of life but personal sacrifices short of life. With the Gains-Preservation Principle operating, too, along with the anti-discrimination condition, it carries out this resistance to the end, in detail. It stops resisting only when the Revisionary Process hits upon a policy that need not be resisted. Finally, so far as the results of policies go, at least a large measure of distributive justice, if not the whole of it, is achieved by meeting everybody's needs, and any advance toward this state of affairs is an advance in distributive justice.[30]

Utilitarianism recast captures important aspects of justice that do not directly figure in its operations.[31] Honouring contracts was a defining aspect of justice for both Hobbes and Hume. It is difficult to believe that there is a Matter of Need concerned with making or keeping contracts. On the other hand, the institution of contracts may connect with meeting needs by being an indispensable feature of arrangements for meeting them, for example, of arrangements for coordinating private productive enterprises. The justice of keeping contracts will not be an operational feature of utilitarianism recast; that is to say, it would not be a feature that applied with it in every situation. However, it would be fully justified by its empirical indispensability when it was indispensable, as would any rule indispensable in this way in given circumstances. The justification would be weighty enough if it were happiness that was at stake; it is even weightier, if contracts are indispensable to meeting needs.

Again, it is an important aspect of justice that people not be unjustly accused of derelictions and that they have procedures available for exculpating themselves. If occasions for exculpation should arise, they will need the procedures, and this will be an important need. This will not rank as a Matter of Need, like the Matters on the basic List, that will have to be provided for in everybody's case continually through life or at least in some phase of life that everybody passes through. However, it might be one feature among others of a legal system – a system of rules or of natural laws – that performed an essential function in the continuing organization and policies of a society that adequately met needs.

I surely have not treated all aspects of equality and justice. Should others be brought up, however, I would make a committed effort to treat them in the same way. If they could not figure directly, logically, in the operations of utilitarianism recast, then I would consider whether they could not figure among the empirical conditions of carrying out the operations and achieving the results (keeping them, too).

Some moral considerations, I believe, would escape the reach of utilitarianism recast. Although the conditions of its operation do something to safeguard respect for human dignity, and the presence of democracy as an empirical condition of its success does something more, there may be some shortfall in demands for human dignity. Moreover, sociability and a common purpose, as they figure in natural law theory, do not fit so easily into utilitarianism recast. Utilitarianism recast carries over from utilitarianism before recasting a certain indifference to both. Insofar as people meet their needs in social cooperation and in the pursuit of a common purpose, utilitarianism recast will value sociability and a common purpose, as would utilitarianism before recasting if sociability and a common purpose served pleasure similarly. Yet if everyone with whom a policy is concerned gets optimal pleasure isolated in a personal pleasure-cell, that suffices for utilitarianism before recasting, unnatural as such a result may seem. Utilitarianism recast, if it continues to recognize a need for companionship and a need for social acceptance and recognition will not be quite so ready to accept a personal-cell solution. However, it would not be troubled by having a very limited need for companionship to deal with – say, one friend, seen at lunch every six months. By contrast, natural law theory would insist on having people brought up in a way that fostered companionship and sociability – that made the most, if you like, of a natural disposition developed in this way. Simultaneously it would insist, too, that the motivation for meeting other people's needs – historically always a problem for utilitarianism – originates in the same sort of upbringing.[32]

Utilitarianism Recast on the World Scene

Still a project so far as offering a complete ethics go, still a theory under renovation, utilitarianism as I have recast it falls short of what utilitarianism has historically aimed at. Yet in several respects, as I have shown, it does better in offering an effective current guide to policy-making. A utilitarianism improving on utilitarianism recast might reasonably be asked to do at least as well, and maybe some of the features of utilitarianism recast that work well now will survive in the perfected theory. One feature that looks especially likely to survive is the priority given to meeting needs, which makes a crucial difference to the application of utilitarianism to the world scene.

Historically, utilitarianism has argued nobly for comprehensive attention to everybody (every sentient being, in fact) affected by the actions and policies to be evaluated under its auspices. But this turns out to be very demanding, imposing obligations to promote the well-being of the whole world population. Worse, the obligations do not discriminate between utilities; they bind people with the resources to do so to assist others to greater satisfactions from optional, even frivolous, pursuits if the transfer of resources will raise the overall utility score. Thus, there emerges a demand for altruism, as altruism is now understood by economists and philosophers: altruists give as much weight (or more!) to the preferences and satisfactions of any other persons as to their own. Utilitarianism, on the received understanding, calls for such altruism, and this redoubles the exactingness of the demand to serve the whole world population in deciding upon actions and policies.

The conception of altruism demanded by utilitarianism recast is much easier to accept (and, I would claim, more in accord with traditional notions about compassion and benevolence). The Principle of Precedence, which is the vehicle for bringing to bear the demand for the altruism, binds people to give priority, once their own needs are met, to meeting other people's needs. What is to be done to accommodate other people's preferences, once their needs are met, is another matter. This is the position taken both when the Reference Population, whose needs are at issue, is the same as the Policy-Making Population (in both cases, say, the population of Canada) or a different population (say, as opposed to the population of Canada, the population of Ethiopia). No doubt someone involved in efforts to promote the well-being of any Reference Population, abroad as well as at home, would not stand in the way of having their preferences heeded as well as their needs met and, in a friendly spirit, be willing to offer some assistance. The moral urgency of doing so, however, would fade away once the issue had shifted away from meeting needs to assisting the members of the Reference Population in the superstructal dimensions of utilitarianism recast, where only preferences and packets of discretionary income are at stake. Indeed, the distinctive urgency that utilitarianism recast lends to meeting needs tends to fade away when matters of need with relatively less firm claims to figure on the basic list come into the picture or when more liberal standards are adopted of minimal provision for matters of need anywhere on the basic list. In these respects, utilitarianism recast makes a much more plausible and acceptable demand upon the people who subscribe to it.

It is not, or should not be, an indiscriminate demand. Transferring funds abroad, even shipping material provisions for needs, often may not be the best way to give effective aid. The best way may be a combination of indirect measures: standing out of the way of letting people help themselves by protecting the position of their farming in international trade (enabling them to go on cultivating their own food and when they have crops to export giving them easy access to markets in the rich countries); preventing kleptocratic elites from diverting aid in funds or provisions into their own hands; preventing those elites from selling off the resources of their countries for their private benefit.[33] But if such a combination of indirect measures is the best way of meeting the needs of the population in Ethiopia or any other country beset by difficulties in meeting them, that is what utilitarianism recast firmly recommends.

Envoi

These restorations, repairs, and renovations give the attractions of Bentham's Master-Idea a more convincing cast than ever and bring its unhappy career to a happy end.

When I was beginning in philosophy, I made my way to Oxford, after an appropriate preparation at Cornell, and found myself studying and practising ordinary language philosophy in its all too brief heyday. I took instruction from J.L. Austin, who was propounding, and himself setting an example of heeding, the maxim that before embarking on innovative theories about concepts, philosophers should look carefully first at how the concepts (and cousin-concepts) worked in ordinary language. I think what I have done in my treatment of Bentham's Master-Idea is show that by disregarding Austin's maxim, chiefly by ignoring the census-notion (which Austin liked when I brought it to him), ignoring along with this the affinity between the census-notion and inquiries about meeting needs, and ignoring the policy-making process with its Revisionary feature, utilitarians (abetted by their critics) have produced a monster that matches or surpasses anything else that philosophy has done in disrespect of ordinary language. Fortunately, utilitarianism can escape from the monster and the labyrinth in which the monster resides. The restorations, repairs, and renovations that I have expounded in the present book give the attractions of Bentham's Master-Idea a more convincing cast than it has usually borne and bring the unhappy career of the Idea to a happy (if not entirely tidy) end.

Notes

Introduction

1 See Scheffler, *The Rejection of Consequentialism* (Oxford: Clarendon Press, 1982); and for a succinct and lucid synopsis of the disputes, his introduction to the anthology that he edited, *Consequentialism and Its Critics* (New York: Oxford University Press, 1988).

2 See Williams's contribution to J.J.C. Smart and Bernard Williams, *Utilitarianism For and Against* (Cambridge: Cambridge University Press, 1973). In chapter 3 of this book I shall discuss at some length a famous example that Williams puts forward in his contribution; but, consistent with my emphasis on public policy-making, I shall have little to say directly about Williams's concern with personal integrity.

3 Goodin, *Utilitarianism as a Public Philosophy* (Cambridge: Cambridge University Press, 1995).

4 Shaw, *Contemporary Ethics* (Oxford: Blackwell, 1999), 38.

5 Shaw, *Contemporary Ethics*, 13.

6 See the writings cited following Ross Harrison in chap. 3, n. 17, below.

7 Mill, *Utilitarianism*, 4th ed. (London: Longmans, 1871 [1861]), as reprinted in the University of Toronto Press edition of Mill's collected works, Vol. X, *Essays on Ethics, Religion, and Society* (1969), chap. 2, 214.

8 Goodin says that 'the Greatest Happiness' was 'the phrase favored by Bentham and his nineteenth century friends and foes alike, supplanting the 'earlier, careless phrase – "the greatest happiness of the greatest number"' (*Utilitarianism*, 3). Fred Rosen corroborates this point, at least as regards the shift by Bentham (Rosen, 'Individual Sacrifice and the Greatest Happiness,' *Utilitas* 10, 2 (July 1998), 129–43, at 131). However, I doubt whether the supplanting was thoroughgoing, or that many people

even now under stand the earlier slogan to be 'a mathematical impossibil-
ity,' Goodin's somewhat obscure account of its defect. (See below, the
citation of Edgeworth in chapter 4, n. 19). Bentham himself was using the
slogan at least as late as July 1822, in an addition of that date to n. d,
chapter 1, *Introduction to the Principles of Morals and Legislation* (London:
University of London Press, 1970 [1789 and later]).

9 There is a hint of the importance of something like the Revisionary
Process in J.S. Mill's statement toward the end of chapter 2 of *Utilitarianism*, 'The corollaries from the principle of utility, like the precepts of every
practical art, admit of indefinite improvement, and, in a progressive state
of the human mind, their improvement is perpetually going on' (Toronto
edition of the collected works, Vol. X, 224).

10 Nor do I go far from Bentham himself: Rosen cites Bentham as stressing
(in his *Codification Proposal* of 1822) the universal importance of 'the four
most comprehensive particular and subordinate *ends*' associated with the
principle of 'the *greatest happiness* of the greatest number,' namely,
'*subsistence, abundance, security*, and *equality* (Bentham's emphasis). Rosen,
'Individual Sacrifices,' 136. 'Equality' stands in the way of naked aggrega-
tion. Subsistence and security will figure prominently on any plausible list
of basic needs.

11 And for other sentient beings, when due attention is paid to them. I
acknowledge the presence and importance in Bentham of this larger
notion of utilitarianism, but I have nothing interesting to say at the
moment about how utilitarianism recast as I would recast it would treat
other animals, except that I do not foresee any intractable problems. We
are already counting the numbers of animals in other species endangered
by reckless human policies. I do touch upon the sufferings of animals in
an example discussed at length in chapter 2 (see pp. 63–4).

12 Nor does Bentham treat it as indissoluble. Rosen and Gerald J. Postema
(in a response, 'Bentham's Equality-Sensitive Utilitarianism,' *Utilitas* 10, 2
(July 1998), 144–58, on somewhat different grounds and somewhat
different textual evidence), both argue that Bentham was concerned not
with aggregative scores of group happiness, but with the distribution of
happiness to the widest possible extent to members of the group. I go no
further myself than to say that in some texts (to be cited below) distributive concerns are dominant. Even this, however, lends powerful support
to my contention that at the bottom of Bentham's thinking there is a
Master-Idea of which the use of the census-notion supplies an alternative
interpretation.

Chapter 1

1 Judith Jarvis Thomson, *Rights, Restitution, and Risk* (Cambridge, Mass.: Harvard University Press, 1986), 255. As I have belatedly realized, Thomson actually writes 'Hedonistic,' though she inspired me to think 'Hedonic,' with which I shall stick.

2 David Hume, *A Treatise of Human Nature*, Book III, sec. II (London: Penguin Books, 1984 [1739, 1740]).

3 'Act-utilitarianism' and 'rule-utilitarianism' are Brandt's terms. See Richard B. Brandt, *Ethical Theory* (Englewood Cliffs, N.J.: Prentice-Hall, 1959), chap. 15. I follow Smart in adopting them. (See J.J.C. Smart, 'Extreme Utilitarianism: A Reply to M.A. Kaplan,' *Ethics*, 71 (1960–1), 133; and *An Outline of a System of Utilitarian Ethics* (Melbourne: Melbourne University Press, 1961), 2–5. I do not subscribe to Brandt's definition of rule-utilitarianism; see *Ethical Theory*, 396–7. The case for rule-utilitarianism (as I have characterized it above) does not, it seems to me, presuppose that there is a complete set of ideal prescriptions that is to be adopted on utilitarian merits exceeding those of other sets. (There is, so far as I can see, no trace of this presupposition in Smart's treatment either.) I treat act-utilitarianism and rule-utilitarianism as doctrines about how the Principle of Utility is to be applied if thoroughgoing application of it is sought. Rule-utilitarianism contends that direct application of act-utilitarianism fails in some possible circumstances (though not in all).

4 (Oxford: Clarendon Press, 1995), 37.

5 This is Smart's epithet.

6 Cf. Henry Sidgwick's argument that utilitarianism must be brought in to repair the defects of common-sense morality. *The Methods of Ethics*, 7th ed. (London: Macmillan, 1907 [1874]), Book IV, chap. V.

7 See G.H. von Wright, *Norm and Action* (London: Routledge, 1963).

8 As stated in the Acknowledgments, 'The Choice between Utilitarianisms,' *American Philosophical Quarterly* 4 (January 1967), 28–38.

9 Cf. Rousseau, *Du contrat social*, livre II, chap. III, in *Oeuvres complètes* (Paris: Éditions du Seuil, 1971 [1762], 161.2.

10 For the purposes of the discussion in the present chapter, I follow Brandt and Smart in waiving inquiries into the difficulties.

11 Brandt, *Ethical Theory*, 389–91.

12 J.J.C. Smart, 'Extreme and Restricted Utilitarianism,' *Philosophical Quarterly* 6 (1956), 344–54, at 350–1. As the phrase 'gas-cheat' implies, originally, in both these examples a rule prohibiting the use of more than a

ration of gas or of water are at issue. Consistently with my approach leaving rules aside for the time being, the examples are to be understood here as simply involving uses of gas or water great enough to raise questions about additional burdens on the community supply.

13 *Summa Theologiae*, 1a2ae, Q. 96, art. 6.

14 The suggestion was made by one reader of this book in manuscript.

15 A student, Vladislav Stoychev, brought up this example.

16 This was the phrase that a student (Brandon Butler) used to express his reaction on first encountering the idea of the Community-in-Session.

17 As a sophisticated champion of act-utilitarianism, Smart gives these imperfections a great deal of weight. His act-utilitarians are superior to ordinary men in being rational, benevolent, and conscientious; and even they will do best to act by 'stereotyped rules' in many circumstances. Cf., for instance, *Outline*, 4, 29–31.

18 Cf. the list of advantages of going by the rules enumerated by William H. Shaw, *Contemporary Ethics: Taking Account of Utilitarianism* (Oxford: Blackwell, 1999), 145–58.

19 Cf. John Rawls, 'Two Concepts of Rules,' *Philosophical Review* 64 (1955), 3–32, at 16. The moral rules that will figure in my discussion may or may not have the same content as rules of traditional morality; and they may or may not be clothed with the extensive institutional vestments that Rawls, discussing traditional rules, has ascribed to 'rules of practices.' On the other hand, they are more than 'summary rules,' if these are understood as merely indicating as defeasible guides to present personal decisions the tendency of past experience. In all cases, they are designed to forestall the operation of personal discretion. Shaw, *Contemporary Ethics*, 150, includes among the advantages of having ethics work through rules that it is easier to monitor whether people have been acting in accordance with the rules than whether they have been making decisions on utilitarian grounds.

20 (Oxford: Clarendon Press, 1965), x; cf. ix, 25.

21 Scanlon, 'Rights, Goals, and Fairness,' in S. Hampshire, ed., *Public and Private Morality* (Cambridge: Cambridge University Press, 1978), 93–111. I discuss the third objection at the end of this chapter and the second one later in the book (see chap. 4, n. 12). Scanlon may have in mind a conception of rule-utilitarianism less like the one that I characterize and work with in this chapter than like the one that figures in the definition given by William H. Shaw in his *Contemporary Ethics* (164): 'Rule utilitarianism maintains that the utilitarian standard should not be applied to individual actions, but should instead be used to determine the appropriate moral rules to follow;' and, moreover, that 'an action is morally right if and only

if it accords with that set of rules, the general acceptance of which would result in more happiness than any alternative set of rules.' But even with this conception Scanlon does not put forward a case to answer: either there are actions that fall outside the rules and may without trouble be left to fall out or there are not. In both cases, there are places for act-utilitarian reasoning. In the former case it establishes whether the actions can indeed be left out without trouble. In the latter case it has to do with the actions of choosing rules in the first place, but it can always be invoked in the face of a challenge to vindicate any rule correctly chosen.

22 Smart, *Outline*, 43–4. It is assumed that V, the total (increased) benefit, equals 0 when $n = 0$; and that V is not then maximized.

23 Richmond H. Thomason has supplied me with the following illustration of a mixed strategy solution, which is typical in indicating how the chances of a disaster remain but are minimized:

Consider a community of three individuals. Here,

$$E(p) = \sum_{i=0}^{3} (3/i)\, p^i (1-p)^i (a.i + f(i))$$

$$= (1-p)^3 f(0) + 3p(1-p)^2(a + f(1)) + 3p^2(1-p)(2a + f(2)) + p^3(3a + f(3)).$$

I have added the values of f in this equation, since I am thinking of f as a function which gives the utility to the community, positive or negative, of a certain number of people performing a given act. In the cases which interest us, f will be nonpositive and decreasing (or at least nonincreasing).

Let $a = 1$, and let f be given by $f(0) = 0$, $f(1) = -1/9$, $f(2) = -2/15$, and $f(3) = -7$. One can imagine situations which would give something like these numbers; say, three homeowners, each with electric dishwashers. If one or two of them use their appliance in a given time period (say, after the dinner hour) there is only a little general inconvenience, say, a slight dimming of the lights, but if all three wash at once, the fuse blows on the main line, and someone has to go out in the cold to replace it.

The value of p which maximizes expected utility (i.e., $E(p)$) here is $1/4$.

If the three individuals spin their wheels, in an average run of 64 days none will wash 27 days, 1 will wash on 27 days, 2 will wash on 9 days, and all 3 will wash (and consequently blow the fuse) on 1 day. Total utility gained in this period, using Smart's method, will be

$$27.0 + 27.(1 - 1/9) + 9(2 - 2/15) + 1(-4), \text{ or } 24 + {}^{84}/5 - 4 = 36^4/5.$$

24 V represents utility; hence, it already takes into account the impact that various gains and losses would have on the community, given its initial circumstances. A loss of a given size will mean more, one may assume, to a poorer community than to a richer one. Agents in either community may still vary among themselves in the utility or disutility that they place on taking even favourable risks. A positive value of E may be offset in a given agent's eyes by the disutility to him of gambling. See Rudolf Carnap, *Logical Foundations of Probability* (Chicago: University of Chicago Press, 1950), 276.

25 This point has been established in the course of an exchange of views between Smart and Morton A. Kaplan in *Ethics*. See Kaplan, 'Some Problems of the Extreme Utilitarian Position,' *Ethics* 70 (1959–60), 228–52; Smart, 'Extreme Utilitarianism: A Reply to M.A. Kaplan,' *Ethics* 71 (1960–1), 133; and Kaplan, 'Restricted Utilitarianism,' *Ethics* 71 (1960–1), 301–2.

26 The revised version is Smart's contribution to J.J.C. Smart and Bernard Williams, *Utilitarianism For and Against* (Cambridge: Cambridge University Press, 1973), 60–1. Lewis's understanding of convention is set forth in his book *Convention* (Cambridge, Mass.: Harvard University Press, 1969).

27 Kaplan rightly stresses the importance of the concession that Smart makes to him about the assumption of symmetry, namely, that in assuming symmetry of reasoning and conduct a departure has been made from act (extreme) utilitarianism. For in assuming symmetry, Smart takes aggregate effects fully into account; whereas act-utilitarianism takes aggregate effects into account only insofar as they are connected with given single actions – either as known from past actions, and in this way entering the premises of this one, or as expected among the causal consequences of the one now contemplated. 'The rightness or wrongness of an action is to be judged by the consequences, good and bad, of the action itself' (*Outline*, 4). 'The rightness or wrongness of keeping a promise on a particular occasion depends only on the goodness or badness of the consequences of keeping or of breaking the promise on that particular occasion' ('Extreme and Restricted Utilitarianism,' 344). Act-utilitarianism, so expressed, is inconsistent with a mixed strategy solution. Smart wavers between recognizing the discrepancy (in his reply to Kaplan) and refusing to recognize it (*Outline*, 44). In *Outline*, Smart assumes that all the members of the community in which the mixed strategy solution is adopted are act-utilitarians; but they cannot be. They may have begun by being act-utilitarians; but they become rule-utilitarians as soon as they adopt the mixed strategy solution.

28 Commenting on the illustration given above, Thomason says, 'If the three individuals are in communication beforehand and work out an agreement so that two can wash on every night of the period ... (the [period] of an average run of 64 days), $64(2 - {}^2/_{15}) = 119\ {}^7/_{15}$ units of utility will be gained, a considerable improvement over the expected utility to be gained by the mixed strategy solution, which was $36\ {}^4/_5$.'

29 As analysed, for example, in Marcus G. Singer's discussion in *Generalization in Ethics* (New York: Knopf, 1961).

30 Cf. in the Bible, *Book of Judith*, especially chaps. 12 and 13. What I say about the stakes accords with Judith's own report, in her triumphal song about her action. The story in the *Book of Judith*, taken as a whole, is not entirely committed on this point. The people immediately affected by the threat, in Judith's home town, might simply have been enslaved; but this is arguably bad enough.

31 Which, I understand from a philosopher who has worked in business (Jack Stevenson), happens all the time. Philosophers have much too rigid notions about promise-keeping.

32 *Summa Theologiae*, 2a2ae, Q. 120.

33 It is the third of the three 'very serious objections' put forward in Scanlon, 'Rights, Goals, and Fairness'; see n. 21, above, and the passage disposing of the first objection. The second objection, that rule-utilitarians are in no better position than act-utilitarians to 'give a satisfactory place to considerations of justice' will be dealt with in chapters 3 and 4, below.

34 Ibid., 94.

35 Professor H. Chandler Davis of the University of Toronto, Professor Harry R. Pitt of the University of Nottingham, and Dr Richmond H. Thomason, then a student in the Yale graduate school, very kindly assisted in the preparation of the paper from which this chapter derives by providing substantial advice both mathematical and philosophical. An earlier version of the paper was read at the University of Rochester, 5 March 1963.

Chapter 2

1 In Notes published with *The Will to Power* (1888), reprinted in *The Portable Nietzsche*, ed. W. Kaufmann (New York: Viking Press, 1968), 457–8.

2 Joseph Butler, *Fifteen Sermons and a Dissertation upon the Nature of Virtue* (London: Bell, 1964 [originally published 1726]), in the *Dissertation*, 255–6.

3 William H. Shaw, *Contemporary Ethics: Taking Account of Utilitarianism* (Oxford: Blackwell, 1999), 15–16, 67; J.S. Mill, *Utilitarianism*, 4th ed. (London: Longmans, 1871 [1861]), as reprinted in the University of Toronto Press edition of Mill's collected works, Vol. X, *Essays on Ethics, Religion, and Society* (1969), chap. 2, toward the end.

4 Braybrooke and Lindblom, *A Strategy of Decision: Policy Evaluation as a Social Process* (New York: The Free Press, 1963).

5 Tinbergen, *Economic Policy: Principles and Design* (Amsterdam: North-Holland, 1956).

6 Dimock, *A Philosophy of Administration* (New York: Harper, 1958), 140.

7 Lasswell, *Politics: Who Gets What, When, How* (Cleveland and New York: World Publishing [Meridian Books], 1958 ed. with postscript), 206.

8 Hart and Honoré, *Causation in the Law* (Oxford: Clarendon Press, 1959), 64ff.

9 R.G. Lipsey and Kelvin Lancaster, 'The General Theory of Second Best,' *Review of Economic Studies* 24 (1956–7), 11–32.

10 Shaw is another writer who draws upon traffic problems as a source of examples for utilitarian consideration, though not having specialized in the subject to the extent that I have (see n. 11), he does not make so much of it. See, for instance, Shaw, *Contemporary Ethics*, 147.

11 Here and several times further in this passage, I shall draw upon my little book, *Traffic Congestion Goes Through the Issue-Machine* (London: Routledge, 1974), written and published during the time when of all the English-speaking philosophers in Nova Scotia I was the one most expert on current traffic problems in the United Kingdom.

12 For an illustrative list, short in itself, but too long to reproduce here, see *Traffic Congestion*, which also enumerates the many groups and agencies that had parts in discussing the list and weeding it out.

13 Shaw, *Contemporary Ethics*, 29–30.

14 This objection was actually raised in Britain during the discussion of proposals for full road pricing, which might have made such monitoring feasible.

15 This point was made by Daniel Pozza, a student in the seminar who is also a practising lawyer.

16 This point was of special concern to another student, Shaun Gilligan.

17 Cf. H.A. Simon, *Models of Man* (New York: Wiley, 1957).

18 Objecting to any complacency about the operation of the strategy, a student, Brenna Troncoso, pressed this point in the seminar.

19 Ehrenfeld, 'The Cow Tipping Point,' *Harper's*, October 2001, 13–20.

20 Malcolm Gladwell, 'Connecting the Dots,' *NewYorker*, 10 March 2003, 83–8, at 87; quoted from Harold L. Wilensky, *Organizational Intelligence* (New York: Basic Books, 1967), 51.

21 *Utilitarianism*, vol. X, 203–59, at 220.

22 For a careful and deliberately 'unromantic' discussion of the resettlement policy, see Parzival Copes, *The Resettlement of Fishing Communities in Newfoundland* (Ottawa: Canadian Council on Rural Development, 1972). The point about the single jukebox can be found on p. 132.

23 The history of the policies referred to can be found in J.R. Miller, *Skyscrapers Hide the Heavens* (Toronto: University of Toronto Press, 1989). Miller makes the point that the issue of assimilation arose only after the European colonists had ceased to need the First Nations as military allies. See also J.R. Miller, ed., *Sweet Promises: A Reader on Indian-White Relations in Canada* (Toronto: University of Toronto Press, 1991), especially the essay by John H. Tobias, 'Protection, Civilization, Assimilation: An Outline History of Canada's Indian Policy,' 127–44.

24 See Hochschild, *The New American Dilemma: Liberal Democracy and School Desegregation* (New Haven, Conn.: Yale University Press, 1984). See also 'Scale, Combination, Opposition: A Rethinking of Incrementalism,' my critical review of the book in *Ethics* 95 (July 1985), 920–33 (reprinted as chap. 16 of my collected essays, *Moral Objectives, Rules, and the Forms of Social Change* (Toronto: University of Toronto Press, 1998).

25 Someone who (very implausibly) took being incremental as a sufficient justification for a policy might shift to a jurisdiction in which it was incremental and thus try to shift attention away from the non-incremental disasters portending or actually occurring in a subjurisdiction. Brandon Butler suggested at a session of my seminar that here a whole new objection to utilitarianism was opened up by the combination of utilitarianism with incrementalism. But in such a case the demands of utilitarianism in the combination would be ignored.

Chapter 3

1 (Cambridge, Mass.: Harvard University Press, 1986), 257–60.

2 J.J.C. Smart and B. Williams, *For and Against Utilitarianism* (Cambridge: Cambridge University Press, 1973), 98–9, 117.

3 In J. Bentham, *An Introduction to the Principles of Morals and Legislation* (London: University of London Press, 1970 [1789]); J.S. Mill, *Utilitarianism*,

4th ed. (London: Longmans, 1871 [1861]), as reprinted in the University of Toronto Press edition of Mill's collected works, Vol. X, *Essays on Ethics, Religion, and Society* (1969), 205–59; H. Sidgwick, *The Methods of Ethics* [1874], 7th ed. (London: Macmillan, 1907); F.Y. Edgeworth, *Mathematical Psychics* (London: Kegan Paul, 1881).

4 Mill, *Utilitarianism*, chap. II; Sidgwick, *Methods of Ethics*, 432; William H. Shaw, *Contemporary Ethics: Taking Account of Utilitarianism* (Oxford: Blackwell, 1999), 90.

5 Edgeworth, *Mathematical Psychics*, 75; cf. 63–5.

6 Nor is there any sign in what he writes of a suggestion that some members of the population might be tortured just to increase the happiness of others.

7 Edgeworth, *Mathematical Psychics*, 71–3. I am making something more of the text than a strictly literal reading might.

8 Mill, *Utilitarianism*, chap. 2.

9 Sidgwick, *Methods of Ethics*, Book IV. See also Book II, chap. II–VII; Book III, chap. XIV.

10 I owe to Robert Henderson this reference to Hutcheson. In a passage reprinted in Selby-Bigge, *British Moralists*, Vol. I, 122 (Oxford: Clarendon Press, 1897), Hutcheson says, 'If putting the Aged to death, with all its Consequences, really tends to the publick Good, and to the lesser Misery of the Aged, it is no doubt justifiable; nay, perhaps the Aged chuse it, in hopes of a future State. If a deform'd or weak Race, could never by Ingenuity or Art, make themselves useful to Mankind, but should grow an absolutely unsupportable Burden, so as to involve a whole State in Misery, it is just to put them to death.' These are (to say the least) arresting remarks, but they do not perfectly align with the examples that Thomson and Williams bring up – on the one hand, Hutcheson assumes that the Aged gain, too, by their death, not merely by entering a future State; on the other hand, the 'deformed, or weak Race' not only are irremediably useless, but 'involve' everyone else in 'Misery' – not something that can be said of the young man who has come in for his check-up, or said of any of the Indians.

11 William Godwin, *An Enquiry Concerning Political Justice and Its Influence on General Virtue and Happiness* (London: George Robinson, 1793), Book II, chap. XIII; Book VII, chaps. II, V.

12 See above, n. 4. J.B. Schneewind, in *Sidgwick's Ethics and Victorian Moral Philosophy* (Oxford: Clarendon Press, 1977), 139, briefly surveys Godwin's 'radical' utilitarianism; and says, 'Historically it helps us understand' how the utilitarian was repeatedly pictured as a 'monster of abstract rational-

ity, basically selfish, denying the importance of family, friends, country, laws, traditions, replacing the Christian virtues of the humble heart by those of the calculating mind, reducing man to a machine for grinding out pleasures. Godwin, far more than Bentham, must be the original of these portrayals.' This may be so, but a charge that he endorses imposing involuntary life-sacrifices just to promote the happiness of other people is hard to sustain.

13 Schneewind, *Sidgwick's Ethics*, 148. Schneewind describes the objection as 'commonplace,' but however commonplace it may be now, was it commonplace then? One cannot tell from Hazlitt's assertion.

14 See Nowell C. Smith, *The Letters of Sydney Smith*, Vol. II (Oxford: Clarendon Press, 1953), 632.

15 The reliance on the felicific calculus varies in enthusiasm and precision. Ross Harrison has found Bentham himself, in the *Constitutional Code* (Bowring Edition, Vol. IX, 199), reasoning with only the loosest attachment, if any, to the calculus. There Bentham holds that the only end of government is the Greatest Happiness 'of all without exception, in so far as possible: of the greatest number on every occasion on which the nature of the case renders it impossible, by rendering it a matter of necessity to make sacrifice of a portion of the happiness of a few, to the greater happiness of the rest.' He is not being a greatest total or greatest average utilitarian in the first part of this statement; and in the second part he is being a greatest number utilitarian. See Harrison, *Bentham* (London: Routledge, 1983), 233–4.

16 The notion of a precise average happiness score is not in much better shape. James Fishkin has pointed out to me that some current adepts of utilitarianism who have taken the greatest total happiness in the group as the supreme criterion find themselves confronting a problem about replaceability: substituting a person from outside the group – a person created, perhaps, by some science fiction device – for someone in it if the total score is thereby increased. See Fishkin, *The Dialogue of Justice* (New Haven, Conn.: Yale University Press, 1992), 13–17. These utilitarians might think the constraints that come with the other notion, of making the people in a group as happy as possible – the SGSIT constraints – arbitrary, brought in ad hoc just to solve the problem. They seem to me to have got things phase backwards. I would take them by the hand and lead them back to the point in the history of thinking about these matters at which making the people in a group as happy as possible began to be displaced by the other notion of greatest total happiness; and I would try to persuade them that shifting to the other notion was ill advised – creating

a difficulty about intelligibility in the first place and then a host of
difficulties about sacrifices to be imposed on members of the initial set of
people whose happiness invited attention. Perhaps this was the worst
move in the whole pernicious career of the concept of utility.

17 Bentham, *Principles*, chap. IV, section V, item 6.

18 Ibid., chap. XV, sections XVIII and XIX; for the definition of 'unfrugal,' see
section XI of the same chapter.

19 Mill, advocating capital punishment rather than life imprisonment
in a speech in Parliament, concentrates on the prisoner and his prospects of suffering as an individual; Mill argues that life imprisonment
implies a more painful prospect. See 'Speech (1868)' in J. Feinberg
and H. Gross, eds, *Philosophy of Law* (Encino, Calif.: Dickenson, 1975),
619–22.

20 It need not gainsay Bentham's claim to innovation very much to recognize
that he borrowed the root idea of calculation from Beccaria; or that he had
some predecessors (Petty and, even more notably, King) who were
concerned with collecting statistics on the personal welfare of the population of England.

21 In the enormous mass of Bentham's papers there may well be explicit
assertions that imply the same conclusion as my three arguments. P.J.
Kelly, in *Utilitarianism and Distributive Justice* (Oxford: Clarendon Press,
1990), based in part on unpublished papers, intimates as much without
(I think) quite bringing the intimation home to the issue of the present
paper. Paul Lyon has cited to me a passage in *The Rationale of Rewards*,
one of Bentham's published works, reprinted in the Bowring edition,
Vol. II, 89–266, at 252, where Bentham opposes sacrifice. With or without
the addition of explicit assertions, my three arguments retain the interest
of showing what should sensibly have been made of the most familiar
passages in Bentham (and Mill, and Edgeworth, and Sidgwick), though
interpretation and criticism have taken another course. (At this point, I
would like to be able to produce some historical information about how
Bentham's innovation in respect to the general use of statistics led to the
degree of systematic use that became common after, say, the middle of
the nineteenth century. Unfortunately, my researches have not turned up
such information. The historical aspects of statistics treated in the two
encyclopedias of the social sciences are almost exclusively aspects of the
history of the theory of statistics rather than of the history of applications.
I suspect, moreover, that it will be difficult to distinguish Bentham's
influence from the influences of many others. I shall confine myself for

the moment to observing that even if this proves so, it would not imply that Bentham had no influence; he may have had an important influence in creating a climate of opinion favourable to the use of statistics. His influence in this way may have been as important, and as progressive, as his influence in liberating us to treat pleasures of all sorts, playgoing, feasting, dancing, the merrymaking of Christmas, and the whole variety of sexual pleasures, on their merits, rather than under the multitudinous arbitrary prohibitions that various religions have launched against them. Moreover, whatever we make of the historical influence of the felicific calculus in regard to the use of statistics, to see the project of the calculus as a sketch illustrating just one possible way of making them systematically relevant may check us from the heavy-handed literalness with which the sketch – and it is no more – has usually been treated.)

22 Given an easy extension to populations one of which has succeeded the other entirely through a process of natural change (births, deaths from natural causes) BU, it may be noted, can deal with a wide range of future states; and SGSIT, qualified as need be, will accompany the extension. Sidgwick's idea that the Principle of Utility should be invoked to decide whether as a matter of policy future generations should be larger or smaller gives some purchase for Derek Parfit's problems about maximizing happiness in future generations; and because of the difficulty, which Parfit stresses, of disentangling the consequences for any present group from consequences for future generations, maybe BU would have vanishingly little scope if it does not take on these problems. See Parfit, *Reasons and Persons* (Oxford: Clarendon Press, 1984), Part Four, 356–7.

23 One champion of utilitarianism (as he then was), Jan Narveson, remembers having arrived at SGSIT or some statistically equivalent principle at about the time he wrote his book, *Morality and Utility* (Baltimore, Md.: Johns Hopkins University Press, 1967). He does in that book argue that utilitarianism does not license life-sacrifices of the sort in question with the critics' examples, but his argument does not invoke a statistical principle. He uses a principle (stated on p. 158) according to which an action having negative utility is never justified merely by references to other effects that have positive utility.

24 Could you get a gun and turn the tables on the captain? Williams says, 'It is quite clear that nothing of that kind is going to work' (Smart and Williams, *For and Against Utilitarianism*, 99). Hutcheson's cases (see n. 10, above) are clearly forced choices.

25 In my seminar, Brandon Butler pointed out that the Indians might feel so bound to each other as to insist that if one of them were to die, all of them would. People can feel very close and bound to each other, however, without taking this position. The Indians, for example, might think that their village could much more easily spare one of them from productive duties or military ones than spare all twenty.

26 A question not entirely decided by Bentham's seeming to make just this move in the greatest number quotation above, nor decided either by observing that one way of dealing with Bentham's allowance for capital punishment would be to say that at that point augmentation occurs in *Principles* itself. The 'very extraordinary cases' that Bentham had in mind might well be cases of forced choice, with severe reductions in happiness, even loss of life, in prospect whatever one does: he mentions as candidates for capital punishment 'competitors for the sovereignty and leaders of factions in civil wars,' whose names, so long as they live, suffice 'to keep a whole nation in flames.' The interpretation adopted above in the text of this paper, though it preserves a place for SGSIT, must concede that a step toward augmentation occurs with the final comparison, outside SGSIT, of the prisoner's scores with the group scores. Nevertheless, that interpretation is both more conservative and more helpful in explaining why taking innocent lives never came up in the thinking of Bentham and the others.

27 Williams, when he asserts that utilitarianism moves too quickly to solve the problem posed by Sanguinario I, leaves out of account the prior shift from BU, which stands silent in such a case, to Augmented BU; and leaves out of account also the alliance with social contract thinking on the point of the Indians' consent.

28 Brandon Butler brought up a complex case in the seminar, and Dan Pozza aided and abetted him.

29 It may seem distinctly less horrifying (though horrifying even so) to shoot one of twenty, all of whom otherwise are going to die anyway than to shoot a twenty-first person picked arbitrarily out of the crowd of bystanders. How much of the distinction will remain, however, if the twenty were picked out equally arbitrarily? A moment ago, they were free; they had come to town that morning just to sell some chickens.

30 Thomson, *Rights, Restitution, & Risk*, 260.

31 Ibid., 47–8.

32 Ibid., chaps 6 and 7 as well as the Afterword. Chap. 6, as an essay, was published in *The Monist* in 1976.

33 Some time after publishing (and republishing) the writings that I have cited, Thomson published a valuable book devoted to rights, *The Realm of Rights* (Cambridge, Mass.: Harvard University Press, 1990). In it she again takes up 'the Transfer Case,' and treats it with variations that I do not here bring into account; but instructive as her discussion of these variations is, I do not think it affects my argument; nor do her observations – often subtle and illuminating – on the general notion of rights. She has certainly advanced her understanding and ours of how the concept of a right works, but she has not resolved the issue of whether it must be a right rather than some other consideration that saves the young man from cannibalization.

34 St Thomas, *De Veritate*, Q. 17, art. 4; *Summa Theologiae*, 1a2ae, Q. 19, art. 6 and 3a, Q. 64 (I cite these works following at one remove G.H. von Wright in an attribution to him and to St Thomas in Risto Hilpinen, ed., *Introduction to Deontic Logic* (Dordrecht: Reidel, 1971), 12, 34). St Thomas might insist that morality would be quandary free only for anyone who had not herself done something wrong; but it seems reasonable to generalize to quandaries created by the wrongdoing of someone else.

35 D. Hume, *A Treatise of Human Nature* (1739), Book III, Part II, section II.

36 Thus, some grounds for Scanlon's misgiving about utilitarianism leading to injustice in the choice of rules (and, I presume, in other choices) disappear. (See chap. 1, above, n. 21, referring to Scanlon's article, 'Rights, Goals, and Fairness,' in S. Hampshire, ed., *Public and Private Morality* [Cambridge: Cambridge University Press, 1978], 93–111.) A fuller answer will be given in the next chapter, invoking the census-notion combined with the Gains-Preservation Principle.

37 W. Allen Wallis and Harry V. Roberts, *Statistics: A New Approach* (Glencoe, Ill.: The Free Press, 1956), 113–14.

38 Here I am responding to a comment by Sam Fitch.

39 Utilitarianism with SGSIT is by implication a 'prior existence' utilitarianism, which does not allow someone to be discarded from the group in favour of a replacement who is just as happy or more so. But SGSIT is not something that derives from postulating any thesis about 'prior existence.' It is, in the first place, just a requirement of statistical comparison, though in the second place it is a feature of a sensible ordinary approach to comparing groups with a view to increasing the happiness (or some other beneficial condition) of the people in them. To lose sight of SGSIT is to drift away from sensible ordinary comparisons, which support care for what happens to every member in the given group, in the direction of

selecting for proficiency. If you are selecting for proficiency, you can discard inferior performers as you like. The idea of 'prior existence' utilitarianism and the obstacle that it presents to replacing members of the group to get a higher overall score evidently originates with Peter Singer; see *Practical Ethics* (Cambridge: Cambridge University Press, 1979). I treat it here following Eric Mack's discussion (in which there is no sign of SGSIT) in 'Preference Utilitarianism, Prior Existence, and Moral Replaceability,' *Reason Papers* 13 (Spring 1988), 120–31.

40 Compare, in the *Principles*, chap. I, with the first ten paragraphs of chap. II.

41 See *Principles*, chap. II, n. d, section 9.

42 Members of my seminar at Texas, led on this point by Brandon Butler, pressed for amplification on the distinction between utilitarian reasoning and social contract theory and the distinction between social contract theory and natural law theory.

43 D. Braybrooke and A.P. Monahan, 'Common Good,' in L.C. Becker and C.B. Becker, eds, *Encyclopedia of Ethics*, 2d ed. (New York and London: Routledge, 2001), Vol. I, 262–6. Reprinted in D. Braybrooke, *Moral Objectives, Rules, and the Forms of Social Change* (Toronto: University of Toronto Press, 1998), 220–7. Cf. chap. 3, 'Rousseau and St Thomas on the Common Good,' in D. Braybrooke, *Natural Law Modernized* (Toronto: University of Toronto Press, 2001), 54–89. All the attractive features of the Common Good might be supported by utilitarianism; insofar as it supports and draws upon social sentiments and feelings of solidarity it runs hand-in-hand with natural law theory; see Shaw, *Contemporary Ethics: Taking into Account Utilitarianism* (Oxford: Blackwell, 1999), 147. However, natural law theory takes a stand upon the Common Good and anticipates continued vindication by available evidence, while utilitarianism may not be able to deliver the evidence that it would ultimately invoke.

44 Exactly how many is hard to establish. J.M. Winter, in *The Great War and the British People* (London: Macmillan, 1985), 27, gives a figure of 2.4 million. H.M.D. Parker, in *Manpower: A Study of War-time Policy and Administration* (London: HM Stationery Office and Longmans, Green, 1957), 3, gives a figure of 800,000 net of men rejected as medically unfit or for other reasons.

45 A number of people have helped with comments and advice: I particularly thank Judith Jarvis Thomson, Douglas Long, Natalie and Chandler Davis, Lorraine Daston, Ian Hacking, Sam Fitch, Wayne Sumner, James Fishkin, and William Twining; and, with respect to the very last section,

on natural law and the Common Good, my friend and collaborator
Arthur P. Monahan.

Chapter 4

1 This question was raised by Lance Thomas in my seminar.
2 *A Theory of Justice*, rev. ed. (Cambridge, Mass.: Harvard University Press, 1999), 155, 156–8.
3 Or, as T.M. Scanlon would prefer to say, 'Could not reasonably reject.' The difference turns for Scanlon on whether people who voluntarily and reasonably go along with self-sacrifices under a certain arrangement could not have reasonably rejected the arrangement. See Scanlon, 'Contractualism and Utilitarianism,' in Amartya Sen and Bernard Williams, eds, *Utilitarianism and Beyond* (Cambridge: Cambridge University Press, 1982), 103–28, at 111–12. One might go either way, it seems to me, on the issue of making this distinction. It does not seem to be entirely firm in Scanlon's own mind: cf. Scanlon, *What We Owe to Each Other* (Cambridge, Mass.: Harvard University Press, 1998), 153, n. 8 (390).
4 Is ten minutes realistic enough? Strenuous enough? I e-mailed the ROTC office at The University of Texas at Austin hoping to get expert advice on this point, but I got no answer. Perhaps the answer is a military secret.
5 The term 'change of persons' is used in this connection in *A Strategy of Decision* (1963), and I used it earlier in my Cornell doctoral dissertation (1953). James Fishkin, in *Tyranny and Legitimacy*, writing quite independently, gives the same complication extended treatment as an obstacle to relying on principles about 'structure' in comparing policy results (Baltimore, Md.: Johns Hopkins University Press, 1979), chap. 10.
6 Bentham may not have moved along this path at all, or even seen it open before him. The thought that any individual person was moved by pleasure and pain and happier with more pleasure and less pain may have sent him pretty directly to the thought of adding up net balances of pleasure and pain somehow ascertained for all the persons to be considered. (Again, his Master-Idea comes in the company of a procedure that it does not entail.)
7 In the seminar Brandon Butler raised this point, citing a book by Martin Seligman, *Authentic Happiness* (New York: The Free Press, 2002). What Seligman tends to distinguish as varieties of happiness might also be treated, it seems to me, as various bases for happiness falling under one concept, as understood and observed in everyday life.

8 An objection put forward in the seminar by Dan Pozza, in one form or another resonating with several other members of the seminar. In a passage below it will lead, beyond having constraints against discrimination, to renewed recourse to the serial (and remedial) nature of policy-making, and insistence, given that recourse, that the objection about sacrifices of happiness is not to be given any once-for-all answer, but an answer that refers to a practical process for seeking round by round better approximations to an answer.

9 William H. Shaw, in his book *Contemporary Ethics: Taking Account of Utilitarianism* says, 'If utilitarianism appeals to the greater good to justify imposing costs on some individuals, then this greater good is simply the cumulative good of yet more individuals' (Oxford: Blackwell, 1999), 127. 'More individuals' might naturally mean 'a greater number of individuals.' This would accord better with the census-notion (used without caution) than with the aggregative calculus that preoccupies Shaw. But 'more' can be read without strain as 'other individuals,' which fits Shaw's constantly held position better, but allows for sacrificing some people's happiness to promote that of others.

10 The nomenclature may be in the spirit of Bentham. I am not sure that we can attribute the Gains-Preservation Principle to his teachings or to those of the other great figures in the history of utilitarianism – Mill, Edgeworth, and Sidgwick. However, I think they would at least have given it a sympathetic hearing and very likely have found it persuasive once all the reasons for adopting it had been brought up.

11 The following passage on the complications of applying the Gains-Preservation Principle is a response to an objection raised by Richard Arneson at the conference on Bentham held at The University of Texas at Austin in February 1998.

12 Shaw points out that critics of utilitarianism are often troubled by there apparently being no principle of just distribution having independent weight in the theory (Shaw, *Contemporary Ethics*, 124). This is perhaps, at least in part, what troubles T.M. Scanlon in the 'very serious objection' about justice that is one of three he raises against rule-utilitarianism. See above, chap. 1, nn. 21, 33; also chap. 3, n. 36. But why insist on 'independence' if important questions about justice are answered by operating features of utilitarianism, as they are in considering the condition of everyone affected by an action or policy, in blocking involuntary life-sacrifices, and (with the combination of the census-notion and the Gains-Preservation Principle) in safeguarding the present positions of people affected? (The next chapter will bring forward the additional consideration of justice that everyone's needs shall be provided for.)

13 This was pointed out in a contribution to the seminar by Brandon Butler. Other members of the seminar joined him in insisting on the topic of the present passage.

14 There may be a problem about trajectories: successive improvements on one trajectory may cut off the chances of doing even better on another. I shall not deal with this problem here, further than to note that the incrementalism with which (as expounded in chapter 2, above), I suppose, utilitarianism proceeds in application helps by leaving some room to change trajectories when the current one is discovered to be inferior.

15 I mean, specifically, a better answer to generalized objection about sacrifices. The combination of things that constitute the answer leaves open the question which to choose, given a choice of making more people happy, by moving people up from the Intermediate Category, or fewer people unhappy, by moving them up from the bottom, Unhappy Category. Some people will incline to give priority to remedying the condition of unhappy people. My own intuitions have some sympathy with this inclination, but not enough to be decisive. I suspect that different contexts can be described that make priority for the unhappy people less than compelling: suppose, for example, that we have to deal with people who are obdurately unhappy, who time after time have resisted remedial efforts. By contrast, when in the next chapter we get to the subject of basic needs, the priority to be given people lacking provisions for them will be just about unarguable.

16 In the seminar, Shaun Gilligan raised concerns about this sort of question, which deserves more attention than I am giving it here.

17 See *Leviathan*, chap. XXI, par. 16, on military service, not easily reconciled with par. 12 on one's liberty to refuse commands from the Sovereign to take his own life or wound himself.

18 In the Notes at the end of *Mathematical Psychics* (London: Kegan Paul, 1881), n. VI.

19 Shaw holds, as I remarked in my Introduction, that 'correctly understood, utilitarianism tells us to do only one thing, maximize happiness ... it is the total amount of happiness, not the number of people, that matters' (Shaw, *Contemporary Ethics*, 13). The present chapter is dead set against this 'correct' understanding, and does not concede its correctness either in a comprehensive historical view of utilitarianism or in a comprehensive topical view of its varieties. Shaw himself comes out against 'maximizing happiness by increasing the total population,' maximizing objectionable, he holds, because of 'reifying the notion of happiness' (ibid., 33). But is this not just what the aggregative calculus does (at least pending the completion of the project of obtaining a convincing interpersonal measure

of utility), and not only in regard to increasing the amount of happiness by increasing the population? The census-notion fits, without reification, Bentham's Master-Idea, formulated (as I have noted) by Shaw as the idea 'that we can only derive an overall welfare assessment of a given state of affairs based on the welfare or happiness or utility of each individual person' (ibid., 38).

20 Both Fred Rosen and Gerald J. Postema, in the articles cited in my Introduction (see nn. 8 and 12, respectively), give textual evidence of Bentham's concern with the 'extent' to which happiness is distributed in a given population. Postema cites the same passage that I cited in the preceding chapter (n. 15) from Ross Harrison in his book of 1983, *Bentham* (London: Routledge) about aiming for 'the greatest happiness' of all the members of the community, 'without exception, in so far as possible,' and when it is not possible to provide 'an equal quantity of happiness for every one of them,' then 'the greatest happiness of the greatest number.' Both alternatives imply the use of the census-notion. Curiously, in a comment on Rosen's paper, Harrison himself, coming out for interpreting Bentham as an aggregationist, seems to have forgotten the weight that this passage seems to call for; see 'Rosen's Sacrifice of Utility,' *Utilitas* 10, 2 (July 1998), 159–64c.

21 A cartoon in *The New Yorker*, published maybe a decade or two before real space exploration got underway, showed two astronauts, who have just disembarked from their spacecraft, racing toward a nearby tree, under which a man and woman are standing in their birthday suits; a serpent is coiled around a lower branch of the tree; the woman is offering the man an apple. 'Stop! Stop!' the astronauts are shouting.

22 I pass over R.M. Hare's suggestion about 'coordinating' the preferences of different people 'into a total preference which is impartial among them' (cited by Shaw, *Contemporary Ethics*, 83–4, from *Freedom and Reason* [Oxford: Oxford University Press, 1963], 123), which might do without higher and lower personal utility scores entirely, but is too mysterious to make firm sense of in this or any other connection. It seems to ignore the difficulties raised for aggregating preferences by Arrow's theorem in social choice theory.

23 Shaw is typical of writers on utilitarianism – writers pro as well as writers con – in not giving Bentham any credit for analysing differences in the quality of pleasure (*Contemporary Ethics*, 43). But is this not what he is doing – even if he does not finish the doing of it – with the dimensions of pleasure that he enumerates in chapter IV of the *Introduction to the Principles of Morals and Legislation*?

24 Expounded in the standard textbook by R. Duncan Luce and Howard Raiffa, *Games and Decisions* (New York: Wiley, 1957); see especially 19–20.

25 Harsanyi, overriding problems about distribution as well as about interpersonal comparisons, opts for the 'highest average utility' as the utilitarian criterion for choices of actions and policies (see the citation in Shaw, *Contemporary Ethics*, 77).

26 John Broome distinguishes two arguments presented by Harsanyi, one in 1953 and one in 1955, designed to support interpersonal comparisons leading to aggregative scores for good; see *Weighing Goods* (Oxford: Basil Blackwell, 1991), 51–8. Only the first uses the idea of a veil of ignorance.

27 Ibid., 215–18, 219–20.

28 Broome, *Weighing Goods*, 215–18.

29 The alternatives that Broome has in mind are one version or another of egalitarianism. But the objections about sacrifices and victimization, though they may have some implications about equality between persons, are objections consistent with accepting caste or class differences in social status. They may in particular cases turn out to be objections to depriving people of comforts available to people of their status (even if it is not a high one) in favour of making other people, continuing in a higher status, more comfortable.

30 Scores from the von Neumann and Morgenstern approach, for example, are affected by attitudes toward risk, which differ between people. This seems an extraneous consideration. Moreover, it is a consideration that raises a danger of circularity: to determine attitudes toward risk, we may need to have values for some of the objects at risk; but to establish those values, we need to assume something about attitudes toward risk.

31 See, for example, Adam Wagstaff, 'Health Care: QUALYS and the Equity-Efficiency Tradeoff,' in Richard Layard and Stephen Glaister, eds, *Cost-Benefit Analysis*, 2^d ed. (Cambridge: Cambridge University Press, 1994), 428–47, in particular 431–4.

Chapter 5

1 Kenneth J. Arrow, *Social Choice and Individual Values*, 2^d ed. (New York: Wiley, 1963). For the effect of not allowing for the Revisionary Process, see D. Braybrooke, 'Policy Formation with Issue-Processing and Transformation of Issues,' in C.A. Hooker, J.J. Leach, and E.F. McClennen, eds, *Foundations and Applications of Decision Theory* (Dordrecht: Reidel, 1978), Vol. II, 1–16; reprinted in my collected essays, *Moral Objectives, Rules, and the Forms of Social Change* (Toronto: University of Toronto Press, 1998), 331–47.

2 Centrally, his book, *The Rejection of Consequentialism* (Oxford: Clarendon Press, 1986). See also his lucid account of the issues in debate in his introduction to the anthology that he has edited, *Consequentialism and Its Critics* (Oxford: Oxford University Press, 1988).

3 In this statement I combine points pressed in the seminar by Brandon Butler and Julie Lane, respectively.

4 William H. Shaw, in *Contemporary Ethics: Taking Account of Utilitarianism* (Oxford: Blackwell, 1999), leaves provisions for needs out of a list that he gives of 'objective goods' (57), but he brings them in when shortly afterwards he gives a list of 'basic human goods' (64). He holds that for utilitarians there must be some link with gratification; but an advocate of meeting needs can readily concede this point, especially if the link is statistical, with what most people feel.

5 See C.L. Stevenson, *Ethics and Language* (New Haven, Conn.: Yale University Press, 1944); and for discussion of the analogy mentioned here, D. Braybrooke, 'How, Given Their Emotive-Imperative Dimensions, Is Truth to Be Ascribed to Moral Judgments?' *Journal of Value Inquiry* 137 (2003), 341–52.

6 What I called in *Meeting Needs* (Princeton, N.J.: Princeton University Press, 1987) a Selfgovliset – a self-governing set of people with a common language – to make a philosophical point about the empirical linguistic basis for the construction.

7 Ibid., 36.

8 Sen, in *The Standard of Living* (ed. G. Hawthorn [Cambridge: Cambridge University Press, 1987], 20–38, at 24–5), views all needs as relative to the functionings and capabilities that providing for the needs serves (*The Standard of Living*, 25). Robert Goodin (*Utilitarianism as a Public Philosophy* [Cambridge: Cambridge University Press, 1995], 245) and many other writers take a similar view: all needs are relative, and their importance derives in every case from the importance of the goals to which they are relative. I think that this is not so, or that at the very least it is a view that does not fully appreciate the complexity of the issue. See Braybrooke, *Meeting Needs*, 29–33. Is the need to keep one's body intact in respect to the organs of sight or the full equipment of one's arms and legs any less ultimate and foundational than the various goals retaining these bodily features might serve? They are not simply relative to living, but features of living in a way capable of a great variety of functionings; but many of those are less important than having the organs in question. It is not an adventitious need, which comes and goes with any goal that one might choose to take up.

9 All of the named conditions were present in the account given in *Meeting Needs*, but the Gains-Preservation Principle was not given a name there.

10 H.A. Simon, *Models of Man* (New York: Wiley, 1957).

11 Dasgupta, 'National Performance Gaps,' in *The Progress of Nations: 1996 UNICEF Report* (New York: UNICEF House, 1996), 33–4. This is one of a series of annual reports by the United Nations Children's Fund that rank with the annual reports of the United Nations Human Development Program in pressing forward for public policy purposes social indicators unequivocally related to basic human needs. Dasgupta does not allow enough, I suspect, even in application to Third World countries, for the expenses of meeting needs in very populous societies, where massive public works must be carried out and maintained if pure water is to be provided and sewage disposed of hygienically.

12 Indeed, in the chapter in *Meeting Needs* on 'The Expansion of Needs,' I endorse amending the Criterion to embrace 'the full development of human personality,' a notion that should make room for autonomy. I shall return to the issue of expanding needs and amending the Criterion later in this chapter. See Brock, 'Braybrooke on Needs,' *Ethics*, 104, 4 (July 1994), 811–23.

13 *Globe and Mail*, 2 August 2003, F2.

14 See, for example, Fishkin, *The Voice of the People* (New Haven, Conn.: Yale University Press, 1995).

15 See Brock, 'Braybrooke on Needs.' In one of his contributions as a student in my seminar, Douglas Marshall looked this article up and, after reflecting on it, suggested that I did not have to concede so much to Brock's criticism as I have done. Whether this is so or not, I think the concessions lead to illuminations that I would not have reached without them.

16 In the style of applied argumentation theory as practised by the school of pragma-dialectics at the University of Amsterdam. See various essays and references in F.H. van Eemeren, ed., *Advances in Pragma-Dialectics* (Amsterdam: Sic Sat, 2002).

17 See S.E. Finer, *The Life and Times of Sir Edwin Chadwick* (London: Methuen, 1952).

18 Edgeworth was ready to sacrifice the happiness of 'some of the lower [labouring] classes' to that of 'the higher classes.' But he supposed that there is a limit to the sacrifice 'above the starving point,' where 'the pleasures of the most favoured classes could not weigh much against the privations of the least favoured'; see *Mathematical Psychics* (London: Kegan Paul, 1881), 74–5.

19 See D. Braybrooke, 'Two Conceptions of Needs in Marx's Writings,' in R. Beehler, D. Copp, and Bela Szabados, eds, *On the Track of Reason: Essays in Honor of Kai Nielsen* (Boulder, Colo.: Westview Press, 1992), 119–33; reprinted in Braybrooke, *Moral Objectives, Rules, and the Forms of Social Change*, 15–31.

20 Amartya Sen and others, *The Standard of Living* (Cambridge: Cambridge University Press, 1987), 25–6, 105.

21 Sen, *Development as Freedom* (New York: Knopf, 1999).

22 See the references in the preceding chapter (nn. 26, 27, 28) to John Broome, *Weighing Goods* (Oxford: Basil Blackwell, 1991).

23 I give a discussion parallel to this one of Sen's 'capabilities' approach in a passage of an article forthcoming in *Philosophy*, 'Where Does the Moral Force of the Concept of Needs Reside and When?'

24 In an early writing, Marx says, looking forward, 'To take the place of wealth and poverty as political economy knows it, there comes forward the rich man, fitted out with rich human exigencies. The rich man is at the same time the man who, to live, has need of a totality of human manifestations, the man for whom his own realization is an interior necessity, a need'; see *Economic and Philosophical Manuscripts of 1844* (London: Lawrence and Wishart, 1959), 111–12. The English here is my translation from the French of the *Pléiade* edition. This is the sense in which Marx is to be understood, late in life, putting forward in the *Critique of the Gotha Program* the principle 'From all according to their ability, to all according to their needs.'

25 As G.A. Cohen, detecting an ambiguity in Sen's use of 'capability,' points out in his essay, 'Equality of What? On Welfare, Goods, and Capabilities,' in Martha C. Nussbaum and Amartya Sen, eds, *The Quality of Life* (Oxford: Clarendon Press, 1993), 9–29, at 19–20.

26 He does so, much more freely, in *Development as Freedom* (see, e.g., 64, 73, 132, 148) than in *The Standard of Living*.

27 The qualification about 'contingently reduced expectations' heeds a caution emphasized time and again by Sen in *The Standard of Living* (e.g., 10–11). Shaw cites Sumner on happiness, but does not bring forward Sumner's provision for cautions like Sen's. See Sumner, *Welfare, Happiness, and Ethics* (Oxford: Clarendon Press, 1996), 160, 166, 171, 172.

28 Rawls would have the social minimum meeting needs adjusted to take into account a just rate of social savings; see *A Theory of Justice*, rev. ed. (Cambridge, Mass.: Harvard University Press, 1999), 251–2. This adjustment could be one topic of discussion and negotiation under the schema,

with discussants' being mindful of the demands to come up, in due time, in the second stage of the program of utilitarianism recast.

29 Vladislav Stoychev brought up this example in the seminar, and the other members joined in a vigorous discussion of it.

30 Further reducing the difficulty about justice felt by Scanlon. See above, chap. 4, nn. 3, 12.

31 Yet more provision for meeting Scanlon's objection about justice. See ibid.

32 See chapter 8, on moral education, in my *Natural Law Modernized* (Toronto: University of Toronto Press, 2001).

33 For these points about the direction of aid see Thomas Pogge, 'Global Justice,' *Metaphilosophy* 32 (January 2001), 6–24; and Paul Gomberg, 'The Fallacy of Philanthropy,' *Canadian Journal of Philosophy* 32, 1 (March 2002), 29–65.

Acknowledgments

Pride of place in my acknowledgments must be given to the students who worked with me during a graduate seminar at The University of Texas at Austin in the spring term 2003 through an advanced draft of this book: Brandon Butler, Shaun Gilligan, Julie Lane, Douglas Marshall, Daniel Pozza, Vladislav Stoychev, Lance Thomas, and Brenna Troncoso. I had thought the book finished, except for a little polishing here and there, in the draft that I submitted to them. They taught me differently and led me to many substantial improvements. I have acknowledged here and there in the various chapters of the book their most salient individual contributions; but doing so may distract from the continuous improvement in the text that they elicited during our joint effort. I am deeply indebted to them all; and deeply grateful. Subsequently, two philosophers, asked to read the manuscript for University of Toronto Press, encouraged me by thinking well of the book as a whole, and helped me by raising questions; dealing with the questions has significantly improved the text. I earnestly thank them, too. I thank Sharon Sutherland for a last-minute critique of chapter 2, which has incited some important revisions in the chapter. Further acknowledgments to colleagues will be found in the several chapters of the book and in the Notes. I am glad to have the opportunity to renew my thanks to them. The chapters originate in earlier works that I have published, but they have all been substantially revised for my present purposes. This is so, even in chapters 1 and 3, where I carry over unchanged many passages from the originals and, short of some additions at the end, keep their overall form: respectively, an article, 'The Choice between Utilitarianisms,' *American Philosophical Quarterly* (1967), and an essay, 'Liberalism, Statistics, and the Presuppositions of Utilitarianism,' first published in the collection of my essays *Moral Objectives, Rules, and the Forms of Social Change* (1998). (Full bibliographical information about these and other sources are to be found in the notes about copyright at the openings of the relevant chapters.) The latter fits better, as an essential ingredient in the overall argument, into the present book than in the former one (which, of course, has no overall argument). I would have saved it for the present book had I known that I would get around to writing such a book; but it seemed prudent, as I approached the mid-point of my eighth decade, with 'Time's wingèd chariot' hurrying nearer and my energy not sure to continue unabated, to make certain of publishing the essay by publishing it then. Chapter 2 is based on Part Four, 'The Rehabilitation of Utilitarianism,' for which I was mainly responsible in the book that C.E. Lindblom invited me to join him in writing, *A Strategy of Decision: Policy Evaluation as a Social Process* (1963); the chapter also draws briefly from 'Scale, Combination, Opposition: A Rethinking of Incrementalism,' a review-essay in *Ethics* (1985). Chapter 4 draws on the treatment of the census-notion in *A Strategy of Decision*, in my book *Meeting Needs* (1987) and in the essay that I contributed to the anthology put together by Gillian Brock, *Necessary Goods* (1998). Chapter 5, on needs, is based on *Meeting Needs* and on the essay in the Brock anthology. I have permission from all the publishers concerned (and from C.E. Lindblom) to make the use that I have of these materials. The University of Texas at Austin has made available a subsidy to publication from the research funds attached to my chair there, sparing University of Toronto Press (and me) from having to seek a subsidy from Ottawa.

I wish to thank Brenna Troncoso not only for her contribution to the seminar, but also for her fireball research assistance in Austin. I have also had research assistance from Darren Bifford and Adrian Neerin in Halifax, and I thank them, too. 'Fireball' is a correct description of Brenna's research assistance, but also a joke between us; a fuller and therefore juster description would mention her ever-readiness, promptness, judgment, and consideration, all extraordinary and all of great advantage to me. I must also thank Patrick Couture, the computer technician for the Department of Government at Texas, whose office is just across the hall from mine. He has had to put up with a noisily fretful computer-user. When on occasion the fretfulness has given way to a rational request for advice, he has furnished quick and efficient help.

There are a number of people at University of Toronto Press whom I should thank for encouragement and help: Ron Schoeffel, who as editor-in-chief started up with me the series of books of which this is the third; Len Husband, editor for this book and in prospect for a fourth in the series, on some achievements of analytical political philosophy, maybe editor for a fifth book, about absurdities in politics, not part of the present series; Frances Mundy, the managing editor for the present book; and Catherine Frost, who did a meticulous and challenging job on the manuscript as copy-editor.

It is common and laudable practice for authors to thank their spouses, and accordingly I thank my wife, Michiko-san, for providing, along with her children and grandchildren, the affectionate family life that has sustained my morale as a teacher and writer. My own children, scattered across the continent with their families, live too far away to keep such close company with me, much as I love and honour them, too. Only one daughter, Linda, was available in Austin to proofread the present book with me and help me prepare the index; I thank her for the care and perceptiveness that she brought to the task, and as well for making the work fun for us both.

D.B.
Austin, Texas; Halifax, Nova Scotia

Index